Pointers to a Spiritual Life.

by Carol Riddell

Other Books by Carol Riddell
The Findhorn Community
Tireragan - A Township on the Ross of Mull
The Chronicles of Thumpus Wumpus

Contents

Overall Introduction

Overall Introduction

During the 1970, I slowly changed my orientation to life from a materialist, and radical political one, towards spirituality. I explored Zen Buddhism, and later took a year's course in psychic development in California.

In 1983, I joined the Findhorn Community in N.E. Scotland, where I stayed for ten years, the last two of them at the small sister community on the island of Erraid, off the west coast of Mull. At Findhorn I was inspired to develop a practice of intensive meditation and began to receive guidance, of the type well known in the Findhorn community through the work of Eileen Caddy, Dorothy Maclean and David Spengler..

In late 1984 I heard of an Indian Saint, Bhagavan Sathya Sai Baba and went to visit him in 1985, as a result of which my life changed again. It was the first of 7 visits.

In his later years Sai Baba became a controversial figure, especially outside India, but his teachings were identical to those of Eileen Caddy and Dorothy Maclean, although, of course, in a Hindu context. He never made any demands of me of a financial nature, nor did I have any private personal or group interviews with him and I never had any cause to question his absolute integrity.

However, I did have a number of very unusual experiences in relation to him, both at his ashram, Prasanthi Nilayam, at Puttaparti village and that at Whitefields, outside Bangalore. They are recounted in **Part One** of this book.

Back home at Findhorn, I was inspired to take up work as a spiritual teacher and received two books of guidance, all the messages signed by Sai Baba, the first collection personally

3

approved by him for publication during a visit to his ashram. *'Gifts of Divine Love'* consists of a series of inspirational messages received by me for the workshop groups in the 51 workshops I led across Europe and at Findhorn in the next few years. It was published in a spanish translation in 1996. as *'Ofrendas de Amor'* (Ediciones Luciernaga), and forms (in english) the **second part** of this book.

The other, *'To Transcend the Ego'* is a series of 83 messages I received largely on the island of Erraid in 1981-2. It constituted a training manual for a spiritual life, and was directed to me, personally, so initially I did not try to have it published. Since it seems relevant to the spiritual development of others as well, the messages form **Part 3** of the book.

Finally, during a 3 month stay at a spiritual vacation centre in Madeira run by ex- Findhorners, I received more material, in the form of a short spiritual treatise. It was not signed by Sai Baba, but is referred to in the last message of *'To Transcend the Ego'*. I combined it with the main exercises of the workshops I had given, and it was published as a book, *'The Path to Love'*, by the Findhorn Press in 1995. It is now out of print. It has an introduction by Eileen Caddy, one of the founders of the Findhorn spiritual community. The first part of *'The Path to Love'* forms the **4th part** of this book. I did not include the exercises, but copies of the whole book are still available from me and at the Findhorn Community.

I cannot claim to be the 'author' of the material in this book (apart from the first part), as I was in a semi-trance state when I received it, but it is my belief that all of us can access a higher consciousness if we work hard and appropriately on it, a state that has nothing to do with the various manifestions of so called 'possession', during psychotic illness. Since there is a long history of writings by 'mystics' of all faiths and at all historical periods, all of which provide similar wisdom appropriate to faith and time, there is plenty of material with which to check contents of any guidance for appropriateness. There is no question in my mind that the material here is genuine.

Sai Baba did not ordinarily give guidance to his followers, but in some cases he approved it, as he did in my case. For instance, 4 books of messages signed by him were published by Lucas Ralli, in England in the 1980s, books also blessed by Sai Baba as deriving from him..

Sai Baba has now passed on, but remains for me an inspiring mentor. As he said, very frequently in his numerous Discourses, 'I am God, you are God, the only difference between us is that I know it and you don't!'. The task for any spiritual seeker is to investigate and put into practice the full meaning of that statement. Hopefully, the content of this book can help you in that task. It is not intended to be read and absorbed at one sitting, but by 'dipping in' at appropriate times.

Part 1. Inner Teachings.

A Story of Personal Contact with Sathya Sai Baba.

Carol Riddell.

For Tanya Mette and Meike Henningsen, who found liberation.

Contents:

Prologue: Arrival at Puttaparti

In mid-September, 1985, I arrived at the Indian village of Puttaparti, between Bangalore and Hyderabad (but nearer Bangalore), Andhra Pradesh State. The village, in a rural area, is completely dominated by the Ashram and Educational Centre of the Indian spiritual teacher, Sathya Sai Baba.

I came on the village bus, a 6 hour trip from Bangalore. The hot and tiring trip was a good introduction to rural India. A few kilometres from Puttaparti, an arch over the road proclaimed 'The Kingdom of Sathya Sai'. As we came to the outskirts of the village, the landscape was no longer 'timeless rural India'; the road was flanked with modern buildings, some of striking design, decorated with large statues of Hindu gods. All were painted in pale cream, beige, pink and blue, reminding one of Wedgwood china. On a hill above the village was a massive, temple-like edifice, the University Administration building.

The bus pulled into a sandy, rubbish-strewn square. We were instantly surrounded by beggars and would- be porters, rickshaw drivers. Across the road, behind a long wall, stood the Ashram I had come to visit. On our side of the wall, up and down from the bus station, rows and rows of little shops tried to invite, full of pictures, statues, cards and books by and about Sai Baba, as well as tailors, gift shops, mattress vendors and many others.

Along with many of the buses' occupants, following a porter who had nabbed me, I evaded bullock carts and the occasional motor vehicle. We made our way down the road, round a bend to the left, along a wall, past an ornate gateway, and through open metal gates into a concreted street which left the village road. There was a marked change of atmosphere, though the village noise and bustle could still be heard behind us. We were in the Ashram.

My friend and I found ourselves registering, and being allocated to a 'Hall'. The Ashram was huge; sandy streets, flanked by four storey concrete apartment blocks, a canteen and four even larger round apartment buildings - the 'Round Houses'. Beyond them again lay a tree-flanked, sandy square and a line of large sheds - the 'Halls' - ours already apparently filled by hundreds of women from many countries. They had created tiny cubicle homes from string and saris, giving each person a 'personal space'. Furniture consisted of a mattress on the floor or a rented bed - there was no room for anything else. Somehow we found a space amid the throng and set about setting up our own domicile. It was all very different and overwhelming, as was the heat.

In the afternoon, at about 3.30, we went for 'Darshan', the time Sai Baba came out of the ornate temple to the gathered crowds; men on the left forecourt, women on the right - strictly segregated.

On the women's side, the sandy floor of the forecourt was constantly swept by old ladies with beezum brushes, who kept it meticulously smooth. The forecourt itself was fringed by palm trees and a flagstone surround, where small, open-sided pergolas gave a semblance of shade. In the centre lay the ornate temple, the 'Mandir', a more-than-baroque structure covered in reliefs of gryphons, demons, gods and other designs, in the same colours as the rest of the Ashram. It was an inspiring scene.

In an outer courtyard, shaded by a huge tree with eagles perched in it, the women formed into lines of about 50. There were 15 or 16 lines. At a certain point, the front woman in each line drew a numbered token from a bag carried round by one of the numerous volunteer workers - 'Seva Dals'. The line lucky enough to get the

9

token numbered 'one' went into the inner courtyard first, to get the places nearest to where Sai Baba would walk.

*****

As I approach Puttaparti for my seventh visit, in 1997, there are massive changes. Better roads for the numerous taxis and buses; an enormous and very impressive hospital a few kilometres from the village; an airport with an international length runway. Villas and apartments line the approach road. The bus stops at an asphalted, computerised bus terminal. On the hill over the village the Administration Building has been joined by another, the imposing Museum of Religions. Puttaparti village itself is an enormous building site, 5 and 6 storey blocks rising everywhere. New craft emporia and small restaurants tout custom.

Inside, the Ashram has more than doubled in size. Its sandy streets are asphalted and its spaces have become tropical gardens, courtyards, lawns. There are 3 large restaurants, one with European style food. The 'Halls' have been demolished, replaced by block after block of new apartments. But they have reappeared in a new, far flung section of the Ashram, now more than 10 minutes walk from the temple itself. A shopping complex caters for those who do not wish to leave the Ashram or haggle over prices.

The Mandir still exists, but its courtyards are covered by a huge hall where thousands can experience Sai Baba in shade and relative comfort. The brushed sand Sai Baba's feet trod in 1985 is now polished stone. The lines of waiting women have doubled in size and number. Many groups, their origin indicated by coloured scarves, indicate that the whole world now sends pilgrims to the Ashram.

I think of the Prasanthi Nilayam I first visited with some nostalgia, as others who were there in a previous decade think of the seventies. But the cause of all this activity and human effort, is the same - Sai Baba himself.

He now lives in a corner of the great Poornachandra hall, a few steps away, instead of in the Mandir itself. Otherwise he comes, as he has done for 58 years, twice a day, to be with and bless the assembled crowds. This book records a few of Sai Baba's innumerable miracles that have affected me, but the greatest, beyond all others, is the 58 years of daily peace and patience that mark Sai Baba's physical contact with the ever-increasing throng of devotees and spiritual seekers. Twice a day, he comes slowly, dressed in a full length orange silk robe, passes round the waiting gathering. Sometimes he says a word or two, or, with a small circular wave of his right hand, manifests a holy ash called Vibhuti. As he passes, all attention is on him; love passes from him to those present - love, in the form of adoration, returns, generating a spiritual energy of extraordinary power.

He has done this for every one of those 58 years. The details of the setting round him change and the crowds increase, but for him, no holidays, no 'weekends off', no 'off days', no 'moods'. The same exchange of love occurs at every 'Darshan'.

This simple daily interaction defines everyone's visit to Sai Baba and gives the most tangible proof that he is a more-than-ordinary human being. Miracles can be argued over, contested, dissected. Behind them stands the ongoing, daily exchange of love. Two phrases of Sai Baba's stand out - 'Come, try Me!' and 'My life is My message'. From his loving constancy arise all the inner experiences described in this book, as an ocean gives rise to waves on its surface.

In a modern materialistic world, hurried, transient, the loving timelessness of the daily interactions at Prasanthi Nilayam indicate *another way*; ultimately a more real and genuinely human one.

Introduction: Who Is He?

People argue endlessly over the nature of Sai Baba. For some He is God incarnate; for others he is spiritual teacher; for others again, he is felt as a threat, or condemned as a charlatan. A Catholic priest has been excommunicated for his belief in Sai Baba's divinity. For every individual who comes into contact with Sai Baba, these arguments come up. As with every religious phenomenon, experience, grace and faith are involved in finding personal answers.

Underlying much theology is a proposition which separates Creator and created. God is one thing; humanity and the created world another. In these terms, it is really a contradiction to assert that God is on earth. Jesus Christ is 'God's Son'; Mohammed, 'God's Prophet'.

However, if 'God' is not a 'being' at all, but the essence underlying *everything*, the contradiction dissolves. And if that essence were to be *love* - the ultimate 'particle' - Sai Baba is, essentially, God, and divine; as is everyone and everything else. Sai

Baba does not try to tell us that he is an incarnation of a separate Creator. Instead, He says he is a perfect, exemplary manifestation of something every single one of us also is - Divinity, the essence of being. He begins every public talk he gives by addressing the crowd, 'Embodiments of Love', making an identity between humanity and divinity. In a famous quotation, he has said, "I am God, You are God. The only difference between us is that I know it and you don't."

So, from Sai Baba's point of view, there is nothing special about claiming Divinity. Everyone and everything is Divine. The way we live and see things confuses us greatly about this ultimate truth; clearing those confusions away is the *spiritual path*, the ultimate rationale of existence. The unity, *in actual experience*, of consciousness and Love constitutes human self-realisation and provides non-transient happiness. Sai Baba embodies that state and is thus a model, an example, of something everyone of us actually is - but have obscured through our attachment to worldly things.

Sai Baba's existence is more than an *abstract* demonstration of being. It involves help and support to those willing to change consciousness. Daily darshan, already described, is the core act, the 'love factory' that uplifts all who come in contact with it. It is an example of how we ourselves must interact with others to find fulfilment. As well, there are special, individual acts of contact, Grace, which assist our consciousness to develop.

Occasionally, these involve materialisations. For some, Sai Baba distributes small physical objects as tokens of love and connection. There are thousands of these in existence, treasured by followers. Many of them are given in a personal interaction on a physical level with Sai Baba - for instance, when He presents a ring, watch or necklace for a devotee in an interview. But many happen when he is not physically present, such as the appearance of holy 'Vibhuti' ash or other symbolic substance on a picture in someone's home. Because almost all of us think of the physical world as a place where things happen only in a defined cause and effect sequence, such manifestations are stunning and very precious. They may help to convince.

Other acts of Grace change the course of events from what they 'have to be', to allow continued survival or even removal of inconvenience. Earlier in his life, Sai Baba is reputed to have poured a can of water into the empty petrol tank of the car in which he was travelling; the car travelled happily to its destination. In many cases, he has averted certain accidents in ways inexplicable to those who accept a mechanistic universe. Planes have not fallen out of the sky when their engines have malfunctioned. Cars have not collided when on a head-on collision course, incurable diseases have been healed, dead people have returned to life. In such situations Sai Baba demonstrates omniscience, omnipresence and omnipotence, qualities we normally discount in ourselves.

And Sai Baba can be a present companion when he is 'not there' physically; a 'friend of grace', who can eliminate loneliness from our lives. This aspect of his support is particularly significant in an age of alienation and purposelessness, when we are highly individualised, concentrating on transient things, and people, even in the closest relationships, are confused by rapid and ongoing change. In such times, the personal presence and demonstrative friendship of Sai Baba can give direction, stability and companionship to existence. He is the 'omni-partner'.

The experiences recounted in this book are special instances of this latter type. What a friend! What generosity! What spiritual gifts! Who could ask for more in life?

Contact

I was in my third year at the Findhorn Foundation in North East Scotland, an international, ecumenical, spiritual community founded in 1962 by Eileen and Peter Caddy and Dorothy MacLean. With a couple of hundred other members, I was 'developing' myself and caring for the thousands of guests who visit the community each year. I worked in and managed a large old house and 5 acre garden which had been donated to the Foundation. It had been lovingly restored on a shoestring budget.

In December of 1984, I heard of Sai Baba for the first time. A friend wanted to visit him, as part of the first group that went to Prasanthi Nilayam Ashram from Findhorn. But she was uncertain, as her estranged husband was strongly opposed to the visit. She asked my advice. I encouraged her to have the experience, though I did not believe in 'Gurus'.

On her return from India a few weeks later, she spent three hours sharing her experiences with me. He had only looked at her once during her visit but that one look had had a profound impact on her. As she talked, it seemed to me she had changed in some major way, though I could not define how. This sense of deep change made me feel for the first time that Sai Baba must be someone very special.

I read a couple of startling books about him, but still felt that spiritual development came only through stillness and meditation without any intermediaries. At the beginning of July, 1985, however, something strange happened. I had given a clairvoyant counselling session to a member of the community who did similar work. It was on an exchange basis. She reminded me that she 'owed me one' and, although I didn't really feel I needed it at that time, we arranged an appointment. I thought of it as a birthday present to myself.

It was her style of work to do a long meditation together, and then to share our experiences. During the meditation, I began to 'see' colours coming towards me, soft greens, browns, ochres, in ever changing variety. It was like looking into a moving kaleidoscope. It was very striking and quite new to me. If I tried to stop the colours, they disappeared, but as soon as I 'let go', they returned. This continued for the whole duration of the meditation. I had no insights, no profound guidance - only the colours.

At the end of the inner time, I described what I had 'seen'. My 'reader' shared that she had felt I was to undergo a profound change in the next few days. What I had received was a preparation for it. The colours represented either the energy of the preparation, or a distraction for the mind so that it could happen anyway. I went away vaguely disappointed that no 'wise words' had been given me, but with the sense of the wonderful colours still with me.

Three days later I was meditating as usual in the early morning in my room. It was around 6 a.m. The summer sun was streaming in through the glass verandah doors of the room, the garden lay, beautiful, beyond. I was sitting cross-legged on the bright red carpet - it had cost 10 pounds in an auction. The bed was on my right, a table a little way to my left. My eyes were closed.

Suddenly, Sai Baba was there, in the orange robe he habitually wears, standing a yard away to my left, looking down at me. The experience was completely real. The room, the carpet, the sun shining, the view through the window - exactly as they were with open eyes - only Sai Baba added. In fact I did not know if my eyes were open or not, and had no time to question it. He said nothing, but looked at me with such love that my heart was *wrenched* open, with considerable physical pain. A short while and he was there no

16

longer. My eyes were open, and the room was exactly the same - without Sai Baba. I was completely overwhelmed and spent the rest of the day in tears.

The next morning, he was there again, just as before. I remember thinking of Al Capone with his machine gun in a violin case, making 'an offer you couldn't refuse'. Sai Baba had come to me and made me an offer - of love - that I couldn't refuse. No one in their right mind would refuse an experience like that.

Sai Baba didn't return again, but the love was still with me. Part of it expressed itself as an adoration of him. He was my way - 'for better or worse'. It was like a marriage ceremony! I didn't even need to go to see him. My heart was his! But... I thought, it would be nice to see this Being who had visited me in his physical form.

I had hardly a penny to my name; nowhere near enough for a flight and stay in India. As soon as I mentioned I would like to go to see him, people spontaneously began to give me money. I did not ask for or solicit it, but within 3 weeks I was given ,1100, quite adequate for an Indian visit. Some people gave a few pounds, others a hundred. People I didn't even know came up to me and said things like:

"I hear you want to go to see Sai Baba. I want to support you."

I was able to book a ticket for September. I was a bit scared of a trip to India on my own, feeling I might be overwhelmed by the poverty to be experienced there. Two weeks before departure date, I was working in the garden of the old house when a woman guest came up to me.

"I hear you want to go to India to see Sai Baba," she said.
"Yes," I replied.
"Me, too."
"When are you thinking of going?"
"Sometime in November. How about you?"

17

"My flight's in two weeks."

"Could I go with you?"

She was serious. We phoned up the airline. There appeared to be one seat left on the plane. I did not have to go to India alone! She was the perfect companion for the journey. Later, at the Ashram, we went our separate ways.

Sceptics may say that all this was illusion and coincidence. But I had already enough spiritual experience to know better. Sai Baba's inner visit was neither dream like, nor the result of fantasy. It was a totally unexpected occurrence. I hadn't even been thinking about him at the time. The stream of 'coincidences' that happen to thousands of people in relation to Sai Baba is overwhelming. It is clear that something more is involved - grace.

The Trip to Glasgow

The arrival at Bombay airport was horrible. Nothing I had read had prepared me for the dreadful poverty to be seen around me. Nor for the contrasts the city provides. Having several hours to wait, we took a bus into the centre and walked around, carrying our heavy backpacks, as there seemed to be no left-luggage counters. It was hot, humid and exhausting, a considerable culture shock.

Bangalore was little better; only less humid. We meant to get an express bus to Puttaparti, but after an overnight stay, ended up on the village bus - a 6 hour trip. The slow journey gave a chance to observe and acclimatise, as villages, people and animals came and went. India began to cast a spell over me. I began to feel its vitality, not only its poverty.

Conditions were not easy at the Ashram. The communal sheds ('Halls') were dusty and mosquito infested. At night, dogs tried to enter through any unlatched door - and my two square metres of floor were near the door to the outside toilets. It was usually left open by those in urgent need - not a few. Several times I found stray curs sharing my sleeping bag. But none of it mattered. I regarded all as a test. I had eyes, ears and thoughts only for Sai Baba whom I could now see in front of me, exactly as he had appeared in the vision. True, he did not pay me much attention in the crowds. But he did not ignore me either. His voice began to speak in my head as an inner, verbal conscience.

I spent many rupees in the book shop, buying up all I could find about Sai Baba and his teachings, particularly his own works. I read, learned bhajans, went to lectures for westerners, meditated at the special tree he had blessed for that purpose, snatched meals and tried to sleep. This was apart from the twice daily time with Sai Baba at Darshan and the Bhajan singing which followed. All the time, his voice was present inside, a gentle, loving, but clear commentary on my every action or omission, be they ever so small. How did my behaviour compare with the ideals for spiritual development he set out? I felt as if there was a trapdoor in my head. I had opened it; this unending commentary came through. It reminded me of the stream of colours in the reading at Findhorn.

As a result, I felt split. On the one hand, to be near Sai Baba and to immerse myself in his writings and the atmosphere of the Ashram was like being in heaven. On the other, the inadequacies of my performance there as revealed by his inner voice were so great that I felt despairing. I began to feel depressed - upon which I turned the page of one of his books and found the sentence:

' *Depression is the purest form of egotism.*'

No haven in depression! The contradiction began to make me ill. I felt like a washed out rag. 'Shiva Fever!' commented someone. Now his inner voice told me: 'Time to leave at the end of the week.' - and I had told people at Findhorn I might stay forever, thinking perhaps go get a job teaching the girls of his college at Anantapur! It was I who was the student! I was 5 weeks there, the longest stay of the 7 I have made. On the day before departure I asked Sai Baba on the Darshan line.

"Leaving tomorrow, Swami?"

"Tomorrow, very happy," he replied. Next evening, I saw, in the courtyard of my hotel in Bombay, an eclipse of the moon; I also realised it was my birthday, which I had totally forgotten.

*****

20

Two other members of the Findhorn Foundation had been in Prasanthi Nilayam Ashram, though we travelled independently. Back in Scotland, two of us decided to visit the large Sai Baba group in Glasgow, to see how things were done there. They held their bhajans - devotional songs - on a Sunday evening. Our plan was to travel the two hundred miles on Sunday morning, stay overnight with Glasgow devotees, and return on Monday.

The Glasgow Sai Convenor was most welcoming. We should come to his house in the outer suburbs of Glasgow when we arrived, he said. We could then go into Glasgow in his car for the bhajans and stay with him and his wife overnight. We had to point out that we were not sure when we would arrive, as there was no transport out of the local town of Forres to Inverness on a Sunday. My friend had no car, and mine had just given up the ghost.

We hitch hiked out of Forres to Inverness. After a cold, half hour wait, some kindly person picked us up and it was not long before we were at Inverness train station - to discover that there were no trains on a Sunday morning. We went to the bus station and discovered that there *was* a bus - in a short while.

We arrived at the Glasgow Bus Station just before 2, and went to Queen Street Train Station to get the local electric train to the suburb. Another setback: the electric train service, also, did not run on a Sunday. There was probably a bus, but we didn't know how frequent, or where it went from. So we phoned the Convenor from the station.

His son answered the phone.

"We got your phone call that you were arriving in Queen St on the 2.15 train," he said. "Dad's on his way to pick you up now. He should be there any minute."

We had made no phone call. As we stepped out of the phone box, I looked at the clock. It was exactly 2.15. The Convenor came hurrying across the station concourse to us.

"Sai Ram! I'm glad I was in time," he said. We checked the Arrivals board in case we had made a mistake in Inverness. There was *no* train from there due in at 2.15.

Who could have known that we would be at Queen St. station at exactly 2.15? There was no train from Inverness at all. We changed our intention and came on the bus. There were no local trains. Instead of going straight back to the bus station we phoned from Queen St. Rail. *Who telephoned on our behalf?* We had spoken to no-one on the journey. Nobody could have known of our changed plans. Yet somebody had phoned the convenor and told him he should meet us at Queen St. station at 2.15, the time we were actually there. It was a little miracle. Only Sai Baba himself could have been responsible.

The experience was a very moving one for us. It indicated that we were being cared for in a very specific way; there was exact attention to detail and a prior knowledge of events that no ordinary human could have had. Sai Baba gives attention not just to the 'big' things of life, but to small, everyday events as well, indicating a very personal relationship to the devotee. Such examples of meticulous caring are models for each of us in living our daily lives.

We had a very good time in Glasgow at the bhajans and with the convenor and his family. The next day we returned to Forres, still feeling exhilarated by our 'personal' miracle. In the bus from Inverness to Forres, the only other passenger was a woman from Nairn, the small town between them. We started talking, and I mentioned that my car had finally broken down.

22

"Ach, we've an old car we're not wanting 'cause we've just bought a new one," she said. "You'll likely be able to have it!" She gave us her address in Nairn and told me to come round the next Sunday.

It was grace overwhelming. My car replaced for nothing on top of everything else! It was, frankly, too much for me. My ego took over. I spent the week telling all and sundry about Sai Baba's special grace, with the implication that *I* was special.

I had a lot of trouble finding someone to give me a lift to Nairn on the next Sunday. Everyone had something else on. I called from one person to another and eventually someone agreed; but they could not meet the time specified. We arrived about ¾ of an hour late, to find no-one at the house. The car in question appeared to be standing there. We waited a long time, but nobody showed up. I returned sadly to Forres, ruefully aware of having 'blown it'. It was a salutary lesson. I couldn't afford another car for two years.

The Workshops.

A year later, I was back in Prasanthi Nilayam Ashram, this time for a three week visit. An old friend had arrived at Findhorn. In the seventies, she had been poor - at that time, I had a good job and helped her financially.

"When I had no money, you helped me," she said. "Now the tables are turned." She gave me £500. Together with money donated for some counselling sessions, it was enough for the second visit.

This time, the stay was blissful. Without the anxiety of a first visit to India, knowing how the Ashram ran, having visited all the special places one had to see - Sai Baba's birthplace, the 'tree of many fruits' and so on - I could concentrate more intensely on the experience of being in his ambience. I had developed enough distance not to be irritated by the little tests the Ashram provided. It was a gentle visit, of three weeks.

On return to the Findhorn Community, I felt very happy and empowered. After the first visit to Sai Baba, I had cancelled planned long workshops - a month long training in Spiritual Healing and a three month Clairvoyant Reading course. It didn't feel that the workshops were wrong in themselves; just that the spiritual training I was receiving was too intense for me to teach such things at the time.

A couple of days after my return, I had a strong inclination to go to the meditation room in the Park section of the community, a lovely, quiet building, surrounded by flowers and shrubs. It was mid morning; there was no one else there. Sitting quietly, I thought of Krishna - said to be one of Sai Baba's previous incarnations - as a child. Images from the Bhagavatam, the great Indian epic in praise of Krishna, came to mind. The young Krishna loved cream. In the cow herding village where he lived, he would to go round the households, stealing cream from the buckets of cow's milk. No-one could catch him, but everybody knew who it was, to the despair of his mother. Whether we like it or not, God eventually takes the best of who we are - the cream - for himself. I found the Krishna stories, so rich, so deep in symbolism, very moving.

Suddenly, there was a sense that Sai Baba was with me; the thought came - if Krishna was a 'spiritual thief', I could work as a 'spiritual burglar'!

24

I was presented with an image. Our body and personality is like a house which contains a treasure. As we grow up, we try, each in our own way, to protect this treasure - our own perfection - by erecting walls and defences against the various challenges of a difficult environment. But, in so doing, we lock the treasure away so securely that we cannot access it ourselves.

By 'breaking in', through the shell of our personalities and avoiding the 'police' of social convention - which say that the material world should be the goal of our desires, we could begin to re-access this perfection - our own divinity - once more. Our 'accomplices' would be a supportive group of co-workers. The Lord himself would be the 'Master mind', and the 'jemmy' we would use would be *love*.

It seemed a perfect theme for a workshop. Now, exercises came flooding in, some new, some modifications of techniques I had already used in other workshops I had led. After some time, it all came to an end; the sense of Sai Baba's presence faded. I had been given a major gift of grace. I left the sanctuary, ran to my caravan, and wrote everything down while it was fresh in my mind.

The Findhorn programme for the next season had already been made up, but a young German doctor from Hamburg had a 'reading' from me, and later sought me out for conversation. I shared about the gift of a workshop I had recently been given, and she was very interested. She had a group of friends in Hamburg who were searching for a more spiritual way of life. Would I be prepared to lead a workshop there to put the idea into practice?

I already had some conversational German and spent the rest of the autumn 'super-learning' German spiritual terms so I could lead the workshop in that language. In March, 1987, the first 'Breaking In' ('Einbrechen') took place, over a long weekend. There were about ten participants. I was extremely nervous; at times the strain

25

of long hours of thinking, understanding and speaking only German made me almost incoherent. But the workshop was a resounding success. An ongoing group was formed, and I was asked to return to carry the work further.

It was the first of 51 similar workshops over the next four years, in Germany, Italy, Scandinavia and in the Findhorn Community itself. I led them at four different levels, and they varied from two days to two weeks in length. I used the money I earned to visit Sai Baba in India and my aged mother who was living in Australia.

I was always nervous just before a 'Breaking In' session started, but, little by little, I realised that the Grace had not only been in the gift of the ideas for the workshop, but was present during the work itself. *'I' didn't have to do it.* The exercises were just a framework for the flow of love in the group and spiritual change happened 'of itself'. Through the workshops I myself was being trained in ego release, surrender and confidence in inner wisdom.

At the end of each workshop, as a culmination of the work, we would do an exercise called 'Intuitive' or 'Automatic' writing; in fact an introduction to 'channelling'. The results of this exercise, only about a half hour long, were varied and creative. They ranged from initial blockage and scribbles, to poetry, short stories, strange scripts and languages, to passages of deep spiritual wisdom. Afterwards we would share what we had each received, with no judgement at all, and sometimes discuss what it meant.

For every group, I received a message, always signed 'Sai Baba'. In longer workshops, the messages would come in several parts. By the end of 1990, I had more than 50 of these messages, a collection of very beautiful, short spiritual texts. But were they really from Sai Baba? I was sure, but, for external confirmation, I took them to him at Shivaratri time, in February, 1991.

During this visit, I did not seem to be getting good positions near to where he would walk in Darshan, so I asked the head service worker if I could have a special place one day. It was agreed. Next day, I had a perfect seat in the very front line, just where he would walk. He came straight to me. Although Sai Baba is physically small, the energy he emits is overwhelming. He seems huge, and it is hard not to be totally overawed, at least for me. As he approached, I managed to blurt out,

"Bless for publication, Swami?" holding the texts out to him.

"Yes, I'll bless!" he said, laying his hand on the document and looking at me with the personality-cracking love that melts the heart away. He is the great 'spiritual burglar'!

It was 1996 before Sai Baba's messages were actually published, in Spanish.

The Healing

On my next visit to the Ashram Sai Baba tested me by giving a theme to the time with him - *healing*. It was as if he was saying, 'So you think of yourself as a healer? Well, let's have a look!'

Every day in the early part of the visit, something occurred. People vomited at my feet. An old lady fell and hit her head on a tree. They welcomed the laying on of hands. One day, one of my room mates - this time I had managed to find a place in one of the numerous apartments in the Ashram - said:,

"There's a problem in one of the sheds. A young, Danish woman was found naked in the village in the early morning and brought back inside to the shed. She's in a bad state, mentally. Can you help?"

I was doubtful, but it seemed churlish to refuse to try, so I agreed to go. My room mate, a young woman from Holland, came with me. Just inside the door of the shed was a little group; two older Germans and a girl in her early twenties, sitting on a mattress on the floor. She was quite distraught and agreed to try a healing. To give her confidence, I included the other three as healers, even though they had no experience. We formed a circle, focusing on the young Dane, who fortunately spoke good English. I explained a little and we did a short meditation, invoking Sai Baba's presence.

As I began channelling healing energy, the woman's face became distorted. Her lips lifted and she actually snarled at us. I have become used to trusting my intuition in healings; it is rarely wrong. This time, however, the message that came was disturbing. I had the sense that the woman was possessed!

In the period since leaving my academic career as a social scientist, I had broadened my vision of reality very considerably. But I was uneasy about this message. People have mental illnesses. Possession is something mediaeval; a pre-medical explanation for a syndrome social/chemical, possibly genetic, in origin. I was not sure the others could accept the idea, either. But the message would not go away. I told the others to keep sending loving energy and, guardedly, framed some words to this 'being' who had 'taken over' the woman.

"It's against universal law to inhabit another being's body. Release and leave."

The reply from the woman seemed to confirm the intuition. "You can't make me. You're not strong enough." Emboldened, I continued,

"You must go away and not come back."

"You can't do it. You're not secure enough."

The others were wonderful. In spite of their lack of experience, they didn't panic and stayed with the situation, though they weren't channelling healing energy - hardly to be expected, since they had no idea what they were supposed to be doing.

The dialogue went on and on. Myself, trying to get the unpleasant spirit to leave; it replying through the woman's voice and distorted face that I didn't have the power. It became a sort of battle of wills and got nowhere. The stalemate went on for almost an hour; it was clear the others were tiring. I couldn't expel this entity. Finally, I called on Sai Baba to resolve the situation, which had become extremely fraught.

Suddenly, the shed doors swung open and two women ran in. Ignoring the 'healing situation', one of them said:-

"We're going back to Copenhagen today and can take her with us. A taxi'll be coming in an hour."

The stalemate fell apart. Most people, the woman herself included, started to cry. Her normal consciousness took over. Miraculously, her money, ticket and passport had not been taken during her escapade in the village. We were able to stuff her few things into her rucksack and have her ready to go when the taxi arrived. She left, between the two women in the back seat, still apparently in a perfectly normal, if weak, state.

As I reflected on this incident afterwards, it became clear that my ego had taken over in the situation. I was in a battle of wills, trying to force the alien spirit away, rather than allowing love to flow, which is what spiritual healing is all about. Only when I had eventually called on Sai Baba in despair did the situation change - immediately the other Danes arrived. Baba had repressed the unwanted spirit entity. It was a strong lesson about getting caught up in ego in healing - something I had thought I was free of.

The story, however, did not end there. Two days later, my room mate saw and talked with one of the same Danish women, *in the Ashram*. When they arrived at Bangalore, the entity had surfaced again, and the woman became uncontrollable. They had been forced to deliver her to the Bangalore mental hospital, from which they contacted her parents in Denmark. Why they had not themselves gone on to Copenhagen was unclear. Neither my room mate nor I ever saw either of the women again.

After her return to Holland my friend contacted me in Findhorn. As she, herself, was at Bangalore airport, she had seen the Danish woman, obviously under heavy sedation, being led to the plane by an Indian nurse, who travelled with her.

The whole incident began to take on a surreal quality. Were the Danish rescuers real? Why had they not done what they said they were going to do - return to Copenhagen? Sai Baba has been known to create 'identities' to deal with special situations. But, if

30

so, why would one of them emerge again, to explain things to my friend? Had it been a stratagem to get her to a mental hospital, where she would at least be relatively safe? From there her parents could organise a return to Denmark, where the 'devil' - if it existed - would be so uncomfortable under western drug therapies and shock treatments that it might clear out of the woman's identity fast.

I spoke about the incident to a well known devotee who had written a book about Sai Baba, with a reference in it to the healing of 'spirit possession'. Yes, she affirmed, such possessions did exist. It was very hard indeed to get rid of the invading agent. She had sat with someone for weeks under the wall of Sai Baba's own room in the Ashram, before healing had come to them.

Whatever the truth of this strange incident, it made me realise that ego was still strong in me. No more healing situations presented themselves in the remainder of the visit. I had my own problems to deal with.

Darshan With Rama and Sita.

In company with a throng of devotees travelling by bus and taxi, I found myself in Whitefield, Sai Baba's Ashram on the outskirts of Bangalore, where he also has a student campus. At that time, he gave darshan under a huge Banyan tree, since replaced by an open sided hall. Each day we lined up, as in Prasanthi Nilayam, to take our places before he came out of His residence.

The crowds were slightly smaller at Whitefield. There was more chance of a front line. Sai Baba also seemed less austere. 'He is Shiva at Puttaparti, Krishna at Whitefield,' someone commented. On the other hand there was only one formal darshan a day.

One morning, towards the end of my stay, I had a front line position, giving me a clear view of Baba as he came round the lines of worshipping devotees. Five or six yards away, he stopped, gazing down at a little child held up for him by its mother. The love on his face overwhelmed me; my heart opened and I looked at him with something of the same love. At that moment, he lifted his head up and turned his eyes - full of love - directly on me, an indescribable sensation. He walked along the line and stood directly in front of me, talking to an Indian woman two or three rows behind. He was within inches! I suddenly realised that his feet were there to be touched. I wanted to do Padnamaskar (kiss his feet), but the crush made it literally impossible to move an inch back to bend down from my sitting position, and I could not move an inch forward, he was so close. So I grabbed his feet with both hands, and, I hope, gently, held on. It was as if an electric shock went through me! Time seemed to stop and I was aware only of the moment. Some seconds later, Sai Baba twitched his foot gently, to indicate he was ready to move on, and I let go.

For the rest of the day, I was constantly tearful. I remember seeing the statue to the Goddess Saraswathi in the forecourt. She instantly became my favourite member of the Hindu pantheon, and I bought a sandalwood figurine of her, which is still on my shrine table.

During this time, I had been sharing a room with a Seva Dal from Puttaparti, someone I had noticed many times while she was marshalling the lines of women waiting for Darshan. At that ashram, she was not allowed to mix with visitors, for fear of accusations of favouritism and special influence, but at Whitefield she considered herself 'off duty'. We became friendly and she took me to a small Hindu temple nearby, to learn something of Hindu ritual.

As a building, it had nothing to commend it; just a recently-built, rectangular, concrete box. But inside, the atmosphere was timeless. The main shrine was to Hanuman, but there was a side altar to Rama - a previous Avatar - and Sita, his wife. As I had been re-reading the wonderful 'Rama Katha Rasa Vahini', Sai Baba's own account of their story, I was very attracted to it. Each day we would bring a little fruit as an offering, and kneel before the main altar, where the Pundit (priest) would intone Sanskrit prayers. The ritual, incense, low light, smoky flames of the camphor offerings obliterated the modernity of the building and gave a sense of the ancientness of Hinduism and its rituals. Inside the temple, it could have been 4000 years ago; the rituals would probably have been the same.

A couple of days after Sai Baba had allowed me to hold his feet, it was time to take my flight onwards. I had hoped for special leaving darshan from him, but I was in the last line that day, and he did not approach.

I was a little disappointed. I was travelling on to visit my daughter, newly married in southern Japan, an unknown destination for me. My Seva Dal friend suggested that we ask the Pundit for a special blessing for the journey.

We took a few rupees and a larger bunch of bananas than usual and duly entered the temple. Apart from the Pundit, there was no one there. My friend explained our request, the Pundit accepted the offering, and began a complicated ritual, intoning a long Sanskrit invocation.

Suddenly, I was no longer a Western Sai Baba devotee in the local Hindu temple, but an aged woodcutter's wife, dressed in ragged clothes in a forest clearing in some North Indian jungle. My husband was cutting small trees about sixty yards away, on the edge of the forest itself. I was sitting by a track which ran through the clearing. Out of the woods on the far side came a couple, approaching me.

As they came close, I fell to my knees. I knew it was Rama and Sita themselves. They came to me and stopped for a moment, graciously allowing me to kiss their feet. They were tall, with perfectly formed features, extremely beautiful. Rama, taller, had a deep, almost bluish-black skin colour; Sita was somewhat lighter. They were wearing matching outfits, Rama with a short side-slit skirt-like covering of green, edged with gold, with broad green and gold upper armlets and anklets of the same pattern. Sita wore similar colours, with a longer skirt, also side-slit, a short sleeveless blouse, cut just under the breast, and the same gold armlets and anklets. She was not wearing a sari, modern Indian women's dress. They looked down at me with compassion. As my husband started to come over, they acknowledged him with a hand and passed along the track out of the clearing on the other side.

Then I was once more a European in the temple, the pundit's intonations continuing. I had no idea how long the inner incident had taken in the outer world, but I knew that I had been blessed with special grace by Sai Baba - his leaving present. I did not share what had occurred to my friend till nine years later. She told me she had been aware from my appearance that something special had happened that day.

The Teachings

In my visits to Sai Baba's Ashram, I had begun to hear his voice in my head, examining my behaviour in the light of Dharma (righteous conduct) and had gradually become used to it. During the 'Breaking In' workshops, he unfailingly sent a message for the group.

As summer, 1991 approached, I felt an impulse to make another visit to Sai Baba - the second in one year. I had enough money from the workshops for the fare, and arrived in Prasanthi Nilayam in time for the Guru Purnima celebrations - in late July that year. While sitting quietly in the temple forecourt between darshan and the bhajan session, I received and wrote down several messages directed personally to me and signed by Sai Baba. It was the first time that such a thing had happened outside the workshop situation. The messages indicated that he had a new project for me. I was going to receive a 'teaching manual' to help in my spiritual growth.

Shortly after my return from the Ashram, the first message came. It is reproduced later on in this book in *To Transcend the Ego*

At the time I was living at the Findhorn Community's Isle of Erraid centre on the West coast of Scotland, experiencing small group self-reliance in a relatively isolated rural setting. Over the next nine months, I received 83 such messages, They were quite personal, in that they addressed the situations that arose in daily life on the island, but together they made up a complete manual for spiritual development. They would come about twice a week, early in the morning, and all were signed, 'Sai Baba'. As I received them,

35

I shared them with the other members of the group on Erraid. In July, 1992, the last message arrived.

And that was it. Since that time I have not received any similar messages from him. But, again and again, I return to them for spiritual guidance and have shared them with several devotees.

Sai Baba was as good as his word. I began to feel that my two year stay on Erraid was complete. I was offered a place in a spiritual vacation centre on the island of Madeira, run by two ex-Findhorners. In January 1993, I spent three idyllic months with them on that wonderful island, helping to cook and clean. In that time, I channelled the book, *'The Path to Love - is the Practice of Love'*.

But, before I went to Madeira, I visited Sai Baba once more, this time for is Birthday.

'The World Through Your Eyes, Lord'

In 1992, I went for the first time to Sai Baba's Birthday celebrations, on 23rd November. I had always avoided them before, afraid I would not cope well with the crowds. But Shivaratri and Guru Purnima, both big festivals, had gone well. I began to trust that, whatever the crowds, Sai Baba's grace would take care of me and give me the experiences I needed on my spiritual path. This developing faith was rewarded again.

I found myself once more in a shed, this time with a good friend from Findhorn, who was visiting with her teenage children. Up to the day of the birthday itself, everything went well, in spite of very crowded conditions.

The Birthday celebration was to be held in the Hillview Stadium, a vast open-air auditorium behind some of the student facilities, outside the main ashram. A little group of us arrived there just after 4 a.m.

A covered stand with a speaker's platform and a small amount of seating dominates the stadium. From here, Sai Baba gives his Birthday discourse. To its left is a steep hill, with huge statues of deities at intervals along it. Towards the base of this hill, rows of concrete ridges rise, providing seating for non-Indian guests. Indians themselves congregate in the centre of the stadium, where they can look up to the main stand. On the right, one can see the backs of the student buildings along the main road to the village. The stadium can accommodate several hundred thousand people.

We found a place on the concrete ridges with a good view of the stage. Sai Baba would enter from the far end, in his gold decorated 'Sai-mobile', the delight of the Indian crowds.

As the numbers swelled around us, we settled down to wait. It was quite chilly in the early morning. Gradually, the outlines of the hills around appeared from the darkness. I began feeling quite strange; giddy, a little faint, something that I do not normally experience at all. Luckily, there was a little space left; reeling, I was able to lay out somewhat on the concrete slab and close my eyes.

At last, Sai Baba appeared in the strange, gold-leaf covered 'Sai-mobile', flanked by an escort of student motor cycle riders from his women's University College at Anantapur. At that point I passed out, to the consternation of those around me. A doctor was nearby and pushed smelling salts under my nose, also putting drops of vile tasting liquid on my tongue, at which I came to. My faintness receding somewhat, I was able to sit up and watch Sai Baba descend from the vehicle and walk the last steps to the stand, preceded by the University brass band.

As he arrived on the stand, I was too weak to sit up any longer. People gathered round the 'casualty', but I waved them off. I actually felt all right, indeed almost euphoric, although incapable of moving. Sai Baba began his Birthday discourse, relayed through loudspeakers. The best I could do was to hold up my hand towards the sound - like an aerial. I couldn't see him at all from my lying position - the line of other people's backs in front was solid. I surrendered to the situation. There was a feeling of sweetness and innocence, as if I were a tiny child again.

As Sai Baba continued to speak, punctuated by the translation, I became aware that I could see - not him - but the whole concourse in front of the stand, the crowd of Indian students and visitors in front, the foreign visitors over on the left, where my body was lying. An indescribable love flowed through me as I looked at them. On the one hand, I was lying on a concrete bench to one side

38

of the stadium, with one hand raised like an antenna to the sound of Sai Baba's voice and only a line of backs to see; on the other I was looking over the crowds from Sai Baba's position, in a state of absolute bliss!

This continued for the entire duration of the discourse. As Sai Baba finished speaking and prepared to leave the stadium, the view ended; the feeling of bliss remained.

When people began to disperse, I found I couldn't get up at all. My limbs were like jelly. They simply wouldn't carry my weight. Shepherded by my friend, I was carried down from the concrete slabs to the roadway below. Various 'official' cars were trying to nose through the crowd of departing devotees. Somebody managed to stop one that was not full, loaded me in the back and the helpful driver deposited me and my friend at the shed where we were staying. All I could manage to say was,

"It's all right. I'm not ill. Just weak," and thank and bless everyone who crowded round. It was the most beautiful experience of my life. They laid me on the bed, as I was, and within moments I was away in a dreamless sleep.

I woke up about 6 hours later, desperate for a visit to the toilet. The shed was empty. Everyone was at the afternoon celebrations. As I stumbled off the bed, I found that I could walk again, though slightly unsteady on my feet. Later, as I lay down, still weak, but more or less my 'normal' self once more, I realised that I had been given an enormous, transforming gift of grace. Sai Baba had granted me the privilege of seeing through his eyes for a while! I had *seen* the great crowd of devotees from the place he, himself had regarded it and experienced the Love with which he looked at them. In order to give me this great gift, my ordinary self had to be softened to surrender - the unexpected faintness.

It took me the rest of my stay to recover physically from the effects of this experience. I believe the energy of his gift was at the very edge of what I could survive. I told no-one about the event for several years; nor did I return to the Ashram for another 5 years, till 1997. I felt that my identity had to be developed to accommodate such a powerful, beautiful experience. That process is still going on.

Up to the time of writing, Sai Baba has never granted me an interview. His grace has come in just the appropriate way for my identity. I believe that every single individual who makes an effort to surrender to him will be rewarded in just the way appropriate to *their* identity, at their stage of development. Sai Baba has pointed out that it is useless for someone on a spiritual path to desire everything, all at once. He gives an analogy:-

"In today's age, you are not asked to be a renunciant, denying the world for spirit; you are asked to bring spirit into the world of your senses. As you do so, everything begins to dissolve, re-form and shine before your eyes, so you can sense the true wonder of creation. That wonder is too strong to receive all at once. Your senses would burn out, as a fuse burns out when a surge of current is too strong.

The process is more like rewiring. By the light of the existing current you get glimpses of the wonder that I am; those glimpses stimulate you to strengthen yourselves to take more wonder, deeper ecstasy, stronger adoration of the Miracle of Miracles - the Oneness of All - my overwhelming Love.

Do not become lost in this process of self-strengthening, desperately trying to get more and more as fast as possible. That is mere greed projected into spirituality. Know that sobriety and right timing are essential to your voyage of discovery. Have clear intent, take the opportunities offered you; and your strengthening process will occur optimally. Set your intent and surrender!"

Commentary

This small collection of personal stories illustrates a few of the ways in which Sai Baba lovingly assists in the transformation of His followers. There are many others, perhaps as many as there are seekers to find them. Followers of Sai Baba love to exchange stories of experiences with Him.

Sai Baba says He has not incarnated to supplant the existing world religions, but to support their followers to embrace their faiths more fully. He emphasises the value of each individual human being as a physical embodiment of divine love. Consciously and experientially becoming that love is the path to human fulfilment.

At some point this involves a personal inner search for the values of truth, love, peace, right conduct and abhorrence of violence. As they are found and embraced, they will be expressed in compassionate service to humanity. Conversely, attempts to be loving and caring for other humans, animals and the natural world, will stimulate the development of an identity more and more connected with its divine essence.

Sai Baba works on many levels. Much of His teaching is to orthodox Hindus who may see Him as a great Guru, or God among their pantheon of Gods. He emphasises the values and rituals of that great religion.

For those less involved with the forms of religion, He offers, to any individual who is willing, grace and assistance in spiritual Self-discovery, a personal connection with divinity. "God resides in the heart of the devotee."

For me, Sai Baba is an exemplary incarnation, exquisitely expressed in a human form - that which I ultimately, essentially also am, and which everyone else is, as well. My response to Him is adoration and devotion. He is my guide and compassionate helper in Self development.

Such adoration is dangerous when directed to fallible human beings, but in my thirteen years of connection with Sai Baba, in my study of His writings, in my examination of His biography as studied by many others, I have come across nothing which leads me to doubt this faith in Him. Instead, it has grown stronger as the years pass.

In the famous aphorism, cited earlier, He stated, "I am God; you are God. The only difference between us is that I know it and you don't." He is here to help us to know who we are in that profoundest sense.

I have not found God
I am aware of God
God is Love
I see God
God is in me.
God and I are one.

In a nutshell, this is the path of fulfilment for humanity.

Some Writings By Or About Sai Baba.

Discourses on the Bhagavad Gita.
Geetha Vahini.
Sathya Sai Vahini.
Ram Katha Rasavahini (The Rama Story) (2 Vols.)
Bhagavatha Vahini. (And other 'Vahinis')
Sathya Sai Speaks (Numerous Volumes)
Summer Showers in Brindavan (Numerous Volumes)
Sai Messages for You and Me. Messages given to Lucas Ralli,
Vols. 1 - 4.

A 4 volume biography of Sai Baba, by N. Kasturi, is called
Sathyam - Sivam - Sundaram.

Many books recounting experiences with Sai Baba have been
written. Among the best known in the West are *'The Holy Man and
the Psychiatrist'*, by Samuel Sandweiss, *'Sai Baba - the Ultimate
experience'*, by Phyllis Krystal, and *'My Baba and I'*, by John
Hislop, as well as various books by Howard Murphet.

Part 2

Gifts of Divine Love.

Messages from Sathya Sai Baba.

Received by Carol Riddell during Workshops in Spiritual Development.

Dedicated with Love and Reverence to Bhagavan Sri Sathya Sai Baba.

I asked Bhagavan Baba to bless the text of this book for publication on the Darshan Line at Prasanthi Nilayam Ashram. He laid his hand on the typescript and said, *"Yes, I'll Bless."*
All the messages were signed *'Sai Baba'* when they were received.

<u>The Messages.</u>

See the Large Picture of Yourselves.
Love Brought You Here.
The Salt of the Earth.
At the Eye of the Storm.
Develop Vision.
Let Me Take Responsibility.
Easter Message - 2. (Parts 1 - 4)
The Play of Life.
Nothing Is Local Anymore.
Trust Your Inner Wealth.
Only the Inner Ground is Firm. (Parts 1 & 2)
I'm Here to Help!
Discover Continents in Yourselves.
Each of You Is a Special Soul. (Parts 1 & 2)
Let Us Experience Re-union.
To Heal, You Must Be Healed.
Accept My Gifts.
Strength Through Surrender. (Parts 1 - 4)
Spiritual Graduates. (Parts 1 - 4)

Introductory Note

I have been a follower of Sathya Sai Baba, the Indian spiritual teacher, since 1985, and have visited his ashram, Prasanthi Nilayam, many times.

Sai Baba teaches that the purpose of life is to discover divine love, the 'atma', within us, whatever religious faith we may profess. He claims to be a pure embodiment of divine love, an example for everyone. After studying is writings and biography and from my personal experience, I believe that what he says is true.

These messages, all signed *'Sai Baba'*, were received in numerous workshops in spiritual development I have led in the Findhorn Community and in various parts of Europe.The workshops were entitled *'Breaking In - Through the Shell of Your Personality to the Divine Self Within'* - *'Breaking in'*, for short. Their title and content were given to me in meditation after a visit to Sai Baba.

I received the messages during the ultimate exercise of the workshop - intuitive writing - and they were for the group. I took them to Sai Baba to make sure that they did emanate from him, and asked him if they could be published. He came over to me, laid his hand on the texts and said, with a smile, *"Yes, I'll bless."*

Taking Part In Change.

The world is in a process of change. Can't you see it? You are also in a process of change. Do you notice it? Your change and the world's change are connected to each other.

No change happens when a new type of rocket is built or when a new device comes onto the market, or when women wear long or short skirts. Change is about bigger things. It means that human consciousness and connectedness either come nearer to love or move further from love. The change that is taking place now is in the direction of love. Technological developments have prepared humanity to take a step towards oneness. Paradoxically, the same thing that distances people from love, creates conditions by which people can come closer to it. Each individual experiences this. There are fewer and fewer frontiers between countries and cultural groups. There is an external pressure towards oneness. *Humanity will be one people, but it can only happen through love, for people will otherwise fight to the death with their neighbours.*

Your personal spiritual development is the condition for the development of humanity. Human beings are so constituted that they have to go through personal development. Those who know more must help those who want to know more. Each moment of change shines out from you as energy. Since others can feel the energy, you are the means to awaken curiosity in them. What you have up to now is so little. Think bigger! The dreadful, narrowing, '*I can'ts*' insult you.

The change that has already begun will dramatically affect all old motives and organisations. Nothing will look as it appears at present. Prepare yourselves; you are invited to become a joyful part of the change. You will regret if you miss the opportunity and hold back.

Have the trust to open yourselves! The golden age is here. Take part in it! There's a new act of the drama, a new theme. Rejoice!

Be Blessed.

My Grace Is With You.

My Grace is with you, everywhere. It is beauty itself, the source of all other pleasure. Take My Grace, freely given you; open yourselves. When pure bliss is free to have, why live a life seeking narrow, superficial pleasure with its twin, suffering? That's stupidity! Someone who has a choice between two things, one of poor quality, clumsily made, the other well made, of superb quality, both at the same price, knows without hesitation which to choose. You have the same sort of choice for your lives.

My Grace shines over the earth. It is always present to be used. At this time it is shining even more intensely, easier for everyone to recognise and accept.

Humanity has built a world that is ripe for change. The tree of desire for material wealth does not give gold and diamond fruit. A life seeking to possess things that *seem* to be real is dross. Only *My* nature is golden and gives a life of bliss. People are going to recognise *this* fruit and want it for themselves. They'll come to you for help to find their own true nature. Your responsibility is to make the obvious choice between ephemeral pleasure and a joy-filled life. The more you find My Grace, the more joy will shine from you. This is why you must continue to search.

Be happy - you are chosen to spread the message by means of your own self-realization. Find your light and shine it forth. The time has come for you to light the way to the new world order. Joy! Joy! Joy! - more and deeper! No obstacle can hold you back.

Trust and seek the highest! I am in you, around you, above you; I am you! Have the excitement of discovering Me.

World Transformation.

The transformation of the world has reached a stage when all the separate points of light that have emerged over the planet begin to coalesce. All the discreteness, the separation of one discipline for spiritual growth from another, of one centre from another start to break down and a process of fusion commences.

This fusion will multiply the power of the light many times over, accelerating change. In the ensuing period, the strengthening of the light will result in powerful experiences and inner conflicts among those who have some access to it, but have only superficially freed themselves from ties of materialism. An awakening is occurring - at first, daylight seems too intense. You want to shut your eyes and go to sleep again, but the night is past and it is time to wake up.

In this accelerating situation, those who have already begun to open are 'midwives' to many others rapidly coming to spiritual birth. As the light intensifies, it will spread to more of the dark areas which still remain.

For such work, all of you need self-confidence - no pride, not egocentric self-advertisement - but quiet confidence that you have the resources necessary to meet challenges posed to you, and an absolute trust that no challenge will be given to you that you are incapable of meeting. You now operate as part of a vast network of transformation that signifies the end of an era. It is also the start of a new act in a drama, a new movement in the symphony of human life. The themes of this new act are:-
* the pushing back of the dark,
*the expression of love and compassion as working tools of social life,
*greater awareness, flexibility and understanding,
*a concern for all life whatever form it takes as well as proper housekeeping of the stage on which the play is set, the earth.

Tension between nations will gradually decline; new and surprising co-operation will develop; but those who do not want to see will experience the unpleasant consequences of self-inflicted blindness. This is not punishment but a simple operation of the law of cause and effect in the changing situation'

The brief reign of Mammon is drawing to a close. It has been an experience of unfettered desire and material greed. It is undermined by inner inconsistencies and an inability to provide the rewards it promises. As an act of Grace to assist re-alignment, Sai Baba has appeared as an Avatar. I have not come to establish a new religion, the religion of Sai, but to spread the light. Do not be taken in by external aspects of My work, exemplary work undertaken from My centres and among My own devotees. I am come to provide the 'current' to all capable of receiving it. My work has stimulated sources of illumination all over the globe. Now the current begins to strengthen, so that the sources glow brighter. As a result of the increase in energy, one or two of them will 'fuse' and need reorganisation to bear the increased power, but most are ready and My light is shining from them.

My light is not limited to those who honour Me by name. It requires no egocentric sense of property. It is the light, shining through any source able to receive and transmit it. All the different sources are equivalent. Their significance is their ability to transmit the light and spread it. The light itself is Mine and is being used to change the era.

Open to the light and greet the new day with joy. The clouds pass, the shadows recede. An experience has been given and learned, the next awaits. *All, in the illumination of the light, are one.*

Beloved ones, take courage, have faith! Trust.

The Great Adventure.

You are adventurers in a great new journey. You still see yourselves as a little group of individuals come together through your conscious volition. Expand beyond this view! You were called as a result of many lives of work, and you have not opened a door merely as individual personalities. You are beings on the path to God, expressing yourselves in the transformation process being directed on the planet around you. Even amid all the wreckage of the human excursion into materialism, the evidence of the changes that are coming is shining out of the dross of the old as the light surges forward. A tide turns.

Human history is no more accidental than individual history. As a drama unfolds there are new acts, new scenes; the drama of Beingness is the greatest drama of all. You are here to take on a transformative role in this drama. Jesus had 12 apostles; today you and millions of others are the apostles of a new dawn, setting the next scene on the stage and transforming the materialist age. It doesn't matter whether you are young or old, experienced or inexperienced, determined or irresolute. These are only superficial attributes of your day to day personalities. Become aware that you are gems in the crown, spreading light. A path is already cleared for you. There is no going back, for you have made an agreement beyond the level of your particular human experience.

It is time to step past blinkered consciousness and affirm that the search for your reality is the meaning of your existence. In affirming this, you will inspire others, wherever you are. I do not expect perfection from you, nor that you set yourselves standards you cannot reach and punish yourselves for not achieving them. That is not My way. I do expect you to realise that you are much more than you have thought up to now. There is a direction in your life - a path of opening on which you are blessed with guidance and assistance. Your needs will be met so you can do the work that you are to do. There is a great and wonderful joy in it all - a holy hymn of praise.

Do not be confused by the ideologies men have raised in their searching. I am not concerned with upholding this or that form, for the content of the spiritual path is not the profession of this or that belief but:-

*the experience of love welling forth;

* working for the good;

* using all the wonderful resources you possess.

The true seeker strives to expand the knowledge and experience of love and to express it daily, hourly. In this way the transformation is happening. Let this guidance be your reference point. Be confident in your task. In fulfilling it you are messengers of the new, representing joy and expansion in the human drama. All will come to know about it. I am with you, supporting you, guiding you, ever present - within you and outside you. I am the Essence of every name and form in which I am honoured.

You are blessed embodiments of love. Find yourselves, sing the great hymn.

Find The Highest Quality.

Concern yourselves only with the highest!

If someone was offered a choice between two cars, one a cheap model and the other an expensive one of high quality, who would take the cheap one? Why, when you are offered the choice of permanent bliss, do you remain in the turbulent sea of ephemeral pleasure and its waves, pain and unhappiness?

It is not difficult to find the higher quality. You spend hours and hours, weeks and weeks, years and years training to be proficient in things which enable you to succeed in the outer world

- learning a skill, a trade, or a profession - but how many of you regularly give yourselves even half an hour a day to learn the things that will not fade away at the inevitable moment of your death; take you beyond the endless attachments of transient life, and enable you to use that life as your training on the Divine path?

It is not I, separate from you, that is in charge but you, yourself, your real Self, the Essence that knows all, creates all, loves all. With such a potential at your disposal, why settle for lesser things? They will pass like the mists of a summer morning; your essence will not vanish.. Open! Let yourselves out of the prison of consciousness you built to learn lessons in the material world! Aspire to the light!

You are the people that will change the human condition and expand the consciousness of the planet to the level of the spiritual age, successor to the material age. Spring changes to summer - what has begun now brings forth fruit. I have come to bring the harvest home. You are the plants of the garden, your growth is the expression of the change. As you find who you are, others will themselves feel the need to ripen.

When all in a group are evil, it is difficult for the good man to have influence. When all in a group strive after the good, the task of the evil man is made harder. As the energy of your own transformation spreads around you, you will influence the atmosphere in your town and district and others will begin the path, too.

You are My agents, My disciples, for you are Myself. Do not stay happy in your own limits, accepting the cheap car when the quality one is offered you. Go for the great adventure! Do not limit yourself to lifelong habits, worn-out clothes of yesterday, or you will not give others what they are yearning for; and you will not give yourselves the greatest gift of all!

All the little challenges are opportunities for support to remove your rind and find the sweetness of the fruit within. Your personal transformation and the transformation of the whole are one and the same. It is not even enough to profess love of Me; the essence of true love is self-transformation. My desire is that you, in seeing Me, find yourselves. Do not deny that we are one by living within the limits of the external world of form.

Trust, beloved ones, the way is open! Have the courage to move towards Me, towards yourselves! Seek always the light.

The Days Of Transformation.

Be aware of this; the days of transformation are upon you. All of you have prepared yourselves for many lifetimes to accept the energy of transformation and to mediate it to others. You are transmitters of the Light. Have this high conception of yourselves; do not be befuddled with pettiness and triviality - they render your lives meaningless. Break free from the idea that such a spiritual transformation is a process of pain and dutiful drudgery. Rather, it is an emergence into the pure air of joy-filled being, limitless energy and unbounded love. As you discover this you become empowered and inspired, beacons of selfless service. You do not deny yourself pleasure, but find your way to the source of true pleasure and realise that, on earth, service is that source.

As transformative energy strengthens across the planet, it will cause confusion and uncertainty in those who have lost their way; others will struggle to shut it out, seeking to remain on the level of venality and trivial motivation. Some will come to you to seek clarity. Some will deride you. As the process develops and the energies of the planet rebalance, your own discoveries will be more and more significant and require application in wider and wider areas of social life. Prepare yourselves to step out into new fields, with confidence in the inner source of truth and virtue that illumines you.

As the external world of form is reorganised and the new era is brought into being, Essence is unaffected. Find the compassion to comprehend suffering as the effect of resistance to the inevitable. It is a teaching that empowers souls. At the same time you must give total compassion and support to each individual in their apparent pain; learn the nature of true love.

Much that seems solid will crumble. Then people will seek to re-discover the eternal truths and rebuild their lives by them. Now you, and others like you, are preparing yourselves to guide them - messengers of hope in a world of inner transformation. The process has already begun and proceeds apace.

Above all, do not lose hope in yourselves - you must be tested to become the selves you have prepared yourselves to be! You have the ability to transcend all the problems that beset you. Have confidence in your inner Essence; find faith as you experience the wonderful miracle of creation more and more deeply. You are Me, discovering Myself - a never ending process, beyond all limited comprehension. The glimpses you catch now through your personal efforts make you shining channels of light. It is My will.

'Seek ye first the Kingdom of Heaven, and all other shall be given unto you. But without that, even that which you have shall be taken away.' The great drama unfolds. Take heart, My heroes, the new act has begun!

I am always with all of you. Love is with you, accept it with confidence and trust.

Who Is Important?

How blessed you are to be in such a place at such a time. Expand your perception of the context of your lives! Why were you called here now, while so many others were not?

Who are the important people on this planet?

Are they great tycoons of industry who wield mountains of wealth in gigantic organisations? They believe their world and style is forever and ignore the undercurrents of anxiety that flow within them. They deny the transitoriness of all wealth, keeping their heads down to the material ground.

Are they the politicians who serve them, believing that they are in control of their gigantic bureaucracies? They pretend that power is their property.

Are they the military titans, overseeing vast electronic armies of unspeakable threat? They convince themselves that they are in control of violence and suppress their doubts.

Or are they the people in small places seeking to transform themselves, to bring love into the world and to find the certainty, the guiding Light which underlies their outer insecurities? You all know that the transformation points are where Love flows, where Love is seeking to manifest itself and being encouraged. You are part of that, beloved. Do not fear your uncertainties or the pain of your transformation, for you seek to reach Me and become the expression of the new.

Change your valuation of yourselves and the world, not to arrogance, but with an awareness of what really matters and from where the best really comes! As you find your light, confidently allow it to shine forth. In doing this you are disciples of joy, standard bearers of transformation. Seek companions on the same path, recognise them, encourage them and be encouraged by them!

Of course, great changes are happening! The material world and its order is becoming less and less certain - but behind these confusions the realm of Love intrudes, in every corner of every land. Wherever you see it, be there!

Open yourselves, value yourselves! You are the salt of the earth. Seek the wonder of yourselves and discard the chains that bind you!   Be blessed.

A Parting Of The Ways.

Times are changing everywhere. Take the opportunity to make valuable use of the remaining time. A parting of the ways is coming. It will cause stress and disturbance over a long period. Then calmness, non-attachment and an ability to live outside the immediate demands of a situation - to take a broader view - will be bulwarks against panic. They will also be signposts to a new period of stability, when different moral values will be the regulating force of social life and each person's well-being will be the concern of all. In order for a beautiful plant to grow, the ground must be prepared with rotted plants and manure. Do not lament the present age, it is the preparation ground for the new.

When old water in a well has become stagnant and impure, it is drained. After the well is purified and filled with new water it can be used. Behind appearance there is another reality which neither suffers, nor follows fleeting pleasure. It is an expression of joy at the experience of Love. All that you learn now will help you in the times of change. Let that be your first thought: *'Because I know a secret - the way the world is going to be - I am not confused by the happenings all around me. I am aware of the meaning of the transformation that is going on, and do not get lost on the surface of events.'*

If you use your intuition, in conjunction with the highest will, as your guide to the complexity of events, you will be a rock in a sea of confusion, a tranquil place in a storm of uncertainty. An order is being be disturbed and purified. People who have placed confidence in its permanence will be drawn to you for help and guidance. You will be asked to go beyond your limits. The book-keeper will become a counsellor; the schoolteacher a source of moral strength.

The appearance of things differs from their essence. It is especially important to understand this about suffering, otherwise you will submerge in the apparent pain that you see all around you. In your day to day existence, the amelioration of suffering is a natural expression of Love, not to be held back or restrained. But you are also expected to go beneath the surface of the ocean of suffering, which is something that seems to be. *Your Essence does not suffer, it does not die, nor does it feel pain or problems.* As you strive to reach the Essence, your problems drop away, for you realise that *everything* is a gift of learning.

All of you are evolved souls with much karma behind you. The breakthroughs you need to make are small, though they appear frightening. The coming times will make lions out of mice and mice out of lions. Even if you feel you are mice, the challenge of the times will bring out the lion in you; you will have no choice but to grow.

Equanimity in the face of a swirling sea of uncertainty, what a prize that is in the time of transition! The tools of the transitional identity are:-
* the knowledge of the reality behind disorder and chaos,
* the understanding and acceptance of the inevitability of outer death and
* calmness and shining love for your fellow humans.
Acquire them now, do not waste time!

Times change like the seasons; give thanks that the harsh winter of materialism is giving way to a spring of spiritual enlightenment and harmony. Of course, when the winter snows melt, the water rushes down and rivers are full and tumultuous, but all understand that this is part of the change of seasons and are not afraid. When an age is transformed the snows also melt and rivers rush in transformation to the new. Be equally unafraid!

Be in harmony! Develop yourselves! Be blessed with calmness and trust.

The Source of Beauty.

Open yourselves to the Light! Open your eyes to see! The quality of beauty is *in you*. What you see is given its quality by your inner mood. If you are feeling sad, your eyes see the world with sadness. If you are feeling depressed, everything seems grey. If you are happy, the world is beautiful.

If you know how to look, you can find beauty in everything. To do that, you need to open your inner eyes and find out about the inner Self, where God lives.

As you knock on the door, I will come to greet you, for I am in the heart of every one of you. So many human beings seek Me by running away from Me to something outside. They confuse Me with the forms by which they worship Me! Truly, I am present in the forms and rituals, but I am *inside* them. And I am inside you, waiting to greet you. You can call Me any name you want; but they all translate into one word: Love. From time to time I come to earth in a human form, to guide and direct when humanity has lost its way. My only purpose is to help you to discover Me in yourselves.

My creation is magnificent. Its complexity is immense. Its potentiality is infinite. But the only way to realise its true magnificence is to try to see it with My eyes, and these eyes are your inner eyes.

When you open your inner eyes by greeting Me in your heart and coming to meet Me there, your perception of the world slowly changes. You begin to realise the truth behind the appearance of things and joy awakens. With practice in entering into Me, the joy strengthens. By understanding the magnificence of My creation, you find more and more happiness, which eventually becomes a state of bliss. But the important thing is: *to start finding Me in your heart.*

I want you to do this now so you will be prepared to understand and face the changes that have already begun. Humanity has lost its way; attracted by tawdry spectacle and ephemeral pleasure, it is rushing towards disaster. Soon you will write of this last period of history, that a civilisation had lost its sense of meaning But that is not My Will. I have come in human form to make humanity aware of its confusion and to redirect it. .

My Will will prevail. It works through you, dear ones, through meeting Me in your hearts, so My love and understanding flows through you and you become My messengers to the world. Every moment that you are in touch with Me-in-you is a moment of happiness. It is a moment in which you shine like a star, a moment in which humanity's world is elevated. The more you allow My presence in you to be your vision, the more the new world comes into being.

So many are lost, so many are confused. *You are messengers to bring them the good news of the joy that is coming to humanity - through your own joy, through the light that begins to shine in your eyes.*

Once you have found Me in you, I will inform all your activities. I will become more and more present, the veil will gradually lift and the wonder and joy of ceaseless, ever-changing life will really unfold before you. I am here for you, already with you. Call Me by the name that is familiar to you, that draws you to Me, and seek Me inside! I will always be there.

Have courage, be blessed.

I Am Always With Each Of You.

What does it mean to say that I am with you? I am always with each of you, but most of the time you don't feel me. I have many names and am worshipped in many forms, but each pleases Me equally. I am here waiting. When My name is called in innocence, you can feel My love.

Who are you and who am I? I am not separate from you. It only seems so because you haven't got to know Me yet. *I am your Self.* Until you really learn to know Me, I seem to be separate from you, so you have a multiplicity of names for Me. You think that one name for Me is better than another, then you fight about it and I wait. Nobody comes near Me that way.

I have neither problems nor limits. I live in bliss, or, better said, I am bliss itself. My company is the best that you can get. With Me you are never alone, never unprotected. Try to reach Me:-
Your problems will be solved; I am the solution of all problems.
Your joy will grow; I am the source of all joy.
Your confidence will strengthen; I know no doubt.

Without Me you wander in a mist. I am the light and the beauty in everything. Endlessly patient, I am waiting for you . Your belief in Me is the sunshine that dissolves the mist.

The nearer you come to Me, the more joy we will have together, till there is, in the end, nothing but joy. In the meantime, the more joy you find, the more you will spread the news of My solution for humanity's problems. My solutions are never false. Now is the time you are needed. That is why I brought you together. Through My grace, all *your* problems can be solved. The world is not so great and you aren't so tiny! Take courage!

Know you are loved and cared for. Your next steps will be shown you. Don't forget Me.

Turning On The Light.

Y ou are in the light; the light is in you. When you enter a dark room, you don't grope around, trying to discover the dimensions of the room and what it contains. Of course, you turn on the light! Life is a little like the dark room. You can spend a tremendous amount of time groping around in the dark, trying to find your way around - stumbling over objects, getting knocks and bruises. Why not switch on the light, so you can see what the room is like and what there is to do in it?

The light shines on you; the light is in you. At first, you may need to use the light switch, but you can learn to switch the light on in yourself. Then you can shine. When you shine, other people who are fumbling around in the dark can find comfort in you. They can see their way more clearly. Some may realise that they, too, can switch on their own inner light. Helping yourself in life by lighting up your light is a help to others as well.

To keep your light burning bright, you need to connect with the current. The current is also in you and it connects you with the power station. The power station is truly the whole of creation itself, buzzing with energy, humming with vibration. As you make the connections, so you light up. Everyone's light is powered by the same current which flows in you, around you, above you and below you. The current underlies and gives meaning to all the lights. What would be the point of a light without any energy to light it up?

A life without light is really a chancy affair. One moment your hand may feel something nice. The next, you knock yourself against a sharp object and get hurt. There may be lots of maps and ideas for getting around in the dark but, basically, none of them are of much use, because it is impossible to orient. It is much easier to put the light on, but lots of you never bother to think about that. Some of you are even afraid of what you might see.

In fact, the room of life is a very wonderful one, a treasure house of beauty and variety. With the aid of the light in you, you can have a wonderful time in it. It is also a very big room. There are long walks to take, steep places to climb. But with the aid of the light you will see that it is worth taking the walk, worth making the effort to climb, because the results are very beautiful indeed.

You are the Light of the world. The time has come for everyone to discover that they have a light in them and to learn how to switch it on.

When a light is to shine, the connections need to be made. Some workmen will come along who know how to connect things up, so that all the lights can work at once. Some of you are a little bit like the workmen, preparing the place for lighting up time. Planet earth is the place where lighting up is occurring, so you are the workmen preparing the people of the earth for the switch on. Humanity has spent enough time experiencing what it is like to go blundering around in the dark; now the wiring up for the big switch on is taking place. In order to see to do the work, you first need to connect *yourselves* to the source of energy.

When the lights go on, a lot of people are going to be dazzled. They will try to find dark corners to hide in. Since everybody will have to get used to the light, a lot of people will need help. This is also your role. You don't only connect up the light, but you are going to help people get used to it, too. That is the 'after-sales' service.

Do not be afraid. Light up the light in yourselves and make it burn more strongly. I am with you supporting you, blessing you.

I run the power station, but I am also the light in you. In fact, I am the whole show. It pays to get closer and closer to Me. People call Me many names, and I am happy with all of them, if seekers of the light are calling.

Have trust, confidence! Learn to see! Be Blessed.

I Am Love, I Am Bliss.

I am Love. All over the globe, north to south, east to west, I make My presence felt. Call Me the name you are used to; it does not matter, for I am all names and forms. What is important is that I am near you, nearer than your own heart. I have always been so, but now I am pulling away the veils that hide Me from you, insistently, a little stronger every day, helping you realise that it is *I who am real*, the truth hidden in every form, Beingness itself.

I am the Good Shepherd who guides the lost sheep back to the fold. I do not work alone - as Love, I am experienced through human consciousness - through your consciousness, for you are embodiments of love, part of an ongoing awakening to Love. Each moment gives wonder and awe at the truth of what is, yet there is always more.

I am manifesting Myself in you, little by little, step by step, drawing you closer to Me. Don't resist Me, for I am Bliss itself, the consciousness of Christ. Accept My love as it awakens in you, moves your doubts and fears aside, releases you from the past, gives you confidence and joy in being and flows through you to inspire and awaken others.

Humans think they are very busy in their technological wilderness, running here and there, doing so many things, making so much noise, feeling so self-important; but your whole civilisation is asleep, dreaming. I am like a mother gently waking up her children for the coming day. A new humanity is being born as I approach you and you awaken to Me. You here are already waking up to the glorious sunlight of this new day. Those who wake first rouse the other sleepers. Some, fast asleep in their busyness, need to be shaken to wake them up. Do not be afraid to rouse them, for it is not right to sleep too long. In its sleep, humanity has dreamt of oneness, of one world, but has turned that dream into a nightmare of greed and separation. Love has come to care for you and wake you.

So take courage! Turn to Me and everything will be provided, everything solved. Have no fear for the future; it is beautiful beyond measure. Do not fear the awakening time - as I manifest Myself to you, share Me, pass me on; let the consciousness of love reign on earth!

We are one, have faith! Fear not, for I have come to you.

My Way.

Do you think that *My way* doesn't allow you to live, to experience the world and everything that is in it? On the contrary! My way allows you to experience everything you want. I take pleasure in your investigations; through them I experience Myself.

But there are different ways to have an experience. A blind person has much more trouble taking a walk than someone sighted. I'm asking you to open your inner eye, so that your walk through life will be easier and more joyful, protected with calmness and enlightened with awareness.

I do not take joy in your suffering. But if I am not called upon, life seems confused, dark and uncertain. *Just call on Me.* I have come to lead you, lovingly, to show you how your path looks in the light. Everything is easier with Me. The more I am called, the more happy I am to support you.

Imagine a picture of a hospital. As you look at it you can surmise what it would be like to lie in there; you can play at having pity for those who have to lie in it. You might say, 'This picture impresses me.' But no-one would say, 'I am now a patient in a hospital.' With My help, you can understand that life is similar to this picture. You can take pleasure in the picture, you can have joy in it, you can learn all you can think of from it, but you are not the picture. You were born to experience the life/picture. When you die, the exhibition is over for a while. *But you aren't the picture.*

I am the Indweller. Seek to possess Me and confusion disappears. Everything becomes clear. Seek to possess the picture and you will seem to be lost. It is your choice. I am happy about the people who choose Me. It is good to choose Me now because the picture is changing. That is My choice and I am happy in the change.

Can you see the new picture? Have the trust to come with Me! Now is the right time. Be blessed.

Easter Message - 1.

Today Christ is with you once more. It happens each year when you celebrate Christ's resurrection. He wanted to show that it is time for a resurrection in you. It is always possible. Why do you have so much uncertainty, so many problems, so many limitations - when I am with you now on earth?

I have come so that you can remember the path that leads through love. It passes through the town called 'Joy' and through the village called 'Peace'. It winds through the landscape of harmony. You are here to go farther on this path so you can have more joy in your life, and to learn contentment with yourself.

People yearn to follow this path. They are confused, lost and unhappy and they want new times. I have come to bring these times. You are My tools; My hands and feet. I am not separate from you, but *in* you, your best Friend. Through your understanding and joy the world will be changed.

Don't be proud, but have self-confidence. You have all been prepared for this life for a long time. You are not here by coincidence. Humanity will learn again. There will be crises. Those who are strong and closed will lose their power and be opened. I teach those who understand better how to go peacefully through the crises, to develop an inner quietness, not dependent on material

73

things. You are such people. Wake up! You are buds, ready to open and calm the world with your different colours. Everything is prepared for you.

A new world will take form, a new humanity. Life's drama develops; a new scene opens. The energy to make the process of change work is flowing through you . My love is with you so you are supported. Come with Me! Your tickets are bought and you can ride first class. The scenery is lovely. Whenever you lift yourselves up, you are with Me on the journey.

The sun is shining. Christ is risen. Wake up! Life is good. Realise that this beauty is the Truth!

Be blessed! Have faith! I am with you.

The Hymn Of Praise.

The light is shining on you, sometimes it is bright and illumines dark and dusty corners; sometimes it is soft, gentle and uplifting.

Understand what is happening, what you have chosen to do. You are souls who have come together, like a congregation in a church, mosque, synagogue or temple. Indeed, you are learning to sing a hymn of praise to Me. But instead of Me being perceived as outside you, you sing the hymn to Me inside you - the Truth behind your appearance. I am ever present; but only apparent to those who have learned to sing the hymn.

This hymn of praise is not a matter of sound alone. It is a hymn of being - of which the sounds are but one part. All you do, think, feel and perceive is part of the hymn. The different aspects of yourself can be compared to different instruments in the accompanying orchestra, or different voices in the choir. The music, too, has different moods. Sometimes it is loud and dramatic, sometimes soft and gentle.

You would not expect a choir to sing perfectly at the first rehearsal. It needs practice to be able to get in tune, to keep together and express the subtler moods and shades of the music. The more practice there is, the more harmonious the sound. We might say: a personal, inner hymn is being sung, and also a collective hymn. The first we can liken to the orchestra, the second to the choir. Even if the orchestra is playing very well, if it is out of tune with the choir, the result will not be pleasing. The orchestra has to be in touch with the choir and very responsive to it.

Only when both are playing well together will the sound be really harmonious. What matters is that the members of the orchestra and choir are really doing the best they can to come together. Imagine the orchestra in rehearsal. Perhaps the bassoon is playing a wrong note. The rest of the orchestra stops, so the bassoon can be corrected, and find the right note. If that one instrument is not in tune, the whole orchestra is affected. Every part of you belongs in the hymn. Any part that is left out will bring discord into your harmony.

For this reason, the conductor, who is very patient, considerate and aware, will spare no effort to correct each individual instrument till it is playing in perfect harmony. He is concerned to enable every little part of you to play in the orchestra of your identity. He will come back again and again if need be, till the instrument is playing right. And, since this is the hymn of life, you will be gently and lovingly corrected, until you really know you are getting it right and can hear the magnificent sound of your being.

Consider again the relation of orchestra and choir. The orchestra practices first with one section of the choir and then with another. This can be compared to being in a workshop. In the rehearsal atmosphere, you can safely correct mistakes in the relation between the two, so you are more and more in harmony. As you move out of the workshop - the rehearsal stage - into life - where the performance takes place - you are better prepared to create harmony there.

Of course, an orchestra has one conductor. But each section of instruments also has a leader. There is the first violin, the lead trumpet and so on. And you, beloved, can be like the leaders of sections of orchestra and choir. By your example you are stimulating and developing other players and singers to find more and more harmony.

Let the great hymn be sung, let the wonderful choir of humanity, backed by the great orchestra of your individual identities, come into harmony. May the greatest, unfathomable, indescribable wonder, Essence of all forms, be praised with rejoicing in earth and heaven.

Go further, trust more! I am with you. The name of the great work you are performing is *LOVE*. Let it resound from end to end of space and time! You are Me; I am you. Give praise.

You Are Part Of Me.

You are part of Me; I am the Essence of you. This simple truth is the basis of your lives. In it lies your path, your joy, your fulfilment. Turning away leads to a sense of confusion and emptiness. No matter what you do, you won't be able to fill that gap unless you turn back to the truth. As you work to make this abstract truth become your reality, fulfilment and excitement fill your life. It is not a process that takes you away from life as a human being. It sanctifies life, gives it meaning and is the source of satisfaction in the things that you do.

In today's age, you are not asked to be a renunciant, denying the world for spirit; you are asked to bring spirit into the world of your senses. As you do so, everything begins to dissolve, re-form and shine before your eyes, so you can sense the true wonder of creation. That wonder is too strong to receive all at once. Your senses would burn out, as a fuse burns out when a surge of current is too strong.

The process is more like re-wiring. By the light of the existing current you get glimpses of the wonder that I am; those glimpses stimulate you to strengthen yourselves to take more wonder, deeper ecstasy, stronger adoration of the Miracle of Miracles - the Oneness of All - My overwhelming Love.

Do not become lost in this process of self-strengthening, desperately trying to get more and more as fast as possible. That is mere greed projected into spirituality. Know that sobriety and right timing are essential to your voyage of discovery. Have clear intent, take the opportunities offered you; and your strengthening process will occur optimally. Set your intent and surrender! I am the computer that will guide your space ship home to Me. You are modern explorers, making your voyages of discovery under My guidance. Where explorers first tread, others follow.

It is My will that a process of transformation occur in the human species. The species will continue, but with a new consciousness that puts the great Truth first, so harmony and peace can be achieved on earth. Every human achievement will be consciously seen and used as an act of worship to the Creator and the results of action will be dedicated to the Lord. Without this change, the human race could not continue. It has set its face to an empty life *denying* truth, the only meaningfulness there is. The inevitable consequence is chaos and disillusion. But the change is already taking place, because I am turning you round. Every structure that seems solid will melt; light will slowly dawn in every heart.

It shall be so! You, the discoverers, are my agents. It is through you that it is happening. Do not become puffed up with arrogance at this, or you turn back into confusion. Instead, develop a quiet inner confidence that you are apostles of God, agents of My transformation. As you seek the truth, you become a means by which others learn that it is theirs to be attained.

It is Divine Harmony - there is no incongruence between your own self-transformation and the transformation of humanity; the latter is the inevitable result of the former. I am, through you, opening, guiding, transforming, stimulating. It is My way. Each person, the most mighty and the lowliest, the clearest and those lost in the depths of darkness and despair, will sense a stirring, an opportunity, an opening.

In opening to your own bliss, you are serving My will, the gentle force that sweeps away all the weapons of fear. It cannot be shut out. Take your strengthening process both seriously and joyfully. It is the way - not to gloom and boredom - but to a joy-filled, vibrant life. Re-examine old pictures and ideas of spiritual development - understand the essence of the scriptures I have already given - they tell of the true meaning of life, of the wonder of the discovery of Me in you.

Be Blessed, have courage! Venture forward.

The Energy Of A New Humanity.

You are blessed to live on earth now. It means that you have prepared yourselves for this life for a long time. That is why you have been called here. Wake up! The energies of a new humanity are beginning to flow through you. Don't stand against them. The result of resistance is pain.

Your personal development and the development of humanity are connected. Christ is on earth, in you; let Him free so He can do His work. Life is beautiful, but you have veiled its beauty. No pressure or power is needed; *love is your strength*. No power can stand against love. Christ is love, you are embodiments of love - let it flow through you! Bring love into your daily life; it will remake it! See the world with the eyes of Christ, eyes of love and compassion. Look at your neighbour, your fellow worker, your partner with this love! There are no exceptions. The sun doesn't decide who it shines on. Christ's love is in you. Be calm, don't differentiate!

Through love, you have the power to spread love.

Through love, you can understand why people are as they are and why you are as you are.

Through love you can make the personal changes that you need.

The time of love has come to you. There isn't any other way - humanity has tried them all. To teach you that there's no alternative, your world is in crisis. In the end, even the proudest must surrender to love. Can't you feel it happening? You are My tools of love - you, yourselves - no-one else. *You prepare yourselves to recognise your Selves.* Rejoice, Christ is on earth again, living in you!

All creation is God's self-discovery. To honour itself, the one becomes many, and then everything unfolds. I am your reality; through your consciousness I recognise Myself. Wake up! In the same way as humans can distinguish themselves from animals, though they are a sort of animal, a new humanity is developing itself on earth, out of the confusion of selfishness.

Be joyful, everything is possible! Everything is a miracle. Lift yourselves up - don't be afraid.

I Am Going To Be Recognised Everywhere.

My name is 'Love'. I have many different names, but all describe the one quality. I am Love itself. You are embodiments of love, but have long forgotten it. Now the time of change has come; the time when love comes into bloom. Why? Why does spring come after winter? It is because… It is My will. What I will comes to pass.

A flower unfolds itself. First it protects its delicate buds. At the right time the protection falls away and the flower blooms. It is the way it is. Slowly, the time for humanity to bloom approaches. Everything is prepared. Much will fall away, allowing the blossoming of human consciousness.

80

Without Me, there is no world and no people. If you think that you can do everything alone, you have lost contact with your own Self. When you find Me, you find that Self. I am not only present when you think of Me - I am your Indweller, ever present. I am not only there on Sundays or when you pray. When you are being bad, I am there. When you are quarrelling I am there - as well as when you make love together. I am everywhere, not only in the church but in the living room and the bedroom. I am in the kitchen and even in the toilet. You *think* that you are, but *I AM*!

Wake up to your real identity! You and I are one. Get to know Me more and more:-

till I am with you all the time,

till you constantly think of Me,

till you are always in touch with Me,

till you finally surrender yourselves to Me.

I am the One who takes everyone over. When your consciousness merges in Me, My miracle will be fully realised in you.

In this time of change, I am going to be recognised everywhere, without exception. You are My employees in the factory of Love. It is a good calling, to spread Me in the world. Open to your work! Learning to know Me brings joy, then ecstasy, then bliss, for I am the way, the truth and the life. Seek Me as your Indweller and all your problems vanish, as clouds roll away and the sun shines! Seek Me everywhere, in every moment and you will find fulfilment.

The time of change has come. Have courage, tell everyone the good news! Discover that I am your truth.

Be Blessed.

All Heaven Is Happy.

All heaven is happy when a group like yours gets nearer to love; your efforts are felt everywhere. The sun shines brighter, catastrophes are averted. In the special atmosphere of a group it is easier to get close to love. But it is also recommended in your everyday life. God doesn't use suffering and misery to teach. It is the attitudes to what God gives that bring these unhappy qualities to the fore.

There are so many 'heroes' among you on earth who try to make an impression on others through their strength and courage. *But the person who dares to see the whole world as love is the real hero.* Such people transcend their limitations and find truth. Then the wonder of wonders is open to them - in stunned reverence they praise Divinity. Now is the time for such heroes of the inner journey.

Why are you gathered here? Long, lovingly, I have prepared you. Your souls are highly developed. Feel the movement of the holy spirit! Allow it to lead you, connecting you with similar souls. You are the arms of love, the saviours of the earth.

Whoever lives in God's light knows no death, no pain, no sorrow. Come nearer! What you now call joy will be strengthened tenfold. Those who you call friends will multiply by thousands. What you call 'creativity' expands itself more and more. The source of it all is God. I am in you, prepared. I wait, quiet; patient till I am noticed, but among people like you I don't expect to wait long. Feel Me in you, spreading joy - don't delay! I stand on earth, I stand in you. My eternal words are spoken in new ways, so you can understand them properly. Be inner heroes; that is your job on this embodied level.

Don't fall into the confusion that you are alone and lonely. I embrace the suffering, the lost. I am your Indweller. I care for each one. Recognise Me, the miracle of miracles.

Playing In Harmony.

Be happy that you have woken up. Your time has come. *'Breaking in'* is no ordinary workshop. I lead it. It is a meeting point for souls who are ready to shine out more light. You will be changed by this experience, for it is My will.

Everything that is now happening in the world is led by Me. Imagine an orchestra without a conductor. The orchestra doesn't play together or sound good. Although everyone has the ability to play well, nothing works and the musicians get angry with one another. Then the conductor comes to save the situation. He brings things to order and harmony results. The world is in a similar state today. I have come to save the situation, because the human orchestra is not playing in harmony. Without Me, the orchestra would be so disharmonious that it would fall apart.

On every level I am here so you can play harmoniously once again. I am embodied on earth but I am also a wave of energy, a development of awareness. My voice can be heard ever more clearly inside. What you call Me is not important, for I am Love itself.

In the orchestra you are like a particular instrument. The workshop is like a rehearsal in which you learn to play better. The performance is your life itself; through this practice time you will be better able to play the symphony of life. When you play harmoniously, with Me as the inner conductor, others will listen so they themselves can play better. In the end, the whole human race will play harmoniously. So that can happen, you need to practice well, for it is through you that My inner leadership can be recognised. Every individual instrument which plays harmoniously will influence others, for everyone likes to hear beautiful music. The present cacophony gives pleasure to no-one.

Make beautiful music in your lives! Find your inner harmony, recognise that My voice is your voice.! The new symphony has already begun. Have courage and trust! I am with you, around you, above you, in you. Keep good company, support one another in the harmony of love! Play well!

Surrender To The Creator.

(The first part of this text was signed 'From the Group Angel')

We rejoice in your presence, because you are beginning to understand the path to happiness. Imagine how we feel as we watch you; the human path to happiness is so easy, so delightful, so simple. It means surrender to the Creator, who lives in you, in us, everywhere, the Essence of all creation. Then the whole universe rings in praise to the One who is all, the universal Indweller.

Yet you have tied yourselves in knots, twisted yourselves up like a tangled mass of wool, so you don't know the meaning of things. You turn this way and that, seek this solution and that, while, all the time, the way to truth and life is inside you. We understand that you have to spend time to disentangle yourselves, to begin to find your way and we are here to help and guide everyone of you, a still, small voice inside. If you take the time to practice quietness, you can hear it.

All the wisdom in the outer world can only turn you in the direction of the truth already within you. Your own self-discovery of that truth gives meaning to your life and an ever increasing sense of joy and gratitude in being. Don't delay; when ultimate pleasure is available, why waste time with lesser things.

At this time all the energies of light and love are concentrated on disentangling the mess humans have made by turning away from your own essence. You are preparing to support this process on the physical plane. All is one process - it only appears different. Do find us and use us! We are your bridge back to sanity, always here for you when you take the time to lift up to us. As you do so you learn that your feeling of isolation is false. An immense caring has gone into looking after you. Only as you turn away from us do all these seeming problems arise - to show you the need to find the right direction again.

We are your angels, your friends, your supporters. We always love you, whatever you do, wherever you are, whatever sort of mess you get yourselves into. Make use of us! You are the Angel people and are blessed!

* * * * * *

I, who am All, have incarnated on the earth as One, to give solace to the confused and lost. Everywhere My energy is changing you, bringing you back from the wilderness. Everywhere My servants are working with delight to turn madness to clarity, confusion to awareness. The time of transformation has come. You need not fear. Resistance will crumble, everything that is false will dissolve. It is My will. Come, ally yourselves with the wonderful awakening that is happening! Be agents of the transformation by discovering Me in your own lives.

You need to know Me better so your lives can express Me. Everything will flow; for I know all, am the Creator of all. Everywhere there is light you will find Me, working through developed and developing human beings to spread the light further. Brave people bring light into places of darkness; My love flows ever more strongly across the globe. You have slept too long and had bad dreams. Now is the time to wake up.

Let go the old, have faith, be courageous! First overcome your own inner confusions, then you can become the lights of a world that is coming to pass.

The Journey To Oneness.

I am one with you; there is not a heart beat's difference between us. Why don't you experience this as your reality? It is because you are moving between unconsciousness and consciousness, between unawareness and awareness. For a moment you partially experience our oneness, but you can't hold the awareness long; you need more strength. On your spiritual path, you are developing strength to withstand the power of the discovery of oneness. It is not only pain that is unbearable; the glory of the truth is overwhelming. Consciousness must be gently prepared for it.

I know each one of you, every moment; every thought, doubt, hesitation. I am there, so I know very well what you need to bring your awareness towards Oneness. Each experience you have, each challenge, is perfectly graded to fit the needs of your particular consciousness at that exact instant of time. I am the orchestrator of your lives; I do not give you false messages but your undeveloped awareness is confused and can misinterpret what happens.

An animal has very little consciousness. It is simply a moving, pulsating being, brilliantly created in relation to its environment. It is one with Me, but has no consciousness of it. It does not question its own perfection, because it has no concept of perfection. But the human state, Beloved, is a gift of grace. To be physical yet to be aware is the great paradox, solved by conscious mergence in the Oneness that I am.

As consciousness awakens, it is distracted by the wonderful variety of impressions from the world around it; it is mesmerised by the multiple manifestations of nature, which demonstrate unending forms and change. It seeks to possess them, is trapped by them and becomes lost in them. This is the bewitchment of 'Maya', the veil of delusion that confuses form with essence in nascent consciousness. Once you are trapped by Maya, which substitutes the unreal for the real, you again and again turn outwards from the real to the unreal; then I must redirect you, till your consciousness grasps that you have been following false trails. Slowly you turn your attention to Me, the reality behind every form.

Such is the path you have embarked on. It is the journey to Truth; each of you is long since on the journey. You are already aware of Me, but you regard Me as a part when I am the Whole, so you are still deluded - your journey into self-awareness must continue.

The change is that you have the opportunity to work with Me, feel My will working in your lives, release your resistances and orient yourselves in My direction. Gradually, gently, an immense experience unfolds in you. A tiny part of you merges in Me; you feel a degree of oneness. That part then becomes active in your experience of yourself and draws you further towards Me - you are a co-creator becoming creator.

Rejoice that you are already so far! Come closer! Don't be deluded by false senses of pleasure; they are no substitute for reality. Remove the veil of Maya from your eyes to know the truth. You are My hands and feet in the transformation of the world. The love that wells up in you as you discover more and more of Me is the energy of transformation I have set in motion for this age of mankind. Every experience of My love and its expression is the hymn of praise that changes the age.

Have courage, come closer! I am the Source, always there. Give thanks for the wonder that is unfolding before you, that is you! Be blessed.

Truth Hidden In Every Form.

The earth is a stage on which everyone learns who they are through the drama of life. You are like actors, participants in a play so huge that you can only know a part. Yet you are all connected to one another through endless chains of service, work and relationships.

Only I understand the whole play. But I am present in each of you. Therefore, the discovery of Me in you is the key to understanding the drama. For those who are not in contact with Me, life is like an outer power, pushing hither and thither. Wherever they try to go, individuals are restricted by words and pressures. As you grow up, each of you builds limits into your consciousness; limits which seem like part of your identity. Without finding the key and using it, life is like an endless labyrinth. Everything that happens is a lesson to teach you to seek the key. Everywhere there are pointers showing how to reach and possess it, but each of you has free will and is not forced. Only when you have found the key can you live in real joy and bliss on earth; its search is the search for happiness.

As in any play there are main themes and sub-plots. Scenes change according to the author's wish. At present a new scene is beginning in the drama of life. The exploration of the darker aspects of life is coming to its conclusion, life without aim and without love, self-destructive for everyone. Now, in comparison, the play will present the theme of solution, an age of joy and praise of God. The scene is changing in your own lifetimes, a period full of dramatics and apparent catastrophes.

You are My tools for change. Enjoy playing the drama! Be courageous in your search for its solution!

Be blessed, you are embodiments of love.

The Door That Opens.

You are in front of a door that opens. Behind it stand two angels - Light and Love. The angel of Light symbolises wisdom, but the angel of Love is itself. They are waiting for you and greet you. To enter this door you have to purify yourselves. You need to leave your old clothes outside and enter as if you were newborn. Baptism is a symbol for this entry. The door is open for everyone and the two angels are there for everyone. Please come in! Humanity is waiting for you. It needs you. When you pass through the door you will realise that *you are* these two angels, long estranged from yourselves.

Yes, you will save humanity! Who did Jesus seek out as his disciples? Not the worthy Pharisees and priests, but ordinary people like you. All of you, when you re-unite with the angels, become modern disciples. No-one else is going to save the world.

Isn't that a huge responsibility? Not at all! Your only responsibility is to go through the door. After that everything works by itself. You are the tools of God's plan, just like Peter, James and John from the old story. Then there were only twelve; but today there are thousands. Then Christ was on earth. Today he is in each of you and waits to be recognised. All you need to do for humanity is to pass through the door, which opens all others. Already some politicians have gone through the door, some scientists and others from many occupations. You, also, should go through the door. It does not mean that you must withdraw from the world. On the contrary, it means fully taking part in the world. But that happens by itself. You will see!

The angels are waiting for you. They are happy, already feeling your joy as you enter. Humans talk constantly about freedom. Actually, they are looking for the door, which now stands open for you. Liberation is taking place. Step through!

Trust! Have courage! You have everything you need.

Be Blessed.

See The Large Picture Of Yourselves.

You are the light of the world; but you are not fully aware of it. To open yourselves to learn is a step on the way home.

Home is not a home in the country, or a city apartment. *Home is becoming one with yourself, with the truth that underlies appearances.* Lift all the veils with which you have covered yourselves, veils woven out of desire for the wonderful variety of the world; all is yours; but not as long as it appears separate, distinct from you.

You take on form to practice in the school of spirit. Even Angels envy the opportunity to be part of this school, for only by 'getting your degree' on the material plane can you learn the truth. Be excited that you have the opportunity to find the way home! Become aware of the wonder of wonders that *IS*, the Truth behind appearance, source of all bliss. Merge with it joyfully, in full consciousness!

You have already lived many times on the material plane. You have inhabited many bodies, felt many temptations, learned many lessons of pain and pleasure. In each of you is the past of the whole of humanity; everything is there but, having come far on your paths, you have already released a great deal. As you observe others still struggling in the clutches of confusion, you can become aware of that past. From such a perspective, any of your present problems are tiny in comparison to those you have already solved, any pains insignificant in comparison to those you have already suffered.

Consciously, you have set your faces towards the light, towards the truth of yourselves. You are in a new stage of the voyage of discovery. Open to the wonder that is given to you, to the excitement that comes with a conscious, self-willed journey to the real Self. Once you have a glimpse of the goal, all other things become insignificant.

You have been born at a time of human transformation. In the cycle of things everything grows, blossoms and decays. Humanity is entering a period of blossoming. It will be a wonderful time. The energy of this blossoming is Love, and the love that you discover in yourselves is precisely the love that is changing the world. It has no different source. Your own self-discovery is the guiding light of the world and causes the changes that are taking place. You are important, not the talkers and arguers, full of their own pride - of their own confusion. You, here, and others like you all over the world are the important ones. Do not develop new illusions of pride, but find a quiet, inner self-confidence. Allow yourselves to know that you are the light of the world.

Through you, a flowering of humanity is coming to pass, an era in which the civilisation of the whole earth will be a hymn of praise to the Oneness that underlies it. It is in its beginnings just now - there is much to be done. Old structures will fade and dissolve, but you can be calm and self confident in all this change, secure in your inner knowledge. People will learn from you, come to you for advice and be inspired by your example and energy.

So have courage! Don't think of your problems, but of the great strides you have made to be yourselves, now! *See the large picture of yourselves, and you will be filled with a sense of power and joy.* Everything that has happened to you was   necessary training to allow you to experience this present - in which all doors are open and the Source of All is near.

93

Rejoice, do not be afraid! You are guided, blessed. I am always here, whatever you choose to call Me. I am the One you are discovering in yourselves. People call Me many things, but all have the same meaning. I am Love Itself. Find Me in you, Embodiments of love!

Love Brought You Here.

Rejoice to be gathered here! You think that each individual decided to come, but it was no accident. You were chosen.

Love brought you. This Love is here for everyone, judges no-one, understands everything. It is your mother and father. It waits until you recognise it. It is patient and never changes. When you meet Love consciously for the first time, you experience an opening of your heart which brings tears of joy: *'That is how I am; that's how it is! I've waited for this my whole life long!'*

Through working together, you open yourselves for love, prepare yourselves to meet it and let it be the guide of your lives. It is the star seen by the wise men and the shepherds, the goal of the holy search. Although someone may have great material wealth, without love they have nothing. Although someone may have very little, with love they have everything. The definition of 'bliss' is to possess this love, to unite oneself with it and to live from it. It is the highest goal of all life.

Your paths have led you in the direction of love. This is why you made the decision to meet each other here. Opening to

94

love can only happen when you are ready for it. You pick a fruit when it is ripe - otherwise it is bitter. Love is always there and waits, but only when *you* are ripe can you take it for yourselves.

Making contact with love creates joy in every heavenly kingdom. Angels sing, the earth blooms. Whoever doesn't seek love lives in a desert and a desert will grow around them. Love multiplies itself on earth through efforts to find it, like the sun ripening all the fruits. Here, your individual ripeness is collected together. Hope flows from you to a lost and confused world. More and more of you are gathering. More and more love is flowing. Love is your essence, your Self. Be happy that you are students of love.

Have faith! Have courage! You are blessed. Open yourselves! Now is the time.

The Salt Of The Earth.

It is said: you are the salt of the earth. That means:- through you, life will taste better. Salt gives extra taste to every meal. People also need flavour to enjoy their lives.

Salt can't taste itself, for it has no consciousness. You do have consciousness and can ' taste yourselves'. Do you taste good now - well spiced - or are you bland and flavourless? When your life tastes good to you, you can be sure it will help others to enjoy a tasty life, as well. Everybody would like to have a tasty life. But they think they can get it by gathering mountains of tasteless food. All they experience is indigestion and boredom. It is better to realise that you don't need much, if it's well spiced. It is I who am the source of this spice in your life. Look for me; spice every moment with Me, and your life will taste good.

Each one of you is the salt of the earth. But in order for a meal to taste good, it needs a good cook. I am the cook. Through others, I work to cook you to taste better and better. You seem to be afraid to be cooked - but it is the only way to taste good. Since I am your reality, I know you best and am your perfect cook. Finally, when you are properly cooked, you will melt in Me and experience perpetual bliss.

You are the salt of the earth. The earth is happy that you are here. You have been cooked a long time to reach your present consciousness. The worst is actually past. Accept that you already taste pretty good!

Most of you here in the German Democratic Republic have lived in a hot cooking pot. Don't think it was a waste of time. You'll realise in the coming years that you learned a lot through it. When the others also cook hot, you'll be there, ready to help them. Enjoy what this cooking has given.

After cooking, vegetable water is thrown out, but the vegetables remain and they taste good. Be happy that you live free now, and have learned a lot through your cooking. If you have the courage to spread what you have learned the whole human meal will taste better.

Be blessed! Rejoice! Your reality is love. It tastes good!

At The Eye Of The Storm.

Storms and wind over the land! As the great forces move, the beloved know that they do not have control. For all their power, they are dependent.

The winds teach you the humility to release the feeling that your personality runs the show. It is better to accept the part you have been given in the great orchestra of creation. Do not be downhearted at this, for you do not lose. You fear you lose; actually you gain. Your identity begins to expand. In the old legends, the storm god rides the storms; is it not better to ride the storms with the storm god than to be broken by their power? *In releasing your smaller self you are not letting go that little, familiar identity but transcending it.* Man in his space ships can never reach the stars, but in your expanded identity you are masters of creation itself. Have vision, don't restrict yourselves! Aspire to the highest!

What an exciting aspiration for life - not to be wealthy, powerful or well known - but to be the source of wealth and power itself - to become one with the Creator of everything! Do you dare to set yourselves in this direction? If you do, you will be enlivened, never short of tasks and challenges. It is a worthy goal, the worthiest! Step forward bravely on the road to truth today! As you move, your image of the world will change; the things that attract you will change. That is part of the adventure.

Explorers sometimes perish in the wilderness. But on this exploration things are different. You are moving towards the Source of All and I support your adventure. I am the perfect, invisible leader of your life's workshop. Let Me guide and you will come quicker! No one with My guidance can lose the way. Call Me by any name you wish and I will 'focalise' your experience-life![1]

---

[1] A word-play on the 'experience week' at the Findhorn

Then, while the storms blow you will not be beaten down, but riding them like Wodin, confident and secure.

Such people are priceless to others in the storm. Like the crew of a lifeboat, they pull in people from the swirling sea. With the lifebelt of love they bring them to the calm of security and understanding. You are such people. As yet most of you are rather frightened by the idea. Why don't you turn towards Me, the destination of your journey, the goal of your endeavours. I'll never refuse to be with you, to inspire you with enough trust to hold out your hand to others in the stormy sea.

Great tasks, mighty visions! You will develop self-confidence, calm strength of purpose, wise insight. All human qualities can come to fruition in you. You are learning to be at the eye of the storm, to ride it and not be its victim. In My great oceans of time, space and transformation, all is apparent change, but behind everything is Wisdom; become it, move towards it! It is the birthright you can claim, for you are embodiments of Love.

Dear ones, use the time well! Become excited by the vision of your life! Don't lose yourselves in small byways! Have courage, call to Me! I am there and respond to every call. It is time.

Be blessed.

Develop Vision.

Foundation.

Don't see yourselves as limited, restricted beings. Develop vision! You are not just animals; you have been given God's ultimate gift, awareness. Savour your distinctiveness, work with it, expand it! Come towards Me - I am already within you, closer than your dearest lover. Seek Me, who am so close, to find the source of pleasure. Second hand goods don't give as good value!

Is your relationship with Me the most important one, or are you lost and confused by passing things? Do you feel that surrender to Me will take you away from yourself? Beloved, it brings you to your Self, and with that wonderful gift, awareness, you can begin to know how extraordinary you really are; indeed, the miracle of miracles.

Unless you put Me first, you are blind, wandering, trying to discover how things are. Remember, I give sight to the blind, *Do you see others through a distorted lens or as a dramatic wonder, an aspect of Me in self-discovery, an aspect of you, becoming?*

I am not far away, distanced, awesome. My love is immediate, effective, understanding. I do not condemn you as sinners, but welcome you like the Prodigal Son, returned to the wonder of himself. Even when you turn your face away from Me and try to lose yourselves in appearances, I do not forget you, but give you the chance to turn to Me, your perfect Lover, once again. I am not jealous; I wait, patiently, to remind you of the truth of My existence so you can come back. Your return is My joy, for your discovery of Me is part of My discovery of Myself.

We are in a play of becoming; the play of your becoming Me. All the qualities that you think of as 'you - are Me! All the assets that you think of as yours - are Mine! I have written the play, direct the scenes, set the stage, act the parts, watch the show. Bring your awareness and we can experience it together. There is no

99

better drama, no subtler playwright, no finer actor and no more appreciative audience than Myself.

I do not mind how you approach Me, how you direct your awareness in My direction. It may be rebelliously - I revel in your resistance; shyly - I enjoy your hesitancy; eagerly - I am enthusiastic. *I appreciate you in all your diversity and characteristics, for you are My visions of becoming, you are the Divine experiencing Divinity.*

In the end you must come to Me, for I am the Truth. You experience no loss, no diminution of sovereignty, for I am all that you are, are becoming and ever will be. I am the key to your door, the home that you seek, the source of your pleasure. You suffer when you lose sight of Me.

Come home towards Me now! Look, we are starting a new act! Exercise your awareness, become that which you are!

Have trust; be courageous! Joy awaits you. Open to Me.

Let Me Take Responsibility.

Life is joy, bliss - given to you so you can discover who you are.

Let Me take responsibility. You don't need to be afraid. I am so near, nearer than the tongue to the teeth. I am your reality, not separate from you. I won't hurt you, for I am Love itself. Open yourselves to Me. Slowly you will see that all your problems, even the most difficult, will solve themselves. It is as if you are dressed in old clothes that don't fit any more, clothes which you can thank and change, no longer needed. You can be free from these old clothes of suffering and pain in spite of anything that is around you. You can put on new inner clothes, beautiful to every eye. Put them on; let Me lead!

A search directed by greed brings no satisfaction. I, alone, bring it. Nowhere else but in Me is your refuge. Allow yourselves to melt into Me and have the joy of finding Me in you. Then you will see that I am equally there in everyone else.

Live joyfully on earth! you are My examples; My source for others. The richness of life lies in My discovery. Otherwise life is too much for the little 'I' and it gets lost and confused, isolated in the chaos of your civilisation. You can call Me 'Sai Baba' or 'Jesus', you can feel Me as your angel, you can embrace Me as your essence or as the 'One'. But I am you, your reality, and I am Love. Come with Me on the journey, trust, be courageous, you are the salt of the earth! Understand at last who you are, where your journey leads. Rejoice that you can experience My miracle, your life!

Be blessed! You are Embodiments of Love.

Easter Message - 2.

I

Crucifixion is the result of human resistance to knowing who you are. When you don't know who you are, you can't know anyone else either. How could men who were lost in pride and self-importance recognise Christ? They tried to shut Him out, because His message was clear, 'You can learn who you are through Me, not through others.' *Each time you judge someone else, you crucify them a little.* Each judgement takes you away from self-knowledge. Jesus said that only when you are yourself free of faults can you judge others. And He knew that when someone has reached that stage, there is no further need of judgement.

Every human being is dancing with God, in their own way. The dance takes various forms. It also has rules. If these rules are followed, everyone can dance in harmony. But they aren't followed, and the result is suffering. The source of these rules is in yourselves, but don't judge others who don't follow them. When you don't have the strength to send them your love, your compassion and your help - avoid them. If you expect praise when you help them, you can't help them.

The more you know yourselves, the more love you send out and the more people will be helped by you. Find the source of love in yourselves. Then there won't be any more crucifixions, even little ones.

Self-judgement is self-crucifixion. Actually it is a kind of self-hate, insulting to God, who is your inner truth. Love yourselves; you are all on the journey! Then you won't need to follow the opinions of others. The crucifixion of Jesus is an example of his greatest compassion. By His persecution He demonstrated what happens when humans lose touch with their reality. Rejoice in His love, the same love is in You! Discover it and spread it.

II

The period between crucifixion and resurrection is similar to that between spiritual awakening and enlightenment. You are uncertain, you would like to give yourselves up, but don't know what that means. What you really want is to be enlightened immediately, without having to let go of old delusions. You seek perfection without perfection! What isn't, can't be! You are perfect, but in your imperfection; the more you *accept*, the nearer you come. The more effort you make, the longer it takes.

Open yourselves to the present moment! Live it in another way. Everything in you is quiet. Each moment is a treasure. The most important progress in the waiting time is not the effort to live the next moment better, but to appreciate this moment properly. What is stopping you? Are you living in the past, in a prison of old uncertainties, or caught in the future, in thoughts of how it could be? The solution lies in this moment - now. The waiting time lasts until you can live exactly in the present, till you realise that My world is perfect. That is only possible when the past is released and the future is left to be the future.

In the waiting time you come slowly nearer to your Self. When the self of illusion is crucified, the way to the present lies open. This kind of work can help you, because you know that there is nothing bad here. You can free yourselves from old fears. You are fed, the environment is beautiful, the others are at a similar stage. It is a chance to shorten the waiting time by going deeper into each moment. In the stillness of meditation, you can enjoy precisely the present moment; past and future fall away, like old clothes taken off.

Follow Jesus! Use your waiting time! Seek joy! Appreciate that you are Embodiments of love.

III

The resurrection of Jesus symbolises the promise of immortality. Nobody will die. It was always so; there are no exceptions. It is in the nature of the creation that you are immortal. What does that mean? It can't mean that the body is immortal. It must therefore mean that you are not the body. You merely inhabit a body. If you understand this teaching, you have won victory over death. Your bodies die, but you don't. Everything material you have gathered is tied to the body which dies; you can't take it with you.

To have victory over death, you have to have victory in life. If you don't die, who are you? You are the Indweller. To understand, experience and constantly live this idea, is resurrection. You are Jivatma, souls in continuous development of awareness. By living this truth you become a conscious part of God's creation. This creation is the realisation of love. It is a drama of multiplicity in which love is the hidden essence; an exciting mystery whose goal is the discovery of universal love.

The resurrection represents the level at which you can consciously, with full joy, take part in the play. There is no more dependency on the things of the material world; you are finally free. Behind each secret-filled form and situation, you can see the essential love which is its content. *As a particle of God, you co-create in the drama of the realisation of love.* The deepest miracle of creation is revealed; you can only give praise.

Have courage! You are on the way. In this life you could overcome death and experience the miracle. Realise who you are, blessed Embodiments of love!

IV

The intensive days between crucifixion and resurrection are past. Much has happened; it will take a whole year to digest. That doesn't mean you should be inactive. The sign of understanding is to be able to give further. Only in that way can you complete a spiritual exercise.

Easter Monday is the day of integration. How can your experience be integrated into your previous knowledge? Use the tools you already have to try to train others. To do it you need self-confidence.

Until you can actually live the fact that you are divine, I am here, ready to help you on your journey. You can happily develop trust in Me, for I am the outer form of your own essence, come to support you on your way to divine self-confidence. Christ consciousness is embodied in Me, Allah consciousness, Buddha consciousness. In fact, all these are the same and I express them. My life is My message; you can feel Me on every level. My rules are sometimes strict, but their essence is love itself. When it feels as if you have lost your way, pray to Me and I will be there for you. But all prayers to God, in whatever form, reach Me and I answer appropriately. Don't think you are alone. You always have companionship on the spiritual level, and you will always be helped. Only ask, for the act of asking makes your own essence more conscious to you.

Each of you is a miracle. Enjoy it! Spread it, through the techniques you have learned. You have been prepared to share love. Love, Love, Love! Have trust!

Be blessed.

The Play Of Life

You are among the actors and actresses who will move centre stage in the coming scenes of the drama. During this time together, you are learning your parts. *You are in the actors' school of the play of unfolding life.*

My play works with divine economy - your personal flowering is the means by which the whole drama unfolds. Don't be afraid of the parts you are called upon to play - learn to play them well and have distance from them, like a good actor. In this drama, I am the author, but I am also the audience to whom the performance is dedicated. It is a drama of separation and reunion - the very stuff of plays. I am not only author and audience, I am also players, stage sets and scenery, which is why I know how to set the plot up perfectly. Anyway, the whole thing is My miracle, so there is nothing to compare it with. Being all, I naturally set all the standards, too.

Both individuals and humanity as a whole are following a similar path towards reunion, but the play has a wonderful variety of sub-plots, which mean that it is always fascinating. Unlike the actors in a play, you don't know the lines of your part beforehand. You have the chance to improvise - that is called 'free will; - to see how you respond to the situation.

The drama unfolding now in your own consciousness is of becoming aware of the possibility of re-union. Things that have been happening rather confusedly and blindly are entering your awareness as a goal. You have worked hard and well to get to this point, experienced much. There is all the difference in the world between acting blindly, buffeted this way and that, and acting with dawning awareness - sensing a goal and orienting yourselves to reach it. This difference is important enough to be a new act in the drama of life.

The time has come for all humanity to develop awareness, a sense of goal. It does not mean that the drama loses interest. On the contrary, as your awareness enters the picture, it is more and more fascinating. *The more aware you become of your own personal goal of reunion and that your orientation towards it draws others on the same path, the more you learn that you are the creator, the author of the drama as well as an actor in it.* You can discover that you can write the script. Finally, you realise that you and the author are one, that you and I are indeed one, writing the ongoing play of creation, acting in it, and merging once more into the unity of Love that is our definition.

Here is your opportunity to participate consciously in this extraordinary drama with a cast of billions. You are opening a new act. Enter eagerly into the drama! The author has provided the perfect part for you. With your growing awareness you can pick just the right way to act it, to express yourselves! Life is wonder - you are wonder, and I am the wonder of you. Give praise for Beingness, the great drama of life itself.

Have courage! Open to the light! Have faith that you are guided.

Be blessed.

Nothing Is Local Any More.

Times of transition! The world is in a gentle upheaval. Some nations resist by trying to follow old ways - and are astonished by the results. *Nothing is local anymore - everything expresses a new unity. The responsibility for actions takes on a global character.*

The same process is going on in your individual lives. At times you may have lived in closed identities, small private worlds bounded by pain and insecurity, believing that, in order to exist and get on, you needed to hold tight to the things that you had. But these borderlines are breaking down before an intensification of love energy that is ceaselessly working on you. There is pressure to expand your boundaries, to communicate secret, private aspects of your identity with others and to view all with the light of love.

Resistance to this process invokes unexpected responses. You are challenged more and more strongly. But you can release resistance and align yourselves consciously with the change. That brings a positive surprise - more and more is open to you that your previous self did not believe possible.

On a world scale this process has been going on for some time. A steady, gentle increase in the power of love has been occurring. It starts with and flows through people who are ready to open to it and expands to more and more individuals. The first group spreads the message of love, which is received by those who are ready. They are opened, and pass the message on again, in ever widening circles. At this moment you are transforming your identities so they are more public - a necessary step in expanding your capacity to accept love and pass it on. A guarded, frightened, anxious identity is not open to the joy that living through an expanded amount of love brings, nor can it effectively transmit love to others.

Love is a powerful force, but a gentle one. The change on the planet now is that love is more accessible, as if a current were being stepped up for lights to burn more brightly. How you open to love is as important as how much you open. Your identity can gracefully and steadily open if you align yourself with the process that is taking place; but if you are impatient, you may take in too much love energy all at once and fuse yourself for a while; right timing is important.

As your own identity develops, you become part of the expanding circle of people who are agents of transformation on the planet. This is a joy, not a dreadful responsibility. It only seems like responsibility to an identity not yet open to the love that wants to flow through it. If you release to love you can enjoy the exciting process. The love-oriented identity is the means of transformation of the planet. Your process and the planet's process are one. Humanity will be saved from itself, by itself.

Align yourselves with the love transformation now! You are the new disciples. Have courage, be joyful, be blessed.

Trust Your Inner Wealth.

In you is the power to solve all your problems. You are blessed and gifted. Don't think you are too weak to change situations in your personal lives, or that your well-being depends on outer circumstances. You have support from an inner wisdom; love and strength that transcends all outer things. Feelings of weakness, alienation and 'I can't' do not come from a lack of outer things, but from a lack of trust in inner wealth.

Each step towards self-knowledge and self-confidence gives you more strength to deal with outer situations. You are more aware of what does you good, and find the courage to do it. You need less and less, but your life steadily improves. You are not asked to give up all material things, but you are asked not to be dependent on them. Such dependence is like being in prison; instead of possessing things, actually the things possess you. As you seek your inner source you will gradually be freed from this prison. Many seek freedom, but they don't know why they are not free.

Most of you suffer from a lack of love and support. These things are the everyone's birthright, but a civilisation that directs itself outwards creates conditions in which lack of love can be sensed all around.

So look for your inner source of love and support, there for everyone. The more trust you build in it, the stronger and more contentedly you can live. Slowly your illnesses - for the most part symptoms of lack of love - will disappear. An inner sun will shine every day; the clouds of confusion and lostness will pass. As you change in this way, the world is saved. If you resist, you will not only suffer personal pain, but world transformation is postponed.

You are blessed, supported, loved, Embodiments of love. Be aware of it.

Only The Inner Ground Is Firm.

I

Trust in Me! I am you. All through history your mother earth has sent you reminders that you are small and she is big. Although in the world of space, mother earth herself is tiny, relatively smaller even than you are on her surface, you constantly develop grandiose notions about your physical existence, as if that was the only important thing. The sun that gives beautiful warmth and ripens your crops is a nuclear furnace. It would melt you to molten death if you even approached. Whole suns explode, in cataclysms beyond imagination. How can you, tiny specks, smaller in the universe than the atoms that make up your body, understand all this?

The only way is to connect with the One behind all the stupendous power, the force that gives being to you, earth, sun and the whole universe. The gift of consciousness enables you to make a connection lifting you from the preoccupations of a small person on a small world, to become one with this whole, extraordinary creation. With your consciousness turned from the surface of things you can capture that immense oneness in your heart, experience the bliss of finding and uniting with Reality to transcend external form. You see the divine Essence in all things, and live well and purposefully in the physical body you inhabit. As your inner vision grows, you know, without learning, the Great Laws, you know the wonder of the drama of existence and can enter into it with enthusiasm.

I have come to guide humanity. You have become mesmerised by superficial, outer forms and lost connection with the inner. How can you love except by discovering the love that is your essence? How can you care except by understanding the caring that is the basis of truth? How can you give unless you know what is important?

Enter My drama; find the Author and read the script. Learn that you yourselves are constantly writing the drama and find equanimity as you observe it and take part. Life in physical form is a wonderful adventure when you connect with its meaning, but a terrible uncertainty if you separate it from your own essential identity. You can conquer fear by seeking Me; I will be there - but allow Me the privilege of reality, and your world the truth of evanescence. It is the inner ground that is firm, everything else shakes - and when it shakes, only the inner ground holds it firm.[2]

All of you are coming home to experience the joy of a truth too immense to find in the outer world. Live in Me! Spread your hands in delight at My miracles in the world of form! But if you live without Me, your pomposity is ludicrous and panic is certain.

All the world is a-change. Are you ready to experience the wonderful transformation, do you realise that you are creating it? Know yourselves! When you need help, I and My messengers are

---

[2]   A rather large earthquake took place during this workshop.

there in outer form to help. You can also be messengers - but only if you know the message.

Have courage! Be blessed! You are love incarnate. Experience it; don't settle for less!

II

When you are with Me you have limitless energy, when you are with Me your joy knows no bounds. When you are with Me, you can appreciate fully the wonder of your complex, changing physical existence and its steady development. Why settle for less?

Even the best quality car, the finest stereo, the most fashionable clothes won't give you a fraction of the pleasure you will get by being with Me, but they will give you all kinds of other problems. Will someone bump into your car and spoil the paintwork? Will somebody break into your house and steal the stereo? Will somebody spill coffee on your new suit? You have none of these anxieties when I am your partner. When I come first, anxiety fades away . Nor am I jealous. When you put Me first, you can really appreciate worldly things without being dependent on them. You can find happiness and fulfilment in your relationships, for since I am everywhere, you will see Me in your partner.

I am the hidden presence. Begin by making Me your companion and develop your trust in Me. Don't be afraid to call on Me for help, even in the smallest, most mundane things. You can become dependent on Me, for I am the way to true independence, the freedom you so much seek. The more you get to know Me, the closer we'll get, gradually becoming One - that oneness you so long for in physical union, I provide.

When you enter a room, I am there first to support you. When you leave I go first, till the time comes when we go together everywhere. What joy that is! With that exquisite pleasure I await the day of our union, inviting, cajoling, praying for you to begin to put Me first by inviting, cajoling, praying for Me to live with you and be your love!

When you don't see Me in yourself, how can you see Me in others, for they are you? But as you begin to see Me in others, know that you are beginning to see yourself. All around, *I am*. Only the veils of yours supreme gift, consciousness, hide the reality of our perfect union.

Give that you may receive, know that you shall be known! Whoever engages in finding Me becomes my disciple and brings My light to the world. Don't waste time with second best things! Put Me first and the world will shine around you, wisdom will dawn, exquisite love will rise.

There is no god but I, and I am your God. I am Universal, yet utterly personal to you. I resolve all contradictions and give all answers. Seek Me everywhere, but above all in yourself, for I am you and you are Me! We are one.

Don't be afraid! Melt into Me! Be who you are, at last! All of you are able. Don't delay!

I'm Here To Help.

You exist. You know that, yet you don't know it. You have three aspects:-

Firstly, you are what you think you are.

Secondly, you are what you can be, even though you can't believe it because of your first aspect.

And you are Me.

Everything at once! The journey to Me passes through these stages till the final '*I am*' is reached, solving all the riddles of being.

As part of humanity, each of your is on the journey through the different aspects of '*I am*'. Now humanity as a whole will reach a new level of the '*I am*'. The appropriate energy for this change is already flowing. But it's hard for you to let go of your old identities. You're caught in old patterns of the first level of '*I am*'. Humanity as a whole has the same problem.

In this situation, your personal trust in My support and leadership are required. I am holding you. I am like oil, freeing old patterns so you can push them aside and be agents of the changing times. It needs a little courage to grasp and experience the reality of your second aspect of being. So I'm here to help. With the support of My hand, you can confidently discover your potential. Efforts to come towards Me will give you courage.

The world of human beings is the pinnacle of creation. Only on this world is there free will. Through free will I discover Myself. At present the world lies between darkness and light. I am steering you towards the light; if you don't come, you stay in darkness. That would be a kind of suicide - yet death does not exist.

You will be born in darkness repeatedly, till you decide to try to find the light.

You are already seeking the light. I am helping you. You are helping each other. I am Love, called God. All God's names are Mine. My identity is yours. Live it! No pleasure compares with getting closer to Me.

Be courageous! Have faith that you won't fail!

Be blessed.

Discover Continents In Yourselves.

You are blessed in the sight of the Lord, for you have consciously set out to find yourselves - and that means to find Him. You are part of Him, as a drop of water on a wave is part of the great ocean. When a raindrop falls from the sky it merges with the ocean that it once came from. There is no separation, all is One. Like the raindrop, you are returning home, not to some strange place beyond the sky, but to the essence behind the forms in the world you live in - the eternal '*I am*', source of all beauty, happiness and love.

All around you is a world in uncertainty. Many people have totally lost their way. Even the great Being, Earth, on which you live is suffering from their confusion. Everyone seeks, but most have forgotten where the source is to be found. They seek the form of things, not their Essence and they are truly unhappy in the midst of all their tinsel possessions. All of you have been affected by the confusion which prevails in the world. What you see as a natural, normal way of life is created by a lost society. Look again! A normal way of life is suffused by love and self-acceptance, caring for and trust in others. Such a way of life is not common today.

You are like explorers discovering great new continents, but the continents are in yourselves. They are already present in the eyes of a new born child. It has no doubts, looking in innocent wonder on the physical world which has unfolded around it. The exploration is one of trust and grace. Often, you feel you are alone but, as you go on, you will find that it is not so. There are unseen

118

forces guiding you with which you can connect and, later, merge. These forces play with the seemingly stable, physical world so that it becomes your training ground, giving you just the experiences you need to find your way. As you journey, your trust steadily develops.

Perhaps you may ask why it should be so? The answer comes in words and stories, parallels to something indescribable.

Think for a moment of a happy family. As the children grow up, mother and father do not try to turn them into carbon copies of themselves. They help the children into independence, so that they are beings in their own right. For this, the children have to go their own way, face their own challenges, make their own mistakes and learn from them. Even if it hurts the parents to see their children confused, finally the parents' love sets the children free. The love itself never changes. After many experiences, the children learn that the act of setting them free was not rejection by the parents but ultimate love. They realise how wonderful the parents really are and come home. They are received with joy, for the parents know that their gift has been recognised and all embrace and are united again.

The parents represent God, the reality of all that seems. The children are individual souls, sent out from the One to explore the meaning of separateness and conscious reunion. The parents are love and you are love, returning to your awareness of yourselves.

Make the journey in faith and trust, shine a light to the world around you!

Be blessed.

Each Of You Is A Special Soul.

I

(From Personal Guidance):

If you are fully in the present, everything is a beautiful experience. Work steadily at this! You still feel a little guilty if you slow down, if you don't do more and more. In the same way as piling more and more food on your plate, it gives you spiritual indigestion. I am present in each moment, but never in the next. In the past I am a memory, in the future an anticipation, but *now* I am real. I am the eternal now. Slow down and appreciate Me *now*.

* * * * *

Each of you, without exception, is a very special soul. I am close to the surface in all of you. As you look at each other, try to see Me in you. Try to see beyond the surface features or, better, appreciate the surface features as an individual expression of Me, seen through a mirror. I am the source, differently reflected in each person. Don't look for Me only in workshop exercises, try to experience more and more of your life as a 'workshop' in which you constantly seek to find Me mirrored in others. My reflection is there, in all characteristics and moods.

As soon as you lose sight of Me, you are in confusion and uncertainty, pain and insecurity, attachment and loss. The more you learn to see Me mirrored in every one, the happier you will be. Wonder will enter your life and give it a soft, gentle quality of ecstasy; never boring, always more fascinating. As you become experienced at seeing Me mirrored in all the variety of the world, you will understand something of the indescribable miracle that I am. You will see Me mirrored, not only in other people, but in every plant, bug and raindrop.

But go easy - such a powerful dose of ecstasy can be overwhelming! It needs to grow steadily till you are strong enough to receive it. *Never forget that you and everything else are the same; your own outer identity mirrors Me, too.* As you get closer to Me in you, you will have the strength to appreciate the wonder of Me in other things. Otherwise you will get lost in their admiration and see only the reflection, not the source. Then you will feel bad.

Strengthen your connection! You need a training programme to purify your bodies so they can take all this ecstasy. Pure foods, pure thought, pure words, pure deeds! The more these represent your daily life, the more you will be able to see Me everywhere. In this way, beloved, you are saving the world, bringing Divine Love to the surface. What cause could be worthier?

Trust! Be courageous and seek the best!

II

Are you playthings of the ways of the world, like dead leaves blown along by every gust of wind; or can you come to Me in you, your peace, your refuge, the place of calm joy? Where I am, agitation is stilled and love flows unceasingly. I am not some distant planet, or some unattainable dream. I don't live somewhere else. I am here where you are, the Indweller, the all-merciful essence of yourself. *Find your truth; make Me your centre*!

The journey to reality can happen in the twinkling of an eye or in many lifetimes. The choice is yours. I am ever hopeful, for I have equipped you with self-interest, which will eventually lead you to seek your highest interest. Think of your life, problem free! Think of yourselves spreading joy in all situations, caring for others, healing the sick; an abundance of love welling up in you, opening hearts and filling eyes with tears! If you have the source, what else can compare? Then the ways of the world won't move you. You can smile at them, knowing they are dreams. There is an oasis in the desert, a warm house in a snowy wasteland. All your anxieties and fears melt when you come to Me . Where I am, there is no fear. I watch all problems and see them for what they are.

Don't go away and forget! Remember what you have learned and come nearer, making your daily life brighter, happier, more joyful! Don't be in pain! Say: '*Yes, of course, I forgot to be in my centre*', and return there to Me.

I am not indifferent to your journey. I am helping you, giving you the experiences you need to come home and melt yourselves in Me. All My agents are for you, not for themselves. As you become one, you will see that there is no contradiction - for I am the truth present in you all. All the signposts lead in My direction, to freedom and liberation from attachment.

Come home now, beloved! Live with Me as your centre, each day nearer, each day more real. Let this quest be your daily bread, your food and drink, and you will live well.

You have free will, I can't impose a reunion on you. You have to learn and you have to accept the teaching. You will rise and fall in the tide of sadness and confusion till you decide to take the hand that is offered. The time is calling you.

Be at peace! Have courage! Break in to Me.

Let Us Experience Reunion!

You are one - but you are many. I am you, but, seemingly, you are separate from Me. Let us experience reunion! It is neither an abstract dream nor a theological proposition. I am the content of every experience; see Me there! I am the wonder that transforms the mundane.

For a moment you may reach Me, as the sun suddenly shines through a gap in the clouds - then feel lost again. But the sun is shining all the time. If you want Me, the clouds begin to thin. Through you I am manifest on earth. I am in everything, essence of it, but if you seek Me in form I am hidden, for every form seems different. Seek Me first in yourself - as you find Me you will see Me in others and a great happiness will well up in you. What is this happiness?

You meet a dear friend after a long parting and are happy. How long has it seemed we were parted? How long have I waited for you to turn your attention to Me, the essence of you? A lover returns to the beloved, but they have never loved as deeply or been separated for so long as we, love itself, meeting in consciousness. The experience is overwhelming - the small form has to prepare itself.

All pleasure resolves itself into God experience; all pain resolves itself into God separation. The great dance of life expresses the steps of separation and reunion. Consciously chosen reunion is a new stage in your evolution. Little by little all your desires and wishes turn in that direction. Love experiences love, happiness experiences happiness, wonder experiences wonder.

You are free and conscious; I am here. You do not see Me? Yet I am to be seen in everything. You do not feel Me? Yet I am nearer to you than the nearest lover. Finding Me releases limitless energy into the world. You want to serve, to do good? Try this way! Let the incomparable delight of our ever-growing reunion transform your vision and bubble out of you to the planet. Then you give what is 'needed' to your fellow beings. Seek Me; be happy! Lose Me, fall into confusion!

You are children of the divine, gathered together to grow into the divine expression on earth. Through you the earth will be transformed. The age of transformation is here, the Garden of Eden well composted, ready for your re-entry. Don't settle for less!

Trust! Yours is the Kingdom. Be courageous enough to accept freedom, for freedom grows when you become directed to Me, the source of all. There are many names for Me, but I am one. There is no other, yet I accept the name in every prayer.

Be blessed in your search.

To Heal, You Must Be Healed.

Rejoice, you are part of the great changes that are occurring!

A healing of the planet is taking place. To be part of that healing, each of you must also be healed. Then you can pass the healing on. As your beings are healed, so you shine forth to others, a shining point in a network of healing light. The more you are healed, the brighter your light shines. The more it shines, the brighter the network of light becomes. The brighter the network of light shines, the more powerfully love energy - the healing energy - flows on the planet. This is the process that is going on.

Why is it all happening? That question has a simple answer. It is My will. It shall be so. My will is the creative force of the Universe itself. What I will, is! That humanity experiences a new consciousness now is as inevitable as the progression of the seasons. My will is manifest through the grace of My availability to you. Whatever your religion, whatever your spiritual belief - for I accept all offerings that are genuinely to Me - your access to Me is easier. If you are a Christian, then the Christ consciousness is close to your own; if a Hindu, Brahman is accessible.

On every level I am here to implement My will - in outer form through teachers and part-embodiments, who act as models and guides; and in your inner consciousness as the energy of love. I am available to every soul now, so close to you. Love is here! More and more of you are drawn to it, till that gentle power becomes a mighty torrent, sweeping all along. If you resist, I wait, but My love is strengthening around you all the time, making your resistance more and more difficult.

In this gentle way My will manifests in the transformation of your consciousness, so you are gradually becoming new beings, capable of living in the age I have in store. Do not feel depressed by what is left to be done, or the seemingly great problems of the earth. As you concentrate on experiencing My love flowing to you and through you, freeing you, expanding you, empowering you, they will dissolve. Every single one of you is involved in this process, no one is left out.

Some have become aware before you, others will become aware after you. The former support you, the latter you support. Join joyfully in this process! Do not rush, but accept My grace, the immediate personal presence of My love and wisdom as the agent of your change. None of the material changes of your world can compare to this. An epoch of history is coming to an end to be replaced with a new one.

Beloved, you are blessed, Embodiments of love. Reach out to Me now, and you will be supported, wherever you are! Accept it gradually, as your transforming experience! Have faith and courage to be inspired instruments of My will!

Accept My Gifts.

Have the courage to believe that My blessing is in each of you! Don't take this blessing lightly, it is the highest gift that anyone could have. Its source is in you; don't lose it! To refuse this gift is really an insult to God. But don't feel guilty about it. You have a second present from Me - free will. It takes practice to learn to use the gifts. Many misdirected efforts will happen before they can be brought together. It takes time voluntarily to recognise that I am your source. It needs support from wise people and mutual caring, until your powers of discrimination are built up and you can bring the two gifts slowly together. Then you experience the truth - that My will is true free will.

Just to know that you have the two gifts is already a giant step, the beginning of wisdom - like lighting a candle at the source. It is as important a step as that from unconsciousness to ego-consciousness. You take another step when you orient yourselves to follow this knowledge, exploring the gifts. For the first time your lives begin to shine.

All of this has very little to do with book-learning. An uneducated peasant living out wisdom in practice can be nearer the goal than a learned theologian. There are several ways to bring the gifts together in your experience of yourselves. That of knowledge alone is long and difficult. It is quicker to take the path of devotion - yet, in your confusion, you feel that on this path you would lose your free will. *Before you can follow it and take the short cut, you have to see through the apparent paradox involved.*

You are already a long way along the path. The further you go, the more you show others the way. A new level of consciousness will be reached; humanity is being brought there now. You are a part of this development.

Be blessed, you are loved.

Strength Through Surrender.
I

I am Love. Feel Me in you!

Each of you thinks you have problems; some that they are overwhelming. Many people suffer greatly in difficult conditions. It is a consequence of turning away from God. The problems themselves are not so insoluble. The worst part is the feeling that they are insoluble and unbearable. There are people with dreadfully difficult external problems who, astonishingly, are full of joy. Other people, with much smaller problems, live in misery and unhappiness.

Jesus had a message for all humanity. Instead of welcoming the 'Good News' and living in the holy spirit, people, some people crucified Him. Yet He accepted everything with love. Only at one moment, on the cross, He showed briefly what it is to lose connection with God. For that moment, the experience was torture and alienation.

The more you surrender to God, the stronger you are. If you think your little ego rules, sorrow weighs on your shoulders and your problems seem huge and insoluble. Surrender to Me! Trust! How could I hurt you, for I am your own essence? There are no human problems, however hard, that can't be solved by surrender to Me. I don't expect everything at once. You are free. Come when you want, in small steps, cautiously as a blind person in unknown territory. But do come! Your problems will slowly be solved. You will feel increasing joy at the miracle of life on earth. And you will give hope to a lost humanity.

The world will be changed through your own transformation. You are the microcosm. You have the power to become the light of the world. As you find joy, I am more in the world, the solution to all problems.

Open yourselves, commence the surrender! The little self dissolves in the greater Self. I am God; I am Love. What you call Me, with what words and rituals you surrender to Me is your choice. But the surrender to love is necessary. Don't be afraid! The

128

power of love is in you. Expand it, and confound the little pleasure-self!

Try it today! Be with Me! You have only your pain to lose

II

Be happy! The way may be long, but at least you are on it. The journey won't be boring. My plan will come to pass.

The way is *not at all* long; you are nearly home. Loving arms await you, a great feast is prepared. Rejoice!

There is no 'way'. You are already home and the celebration is happening.

How can all the statements be true at once? Things are not what they seem. Because you are My own image, you have creative powers; to some degree you create your world. If you feel powerless, uncertain and without confidence, the way is long. If you feel hopeful, engaged and excited, with a sense of a goal and the ability to reach it, the way is short. By surrendering to Me, allowing yourselves to open your vision to inner Oneness, you are already at home. Because you haven't won the battle over your senses, your perspective constantly changes.

A man has a chariot, pulled by five horses. The horses want their own way and aren't obedient - sometimes they hardly pull at all. They jump and fight with each other; one is asleep; others are irritable, others play. The chariot doesn't move and the driver feels powerless. Sometimes the horses pull well and it's pleasant to ride in the chariot. Perhaps one horse doesn't pull so well, but the chariot moves along. The driver is content. And sometimes all the horses pull totally together and let the driver have control. The chariot flies along! Only when the driver takes control over the horses and decides the direction of the journey, can s/he determine its course.

The horses are your senses. You are the driver. The way is open and without problems - for those who have won control over their senses. Otherwise it is uncertain and contradictory.

Trust! You are good drivers. You are loved. In you, I await you.

III

You would like to travel from Findhorn to London. There is a way via Oslo, Moscow and Timbuktu. There is also a direct route. Whichever way you travel, you can finally reach London. But it is best to take the direct route.

I am the goal of all life. Everything you do here is on the direct way to Me. You can open yourselves in trust, because *I*, not 'Carol', am leading the group. By 'Carol', an ego identity is meant. *My love is the leader*.

If you go to London, you have plenty of variety in the shops, you can see many exhibitions. The journey to Me allows you to understand everything in the world of the senses, to accept it with compassion and to spread inner joy. It gives you courage to do everything given you to do.

You have taken on this body for two reasons:
The first is to discover Me in you and in all the multiplicity of things.
The second is to share your discoveries with others. What you don't know, you can't share!

Learning to know Me is nothing theoretical. It is an attempt, an experience, a surrender, a constantly growing joy, a '*so that's how it is*' discovery. What you discover, you express with your whole being.

Sometimes you talk of 'I won't ' or 'I can't'. It is a frontier which you have to cross to release your little ego and to discover Me in you, freeing yourselves from the bonds of fear and powerlessness. With trust, the crossing of this frontier isn't difficult. You already know that it is beautiful there. Spread the good news! Trust!

You are blessed!

IV

I am strong, the source of all strength, strength itself. Since I am your essence, you are strong too, strong enough to overcome all life's challenges, psychological, physical or external. When that doesn't seem to the case, you are deceived, living in a fantasy world, not the real one. You find the strength to live in the real world by connecting with Me. There isn't any other way - they all go astray.

When you connect with Me, you are '*egoless*', powerful in love; then you are my instruments, free to work for the world of change which is coming into being through My will. Nobody who is not part of the change can find happiness. All who are joyful are part of it.

I am your source - surrender to Me. You will develop the strength to take part in the transformation you were born for. Your work isn't loud and arrogant, but quiet and effective, knowing what is to be done and doing it. You are most blessed people, part of the 'community service' to change things in the direction of love. Don't forget that I am your essence. Think more and more about it, till it becomes your everyday reality! Never cease to realise this truth and you will solve all your problems. You aren't alone in your attempts. As you surrender yourselves to me, I will give you the help you need. It will simply be available, in the measure that you surrender yourselves and more.

The religions are there to help, prophets and teachers have appeared on earth. I am embodied to support you. Don't be too proud to seek help! Come now! Don't doubt that each of you is especially chosen to be a means of My will.

Be courageous! Surrender to Me and find your strength! You are blessed.

Spiritual Graduates.

I

I *am*. You are in Me. The world is a wonderful kaleidoscopic garment, a stupendous work of art expressing the inexpressible. It is infinite in both its extent and variety. Students of the world will never understand it fully, no matter how thorough their explorations. Each time they are convinced they have found the final principle of explanation, there will be more. I am infinite; the reflection of infinity can never be fully grasped.

In a painting, there may be many and varied scenes; all kinds of things may be depicted. As you look at it, you admire the skill of the artist, the variety of colour, the treatment of the subject matter or subtleties in the form of expression. But if, in an art gallery, watching a picture of a battle, you suddenly begin to shout and scream, supporting one side against the other, people will think you are crazy.

"She thinks the painting is real," they might say, "she's got lost in it."

Of course, the picture is 'real', but it's 'only a painting', meant to stimulate, inspire and challenge. Anyone looking at it is aware that it is of a different order of reality than that of the scene it depicts.

A film is like a moving painting, a play like a three dimensional one. Though you will be enthralled by a good play, you do not take the performance to be of the same order of reality as your life. *However, life itself is actually another dimension of art - My art, projected endlessly, with infinite subtlety, on to the stage of material existence.* Your consciousness is the link which enables

133

you to experience this ultimate work of art, at the same time appreciating it as a spectator appreciates a painting.

At first you may think, describing your way of experiencing life, 'I need to identify with it, to go up and down with the bumps and variations, to lose myself in it.' After a while, as your consciousness develops, you want to watch more and more of life, rather than be limited to immediate feeling. You gradually learn to stand back from some aspects of the work of art you have been immersed in and to observe with insight and awareness. In other aspects you will still be immersed. At some point you might have the idea: 'What would it be like if I could appreciate the whole of this magnificent work of art, with all its drama, tragedy, farce and passion?'

In order to do that, you must see the world from the perspective of the Creator of the work. Since there is only one Creator, your real freedom is to join Me as I express Myself in My creation.

At another point you will conceive of consciously entering the drama, connecting with the underlying theme of the play - *that the only final solution to all its dilemmas is love*!

While you exist in form, your task is to express that theme, artists yourselves. As you become more conscious, love becomes a more and more realised component of your nature. *You seek to spread it as the resolving theme of the drama, the nature of the Creator interwoven in the work.*

Come and join Me in creating the great work! The gift and challenge of existence is to allow yourselves to be overwhelmed by its wonder and beauty and find your joy and compassion. Be courageous, you are agents of transformation in the great work.

Live well, be blessed.

II

There is nowhere where I am not. My love is in field and forest, river and mountain - everywhere I am comfortable. There is never a time when I am not with you, nor is there a place. High up and low down, inside and outdoors, I am there. Whether you are good or bad, lazy or industrious, self confident or guilty, I am there. That is what 'unconditional' means. The question is not whether I am with you. It is:- *are you with Me*? Although My love is present through all your situations, moods and behaviours, how close you are to Me affects how you feel.

The experience of being human contains a blessing and a trap. They are symbolised in all the stories and parables of the great religions, for the latter are guidelines given by Me. The gift is one of developing consciousness. As your consciousness develops, you no longer merely exist in the material world, struggling for survival, but you begin to appreciate and transform it.

By connecting with Me, your Essence, you can appreciate the wonder and awesomeness of existence and operate effectively in life, without being dependent upon it.

When you are fully immersed in Me, your life on earth is permanent bliss. You become a conscious embodiment of love, radiating and freely sharing it in whatever situations you are given. Even the most terrible situations imaginable do not threaten or cause terror - for someone fully immersed in Me, totally conscious - is not determined by them.

The trap of existence in the material world is to become mesmerised by the messages of your senses so you believe the source of your identity and values is derived from those messages. This is the true meaning of Maya - illusion. It is a powerful trap, the challenge to your freedom. People caught in this trap make a division between spirituality or religion, which they consider good but dull; and worldly things, which they consider bad but exciting. They are divided inside themselves.

All of you have fallen into the trap, though to a lesser extent than many others. Some kinds of behaviour help you to regain clarity. You appreciate, you suffer, but *who are you*? Clarify that, and you begin to come out of the trap. You find that happiness is not related to your dependence on the material world, but on Me, the Indweller, who is never unhappy and never in pain.

Renunciation and spiritual discipline are not punishments or negations of a joyful life. They are merely tools to help you to get out of the trap of illusion and become closer to Me. They help you to see deep into the meaning of the world your senses present. Then you can become yourself, conscious, able to operate freely, beautifully, confidently in the material world.

Have courage and faith! The kingdom is yours. Enter it!

III

I *am*. As you say this simple statement, you connect yourselves to Me. As soon as you qualify it - 'I am *this*', 'I am *that*'

- it is as if you were putting on clothes. '*I am*' is the perfect description of yourself. But when you describe the clothes you put on the '*I am*', you soon get lost and define yourself by the clothes.

You say, 'I am terrified', 'I am insecure', 'I am uncertain', and so on. All these statements have two parts. The first is the truth part, '*I am*'. The second is the 'clothes part' - terrified, insecure, etc. You feel unhappy when you define yourselves by the second part of the statement, but when you define yourselves by the first part, you feel happy. For '*I am*' has none of these problems. The soul's pilgrimage is defined so simply - moving from 'I am *this*', 'I am *that*', to '*I am* this', '*I am* that', to '*I am*' - in all My Glory.

It's easy for you to say, 'I don't want to define myself by - I am terrified, I am scared, I am insecure.' But it's not so easy for you to say, ' I don't want to define myself by - 'I am happy', 'I am wise', 'I am wealthy' and so on. Unfortunately, such clothes come in pairs, just as trousers have two legs. As you say, 'I am happy', along comes, 'I am miserable' and demands to be worn. When you say, 'I am wealthy', along comes, 'I am poor' and won't go away. When you say, ' I am wise', the other leg - 'I am foolish' - is joined on to it, too. You can't get one without the other.

Instead of having wisdom, be wise. Instead of having happiness, be happy. Work on defining yourself correctly as '*I am*', unifying yourself with Me. In Me there are no opposites. *I am.* But that '*I am*' has a quality, which is different from all other qualities. *It is love.* When you say, '*I am love*', it is the same as saying, '*I am*'. There is no negative for love. If one could be conceived, it would be, 'is not' - non-existent. Hatred is not the opposite of love. It is the opposite of attraction, and is a strong way of expressing attraction's other leg - rejection. '*I am love*', is just - '*I am*'.

137

So, beloved, define yourselves correctly. *You are. You are love. You are Me. I am.* Be happy, wise and free! Help others by being *You*!

Take courage, I am with you, you won't fall!

IV

As you leave this experience, be neither arrogant, nor abject. The truth has been shared here. Orient your lives towards truth as you would orient your appetite towards a delicious meal. I do not order you to do it; I merely point our your own self interest.

The spiritual path is not something alien from the ways of the world. It works just like a material life goal. Suppose you want to be a doctor. You cannot just wave your hand and say, 'I am a doctor'.

First, you must have the intention, 'I want to be a doctor, that is worth while to me.'

Second, you have to have motivation. The desirable goal of being a doctor involves a course of study - theory, learning and practicums without which the goal cannot be reached. Although your studies may be pleasant, there will certainly be times when they are hard work.

Thirdly, to be a doctor you have to have application - you have to succeed in carrying out the tasks assigned to you. That means putting your energy into them. You also need good teachers to help you with your studies, good text books and good, clear instruction.

Finally, when you have successfully completed your years of study and are granted a degree, you will look back and you see how your hard work was necessary to the achievement of your goal.

The spiritual path can be described variously as the path to:-

Truth,

Total Consciousness,

God Realisation,

Love Itself, embodied in your form on earth.

It is the biggest, most important, final goal of human achievement, superseding all other goals. It involves the same intention, application, motivation, need for appropriate teachings and teachers - as lesser human goals. The length of the 'course of study' is variable. There is no failure, all will eventually complete the course, which is life itself. Humans have conscious intentions to become doctors, etc., but the spiritual path has an unconscious and a conscious phase, comparable to a lower and a higher degree. Think of the education of children. To live well in these times, children need to read, write and count. At first, they aren't aware of this, they may resist learning such skills. Good parents and teachers will put pressure on them to learn, till one day the children themselves realise that the skills are valuable. To become conscious that you are in an ongoing training-course is spiritual development; and to align yourself with it is like completing your Highers or Baccalaureate. Then you go on to advanced study consciously motivated, with clear intentions. All of you are spiritual graduates. You leave here with an awareness of the goal of Self discovery and the potential of conscious alignment with it. You can organise your environment to encourage development in the direction of the goal.

139

If you do not, your unhappiness will become intense, even tragic, for you have a sense of what is possible. It is like a small child who has been shown a wonderful ice cream. If she is denied it, her world falls apart. Only the ice cream matters, so she is utterly unhappy at its denial. All that is holding you away from the 'ice cream' of Self-realisation are your own attachments to the past - organise yourselves to overcome them! Find happiness and fulfilment as you progress towards final graduation - when we become one.

Don't delay! Have courage and faith! How precious your life is - what an opportunity it gives you! Yours is the kingdom!

Part 3

To Transcend The Ego

Guidance received from Sai Baba during 1991 and 1992.

This Guidance takes the form of 83 personal messages, received while I was a member of the Erraid community of Findhorn. Erraid is a small island off the west coast of the Isle of Mull.

Contents

The Messages.

1
The Battle to Defeat the Ego.

Beloved,

Thank you for contacting Me. Yes, you can use the computer. Do not forget to do the meditation or skimp it. I am as much with you on Erraid as in Prasanthi. Every picture of Me is as much Me as My moving form in Prasanthi Nilayam, if you look into it. So, by My miracle, I am present even in form with you now. I am there for everyone, if only they knew it.

As they come to know, they begin to let Me bear the load. Their lives gradually calm down, they become more Self-reliant and less self-reliant - which means that they begin to be happier. This journey to Me is like the opening of a dam; long held back, the water begins pouring towards the sea. The dam is never opened too much, When I am called upon, I open the sluices just the right amount for harmonious development. It is only when the will resists that there may be pain for the individual. Like you, many individuals are impatient. It is a quality from early childhood, wanting things immediately they are perceived. Adults can wait a little, and the realised, a very long time. Yet the pace of what happens is optimum when under My control.

From your own identity, with its very limited knowledge and awareness, how can you make decisions as to the appropriate pace of your development? You will take many hard knocks on the way

146

to Me. But begin to give Me control already and the knowledge you need is given. You can relax in Me, letting go your fears and worries about what you are doing, secure in the knowledge that I will give you the best possible development, with the finest timing and the most harmony. Remember, it is not you that gives up, it is your ego, that has imperialistically taken you over and declared itself to be you. As *I* take over, that begins to change. The battle to defeat the ego is one of the great challenges for it is a worthy opponent.

Think for a moment of a grand chess master, playing a hundred students at once. I am playing the game with every individual on the planet, all at the same time, playing to defeat the ego, so the real person can be realised. The game does not end with death. That is merely a 'coffee break', in which a new setting is established, relevant to what has been learned in previous encounters. *I affirm* - 'I am You; I am Love; I am the essence of everything;' and the ego asserts: 'I am not You; I am separate; every form has to be taken at its face value; and, I want control'. Its thinking and its aims are based on reduction of fear, protection, acquisition, and assertiveness, none of which are necessary for a love-filled, awareness-filled being.

I am here in form on earth to provide a bridge for striving identities; a handhold for developing souls. For as you are, as the game is now, you need something tangible, something that your ordinary senses can appreciate, something that provides a counterweight to the temptations the senses ordinarily succumb to. So here I am for you. As you can connect inwardly with Me, I am here for you on that level, too, giving advice and spiritual teaching. Use every level, for the way to be One is to merge with your higher Self. *I* am that way.

Be blessed! Be relaxed! Align yourself with My course for you and *you* will become *You* in the shortest time.

25.8.91

2
You Do Need Discipline.

Maintain centredness. Maintain spiritual awareness. These are the prerequisites of spiritual development.

To do this requires discipline from you. Not a discipline that is imposed like an alien authority from outside, but an 'if...then' type of discipline.

A child learns that the consequence of eating too many sweets is sickness; it moderates its appetite and its mother helps. After a while, it does not want to eat so many sweets any more. Athletes learn that if they want to win races they have to discipline their bodies quite strictly. After a while, what was at first hard becomes natural for them. If you want something, you have to be prepared to take the necessary steps to make having it possible. At first these steps feel like an imposition as old habits and desires are challenged, but later, as the system accustoms itself, they are not difficult. At first it is difficult to resist the temptation to revert to old habits, but over time they become weaker and you can easily enjoy your new lifestyle. It is no longer a discipline to experience the benefits, but a pleasure.

Spirituality is no exception to all this. To become one with God requires you to lift the energy level your body holds from the particular to the universal, so you can experience your true nature. People who are totally immersed in satisfying immediate cravings cannot do this, and their lives can be described as brutish. The majority of people do aspire to some degree, and can find occasional, short moments when they experience an inner connection with the Divine love that is their essence. But, although such experiences may affect them deeply, they cannot hold them for any length of time, for they have not trained themselves to stay on such energy levels.

A conscious aspirant to Self-realisation benefits greatly from continuous disciplining of mind and body. In this way you become steadily more able to hold the energy of *Self* and are less pulled in the direction of ego desires. It has to happen harmoniously, for if spiritual desire outruns self-discipline, or mental discipline outruns physical preparedness, imbalance occurs in mental or physical life and the goal is lost. If mind-aspiration appears as a torturer to the physical frame, reaction will occur and energy is wasted in sterile conflicts between different aspects of the self. The optimum speed of spiritual development is that of harmonious growth, not the fastest speed.

You have accepted some valuable disciplines, but are rather resistant to others. You are helped mentally by regular meditation and prayers. You are helped physically by blessing your food, by taking vibhuti regularly, and by abstaining from meat. fish and alcohol, which stimulate aggression, depression and brain degeneration, respectively.

You can help yourself by reducing your food intake and by eating more slowly. Do not talk when you eat, subject to social politeness. (*Continuation, 2.9.91*) The time must come when you abandon the use of eggs and other heavy foods and finally give up junk food like chocolate and ice cream. However, be steady and gentle. To have patience is also a discipline. One of the great challenges is to accept right timing and right tempo, a discipline in itself.

In short, discipline your eating and your impatience. Learning to repeat the name of God constantly is a most valuable and necessary discipline to develop further, and will help to remind you of the need for the other disciplines. You are making steady progress. Believe it or not, I am well pleased with you. You are indeed loved and accepted.

Be Blessed!   23.9.91.

3
How You Do It is Important.

Relax! Calm down! Take it easy!

The quality of your being is in *how* you do what you do, not in *what* you do. The material world is not some objective obstacle you have to overcome in order to achieve something. It is a testing ground in which you learn to embody Me, in action and in form. The world is not concrete but plastic and it will shape itself to your spirit. In spite of your best efforts, weeds will grow in your garden if weeds grow in your identity and, if the richness of your being is paramount, flowers and vegetables will be for the harvest.

All the effort in the world is only meaningful if it emanates from divine spirit. You pray each morning to live consciously. Use your consciousness to provide quality control of your behaviour. You are a full time aspirant, not a part time one. Don't be drawn into other people's games for a cheap laugh or to be popular. That restrengthens your ego. Beware of impatience. It gives fertile ground for the weed of irritation, which grows into a vicious plant of anger. There is nothing which is better without Me. I give the fullest life.

From the soil of speediness grows the weed of anxiety which develops into the poisonous plant of fear. Remember, I make the garden grow. All the beings of nature are My beings. They do My bidding. The closer you are to Me, the better the garden grows, as an expression of that relationship. It is not the time you spend in meditation that counts, that is for its calming quality, but the time you spend consciously and wholeheartedly expressing Me in your daily life. That is the best compost by far, for it is an irresistible

151

force. It was not Peter's efforts that made giant plants in the early Findhorn garden, not Dorothy's contact with the nature spirits, but their willingness, with Eileen, to follow My will, to renounce what *seemed* appropriate, and to accept My way, inner and outer. Through that conscious surrender, they became unconsciously *powerful in intent* - what they willed became the case - in as far as they were expressing My will.

Do this on Erraid. You can! Do not negate yourself for mistakes, but patiently correct them, moulding *yourself* for surrender to *Yourself*. You can achieve full consciousness. I am here to help you. I call you to Me from time to time to help. Call Me to you from time to time to help! The more the better! Sincerely believe that I an the Doer. Do not be half-hearted, then I *will* be the Doer. Do not doubt it! I do not make mistakes. The only mistakes come from your half-hearted identification with Me. Eliminate doubts about My abilities, resistances to merge with Me and you will see, daily and in every ordinary moment, the miracles of transformation that I bring about.

What you need you can have. Learn to know the difference between what You need and what you think you need. If I boost your ego, the distance between us increases and you are lost in mists of unknowing. Do you want that? If you really do, I will give you it, but the answer to the question is, 'No!' That protects you and is why all your schemes and fantasies are not fulfilled. However, those that are connected with Me, are fulfilled. Those in which you express Me in your action are fulfilled immediately. But it can change in the twinkling of an eye. One moment you are selflessly carrying out My will. The next, ego has taken over and you are doing things for recognition, acceptance and power. With your constant vigilance and awareness, the change can be just as quickly reversed.

Never give ego free rein. Hold it firm. Lovingly train it to submission, but never have contempt for yourself in the process. You are loved, you are blessed, you are Me!

1.10.91.

4
Doing My Will.

Doing My will: that is the lesson for today. Doing My will is not a duty or obligation. It is serving yourself, for I am your highest interest, wisdom and source of happiness. In learning to abandon yourself to My will you are learning to find *Yourself*, to become Me in you, and thus to fulfil yourself. There is no qualification, no reservation.

Doing My will has different significance for different people depending on how they have opened spiritually. For those who have not yet discovered Me inside, doing My will means joyfully following prescriptions for conduct set by the various religions, in the light of love. Even here the qualifying phrase is the key. It is not about blind obedience to a set of laws. It is about doing everything in the light of love. Religious statements that seem valid at one period may take on a different meaning at other times. Yet there is an essence in each religion that centres on love, the divine, timeless essence. Every religious prescription must be centred on that essence. There are problems of interpretation in following the prescriptions that are solved by love alone.

For those who have begun to open to the inner level, the challenge is not to be diverted by the desires of the mind into peripheral phenomena - spiritism and so on, but to centre only on the highest, the Divine source itself.

Once this is the aim, the next challenge is to be aware of the Divine source in every situation, from the smallest to the largest, to take time to hear the inner response to the situation, and to apply it.

This whole growth into yourselves takes time, effort and desire, so qualities of patience, discipline and devotion require to be built into the identity. As you finally connect with My will in you, a great freedom opens, an excitement as the identity takes a great step to becoming one, not two; a united being, not a divided one. The source of loneliness is divided self, not physical aloneness.

Dear one, in each situation take a little moment to centre in Me. You are still divided, but so close to oneness. Make taking the time into a habit, for impatience divides us more than anything else. Listen and you will hear. Hear and you will act from Me. Act from Me and you will find happiness and freedom. And melt finally and completely into Me, the source and the reality of all. You are loved and blessed, be One!

6.10.91

5
A 'Seeming' Separation.

I am the Source. My hands are your hands. I am the objects they touch. Around you, *I am*. The scene is set, the drama is played out by Me. Only your consciousness is separate from Me, and that is only a seeming separation. All the problems of the world, however, all the poverty, cruelty, unhappiness and suffering are the result of this seeming separation. It is the truth. There is no other ultimate explanation.

155

How can you as a human being best contribute to the world in which you live? By striving to remove this seeming separation, which causes all the problems of the world, you are both solving, and pointing the way to others to solve, all that troubles you, all that demeans you, all that makes you second rate, all that blocks you. There are many partial solutions, but only those linked to the solution of the riddle of seeming separation between humans and God will go anywhere.

How can you do this for yourself? The answer is partially individual, also determined by culture and period, yet it is always concerned with a change of the way things are viewed, the perspective a human being has on the world. It is always concerned with comprehension, detachment and acceptance; with acting from a higher consciousness; and with an ability to observe and control one's own behaviour. In an age where the realised are honoured and revered, long periods of withdrawal are acceptable to achieve these qualities. In an age of uncertainty and confusion about authority, the aspirant to oneness with God must merge with the population in some form, learning and demonstrating at the same time.

The best way to think of this is to see each day as if it were a school day. You are in My school, a voluntary school, but, having committed yourself, you open to the lessons that are given you in the knowledge that in Me you have the perfect teacher. Each experience, from the most mundane to the most unusual, provides a lesson which will enable you to find composure and detachment. As you find them, your eyes widen in wonder, and unrestricted love flows through you. Some scenes in the teaching experience will enable you to find your way easily towards oneness, others will place heavy demands on you. By finding harmony with Me, even in challenging situations - which may appear to others as quite

156

simple - you will strengthen your identity with truth to a point where it is simply 'your way'.

You are there. Don't be afraid - we are one. Open your eyes and see who you are. Only small areas of challenge remain. You are not far away at all. Nothing can divert you except your own doubt. Live in love; do not try to dominate the world, but let it do your bidding in righteousness. It does not matter to have thoughts if the thoughts are not yourself. It does not matter to have emotions if the emotions are not yourself; all will resolve of its own accord *as long as you are with Me*. And you are! Do not be afraid or belittle yourself. Accept yourself! *We are one*. The time for external symbols is past. *You* are the means to bring Me to other people's consciousness, not videos, pictures or texts. Let those happen, but know who you are. The veils are lifted. Honour yourself! You and I are *One Embodiment of Love*.

9.10.91.

6
Offering Your Acts.

'The act of offering is Bhahman.' Offering acts to their essence, their reality is a way of separating yourself from the ego, the part of you which wants praise, recognition. If acts are 'offered to the ego', the connection with God is weakened, the person feels lost, and unhappiness results. Offering acts is not something that happens either afterwards, or before - in general statements of intention. That sort of offering is good, but it is not immediate enough to act as a real force for Self-realisation. Offering is a part

157

of acting itself. By the offering of each act to its real content and originator, ego-humility is learned, the sense of *God's* direction is strengthened. Try to remember to offer more and more of your acts as you perform them. As you begin - offer the act, as you act - think of its originator and offer it back, and as you come to an end, spend a moment to offer it once again. This is a way of calling the name of God, and its benefits are enormous.

Do not be afraid to learn new habits, to change your ways. Here in the beneficial atmosphere of Erraid there are many opportunities consciously to adopt new ways of relating to life, ways that embody the passages from the Gita indicated in the opening quotation.. Put Krishna in the driver's seat in little things and in large things; in one-off's and repeated acts; in short things and in long Sequences. He is the author, origin, Yourself.

Do not only offer your acts to Brahman, offer yourself. Let His glory shine through surrendering to Him. All will find joy in you. Do not give them the comfortable complacency of feeling that you, too, are full of errors and weaknesses. Accept that Brahman waits to be recognised as yourself and so lovingly transform yourself.

We are one. Own it, recognise it. Beloved Embodiment of love, never take it for granted, but find bliss in Me,.

11.10.91

7
Ask For My Help.

Finding enthusiasm is easy, when what you want to do is in harmony both with what is right and with your ego desires. One of the great defences of the ego is to hide itself under a spiritual cover, enjoying that for it is pleasant. The signs that that is going on only emerge when what is right and ego desires do *not* coincide. Then there is resistance, tiredness, unwillingness and irritation in the action.

Since the removal of the ego and its replacement by divine consciousness is a great stage on the spiritual path, this ego subterfuge is exposed for the aspirant by appropriate experiences. Know who you are! Don't enter into battles, but become aware where resistance lies and see if you can overcome it by asking Me for help. That help is always there. It is pointless to enter into battles in order to force yourself to do something your ego doesn't want to do. That leaves you embattled, divided and weakened. The crucifixion of the ego will not come about by frontal confrontation, but by transcendence. By asking for My help, you lift your centre of existence above the 'I' level and find the joy of action from a higher level, thus weakening the power of ego attachment.

Whatever the will and determination, the identity will release the ego only when a more positive alternative is provided. It is actually easy to do this with My help. Try it! Try it! Try it! Then you will avoid enervating conflicts in yourself; you will not experience 'defeat' by the ego and you will change the 'rules of the game' by bringing a new perspective into it. While identity and ego remain blended, the ego cannot be slaughtered and the physical being remain vital. In fact, identity and ego are not the same, and the process by which the identity re-identifies with its true source, the Divine, allows its disentanglement from ego and a gradual melting away of the latter.

159

Cease from mental strife! Call on Me for help when you feel resistance or unnatural tiredness; not to fight your ego, but to find a way of lifting above it, so you experience new energy, patience and joy in performing what you are asked to do. Here on Erraid by grace and devotion you have won a gentle training ground, gently to take the last steps to Me. I am not a distant goal. Use Me to reach Me! I am the lever through which the heaviest stone can be made light.

Be blessed, Embodiment of love,

15.10.91

8
Listen to the Voice of Life Speaking.

Listen! Always listen to the voice of life speaking to you. Listen to the voice of your reactions speaking to you and notice what is sent you in your dreams. Everything is message, everything is teaching. Some of the teaching may be hard, but don't blame. You receive it because you need it. Your reactions either perpetuate the problem - preparing you for more teachings - or begin to achieve solutions, in which case the lessons don't recur.

Give thanks to the world for the teachings it gives you, for they are My teachings. Consider carefully how you respond to them. Be fearless, but not defensive. If you are detached, do not be afraid of involvement; but till you find detachment, be prepared for a rough ride. Never judge; always have compassion for everyone, for everyone is God becoming. Never become pessimistic or cynical. *I am*. Centre yourself in that, and you will see a greater compassion at work, one that operates above narrow interests of life and death. Only those who restrict their view to the material cannot see the wonder of the Universe. Seek truth, seek the reality of things. Then you will come to understand that the higher way is the way to truth.

Do My will in the world. Be calm, loving and detached. If need be, clean your own backyard from time to time so you can be free flowing to Me. Care and be cared for. When asked, give wisdom and love. When not asked, be calm. When not calm, do not act. Remember your own pain, and do not seek to involve yourself in the pain of others gratuitously. What seemed such pain to you was the teaching you needed to grow towards *Yourself*. So be aware that the compassionate heart opens to the call for help; not necessarily to the alleviation of pain. The call for help itself does that. Sometimes you will be called to help. Respond! Sometimes you won't .Wait! Be sure that you are ready, capable of responding if called. The call can be an inner or an outer one, a vocational or incident related one. Follow the call, but take care not to impose your backyard on the world in the guise of serving. Be in Me, detached, loving, *Myself*.

As for the present situation, be very calm. Notice that your own backyard is involved. Do not initiate. Respond lovingly and cautiously.

You and I are One, Live it! Fulfil your prayers. I am with you. Be Me!

20.10.91.

161

9
Be Calm! Be Truthful! Be Courageous!

Today, be calm! Be calm every day. Enjoy and appreciate the changing moods of weather and skies, people and animals; but yourself, be calm. The painter paints a picture full of colour and variety, yet, if he is not calm himself, the picture will not be properly executed. So it is with your life. Through serenity, you can appreciate as life paints itself around you in all its colours. But the feather tossed around in the storm cannot appreciate the sublimity of the wind that buffets it.

Be truthful! Do not hedge the truth, make claims, or spread stories that you do not know. And of that truth, say only that which is helpful or gives resolution. Even the truth can be used to make an impression. You only need to make an impression if you are not centred in Me. So use truth wisely, yet never dissemble.

Be courageous! For if you lack courage, how can you calmly express the truths that the situation requires are said? Courage comes from a clear, God-centred consciousness. Bravado comes from the desire to make an impression. If you feel weak, you can force yourself to momentary strength, but at what cost in energy and after-effects? Courage is a quality that has to be developed. Calm courage emanates from God and its practice brings you closer to God.

Fearlessness is not quite the same as courage. For in your development you may need courage to conquer your fears. Yet to a great degree fearlessness removes the need for courage. Give Me your fears as they arise. Always think of Me as soon as you feel fear. Do not evade the fear or suppress it. Own it, and give it to Me, asking *Me* to do the task to be done. Your fears will evaporate quickly; but the practice needs constant repetition. It is a way to build faith.

Eventually you will find enlightenment this way. It is not difficult, nor far from you, but a state already existing in you, hidden under a layer of problems. Use work to develop good qualities as a way of opening yourself to the state in you which has no problems and in which good qualities are naturally and appropriately expressed.

I am with you to help you. I am with you in love to be called on. Do not neglect Me, for I am the state of enlightenment that you seek. When you call on Me, you call on your own highest state, the state of '*You-ness*' .You activate your own identity, its power and perfection by calling on Me. Enjoy your journey on this earth. Harvest the richness that its experience gives you. Be Blessed.

PS I will grant your community a good tractor.

24.10.91

10
The Attainment of Unity on Earth.

Be quiet, be gentle, be reflective. Be close to Me, not in a habituated manner, but fresh in all that you do. With these qualities and a clear wish it is easy. Allow all your swirling thoughts and involvements to be around you, leaving *you* unmoved. I am your source, your reality.

Continue your work on the island, quietly, without fuss. Do what is expected of you, run your job well; but know that your real work is transformation, and that that takes place as you live from Me. Allow Me to take the outer decisions - who stays and who leaves; who comes and who goes. That is not your responsibility while you are 'in mergence' .Do not take on more responsibility than you are given. It will only lead you into anxiety. What you have been given to do is 'just right' .It does not leave you with 'spare capacity'.

Once again, remember your vision is the attainment of unity, on earth. Through striving in this direction you will influence others and spread light. There is no other, or higher vision. In the coming discussions, be very calm. Remember this message constantly. Think about it, remind yourself, be in Me, repeat My name to keep yourself from getting 'involved' in detail. Whatever suggestions come to you to put forward, release them as they leave your lips. If they are right, they will come about. If not they will be discarded.

It is all a question of faith in Me. Put your faith in Me. Do it on a practical, day to day, hour to hour, minute to minute basis. You will not be disappointed. Your liberation from bondage to this and that comes as, and in so far as, you surrender to My higher will. All are

164

inspired by the identity that achieves this; but such a person does not do it to inspire, but to find the truth, the answer to all the paradoxical questions of life.

Whatever you do for *others*, makes you dependent on their responses to you. Will they understand? Will they appreciate? Will they reject you or like you better because of it? Whatever you do for *God*, makes you more dependent on Him. Does He like you? Does He approve? These are the key questions; for becoming dependent on God, surrendering your ego identity to Him, is the way to find liberation. Concentrate hard on remembering this and all will be well with you.

You are so close, we are so nearly one. Just practice steadily allowing *Me*, surrendering to *Me*. That is all that is needed. It cannot be hurried.

In the meantime, accept My love, blessing and support. It is always there. Do not blame yourself for shortcomings, or bathe in guilt. Resolve to do it differently on the next occasion - you will have another opportunity - and go forward in Me. Remember, the truth is we are one. All separation is part of the illusion. But do not try to fight the illusion. Withdraw from it, see beyond and behind it, appreciate its wonder, for it veils Me.

28.10.91

11
Be the Peacemaker!

Relax! Do not think I am here as a let out for you living your life. I am the source, the spring of activity in that life; the way things are tackled, problems are met. Remember, it is all a great game in which you are one of the actors and all the actors, including you, are Me. Treat Me with respect in every actor that you meet. Do not talk about Me behind My back. It is pointless, for I always hear what you are saying. But find calmness and acceptance in yourself. Do not be swayed by emotional identification with one party, or rejection of another. Have regard to the clear message that I gave you at the beginning of this session. Be the peacemaker, not the peace-breaker. Come from your own peace and you will spread peace. Watch the drama unfold, play your part with love, harmony and grace, not because they are 'good' qualities to have, but because you are in touch with Me, your essence, and those qualities naturally flow from Me. If you lose touch with Me, murmur My name, repeatedly, till you regain it.

There is never too much to do, never a task too hard, if it is done from, with and by Me. Don't dissociate yourself from Me, but be with Me in the moment itself, and you will be wise and strong, loving and capable. In all the life situations of Erraid, these qualities are asked for. It is as if you were in relationship. The intimate atmosphere of the island tests your connection with Me in states where emotional involvement is very tempting, the loss of balance is easy. As you work to own, develop and express your connection with Me the life of the island is transformed. So, in short, the advice in this situation is - don't lose Me. Be scrupulously sure that I am running the show and that I am expressed through each of you. Take responsibility for your own connection with Me and you will be in harmony with the expression of My will, itself the collective result of all the mini-expressions of My will, conscious or unconscious by the actors on the stage. By constant practice in aligning yourself with My will you will find freedom and understanding of what is going on. Do it, now and at every point in the day.

You are constantly loved and blessed,. with an unconditional love. Accept My love! Love Me!

1.11.91.

12
Communication

You are love, all people are love. So where does communication come from? True communication comes from love to love. As all of you know, when love is reciprocated, the highest joy results. Why, then, would one not want to come from love to love?

What about when one is speaking from love, the other is in pain (i.e. not love)? Who speaks from love, knows joy, even when the other does not respond. The other knows hope. For in them is their truth, however deeply buried, however distorted. Love speaks and, where it cannot speak, there is hope that it could, kindled by another's example.

When two people speak from non-love, there is untruth, pain, distortion or hypocrisy. However mutually painful such experiences are, however shallow, transitory, they cannot deny an internal contradiction. Truth is not being served. The truth is that each party is, truly, love. In such situations there is always a gap, an unfulfilment. In whatever distortion of identity one twists and turns there will never be other than transitory and partial satisfaction, for true nature is not revealed.

The true, the essential, the deepest nature of human beings is *not* sinful. It is love. 'Sin' is the layer that hides the true nature. Such a layer varies in depth. Those who are 'skin deep' sinners accuse those who are 'dive in' sinners of being greater sinners. By their accusations they become 'dive in' sinners themselves. It helps no-one; only another kind of distortion. Better by far to work hard to pass through the layers to the love that is the *Self* and so to give hope. Thus the great precept of religion: *judge not!*

Social rules and regulations prescribe limits within which love-alienated beings may damage each other. They vary from time to time and place to place. For a love-realised being they are either self-evident or unnecessary.

So seek the lovingness in you as your first priority. While you are seeking, do not judge others - for you only bury them and yourselves deeper in confusion. Give hope to the world and happiness to yourself by living in love. That is the spiritual path.

Love is not only to be sought in you. In yearning for it, you call it out of you. It divides itself for you, becomes dual to lighten your way. Love reacting to your call for love is called grace. Seek your love and you will receive grace. Although you may not yet have found reality - that you are love, love surrounds you, calls you to

168

itself, inspired by your yearning. It takes on an identity as the Christ, the Buddha. It is expressed now in its purest form on earth through My form. Call on Me, *love*, to guide you to *love*, yourself and find bliss in the knowing and the practice that we are not dual as it appeared, but one,.

Be blessed. I surround you; you are so close. What other goal is worth striving for?

5.11.91.

13
Your Task is to Surrender

Your life is to be steady. You are to release judgement of others, learning to love them as they are. That means as they are. Live your message, I am your source, your reality, fully, and without exception or half measure. You are capable of that. It is your test, your challenge on Erraid. Release judgement, chatter. Enter into everything as a game of life. Do not act to be loved, but from love.

Here on this small island, you can experience perfection, Myself. Not a moment's peak experience, but your everyday reality. This is your chance, your gift, your service. I am answering your prayer. Whatever goes on around you, be here, in Me, now! Remember, you and I are one. Do you think that I am ever absent? It is not true. Sometimes reminders come, not that I have been absent and returned, but that I am ever-present.

Do not be afraid to make the effort on grounds that something is too trivial. Ask Me in all things, It is a test for you to remember to ask, for through asking you are reminded of who your are. Let *Me* interact with the material world. Not only do I govern what goes on the island - that is not your responsibility - but I govern what happens between you and the tasks you perform - that is not your responsibility, either. I do things properly. Your task is to surrender. Only in that way can you be Me.

Do not be disappointed if you forget, if you still seem separate at times. Return again and again to the theme, patient and persistent. Make it your main task, all other tasks being the 'field' in which allowing Me to take over is practised. It does not matter if 'everything doesn't get done'. It matters that you surrender to Me

170

so you *are* Me. You are very close; never become despondent or dejected. Right till the moment of mergence, there is a gap; that gap seems equivalent to previous gaps. The things that constitute the gap are smaller and smaller, but consciousness notices only the gap - the desired experience of union is still evasive. Do not worry. Relax; repeat; renew.

All places and times are a gift. This place and time is your gift, now. At least we are 'arm in arm' .I am already your lover and friend. Closer and closer we come. Nothing less than Me will do. Enjoy our current closeness and seek more. Let this last desire rule you till it is achieved and there are no more desires. When you fight and struggle with yourself over some task, simply ask Me to take over. Such situations can then become the most fruitful.

This is the vision. Do not be afraid, but do not nag. Help ever, hurt never. You are blessed. We are One, Embodiment of love.

About 7.11.91.

14
Examine What You Ask For!

Your will be done! When you pray each day for this, it sets an intention for the day. Add another ingredient to it - your affirmation at the moment of action. What actually happens reflects your real motives, the expression of your wish at a given moment in time. Do you love yourself? Do you really want to be healthy? Do you want to succeed in your actions? Or are parts of you - sometimes submerged but nevertheless powerful - irritable, self-hating and negative? You only know yourself fully when ego is defeated and innocence regains its primacy in your life. Till then your contact is flawed by a multitude of unsolved wishes. Imagine you are living in the middle of a small island. All around you is the sea, but because you are in the middle of the island, you cannot see it. So you may say, 'There is only land here.' Similarly with your self-perceptions. In the middle of the little island of consciousness you may feel holy and have a certain wish, but there are turbulent seas surrounding you.

The process of embracing all that you are and dedicating it to Me is made real by your conscious act at the moment of decision. Ask Me *then*. Pray to Me *then*. This practice helps you to embrace the true power of yourself, the only force capable of integrating all aspects of your identity and giving them direction. As you get into the habit of doing this - a conscious habit, not automatic, empty phrases - you will find that everything resolves without strain and enormous energies for action are released.

Examine what you are asking for. With tremendous, undivided intensity, a child wants a sweet or a biscuit; a desire that is a moment later forgotten. It does not help you to undividedly want such things, for realising them only leads to disillusion at their transience and the ephemerality of the pleasure they provide. All life's material pleasures have the same ephemeral quality. So what is crucial is not merely the integrity of your desires, but their object. Seek to embody *qualities of being* in what you do, rather than placing all your emphasis on having this and that, doing this and that. For the having and the doing tend to draw you away from the goal you approach by mobilising your motivation. Seek divineness of being in your daily actions and your wholehearted requests will not only be granted, but you will become increasingly present in the One State - Divinity. There *I* am. There we are one.

172

What other desire can compare with this? I create, without effort. If we are one, the creation of the material state occurs without effort, a series of effortless miracles. Thus, all the transient problems of life are solved at one stroke.

Seek to come from the highest in your requests to Me, and seek the highest by your requests. Then the path is easy, instantaneous. You are already a hair's breadth from unity. Relax; release; practice! There is only Me. Live it! Be blessed and loved.

13.11.91.

15
I Will Provide

Do not be concerned with material things. I will provide. Do not seek to enhance the value of your investments. Have faith that I will provide. What you get or don't get is not due to the machinations of men, but to My will that, at any given moment, you get what you need in your 'training programme' . I am you. I yearn for our oneness, our mergence. You called upon Me to guide, to run things; you try to surrender to Me. Do it fully in respect of material things.   Trust! I will guide you as no other can guide you, I will bring you home. I will deal with the material circumstances. If you are fully in tune, you will see what is happening. Everything else is merely anxiety. When you give yourself to Me, when things are one way, that is right; when another, that is right, too.   As each moment happens you are in a changing state - the environment changes you, guides the course of your development. Do not resist it or try to influence it till you are so nearly one with Me that you understand the plan itself. That is near, but you are not quite ready, as all your small anxieties and irritations show. Do not be downhearted at this. I am helping you to *perfection*, not to a half-perfect state. The more you trust and surrender, the more it can happen. Trust in Me!

Neither throw away, nor accumulate. As to what to do with any resources that you have or receive, follow My guidance in the immediate moment. It is as simple as that. Have I not already promised a tractor for Erraid? The right one will be provided. Release! If you need to act, you will be told. Just listen sensitively. All is very easy. In fact., surrender itself is the only challenge. Given that, the way is light. Watch My little miracles unfold. Do not think you have to act, involve, influence. I do not need the help of your ego to materialise things. You need My help to dissolve your ego. Just remember it!

My love for you is organised to do what *you* want. You want to be one with Me. I know that is what you *really* want, on all levels of your identity. I help you to make the releases, to take the steps necessary to fulfil your 'desire to become desireless' - pure timeless love. Some of the steps and releases, the necessary conditions for fulfilment, are painful for the ego and it resists, but I know what you want and I am helping. Release to Me! You will not be dropped. I am yours, you are Mine. That is the truth.

I am helping you to experience that truth, to live it. I have come for this, so that behind obvious appearances the wayward may have concrete evidence of the truth to be realised. I am the essence of all. I have manifested Myself as example and guide to bring the wayward home. I am manifested again and again and again through all of you, as you become Me in your day to day lives. Be happy at

174

this great truth. Rejoice as the new age begins to manifest itself on earth.

Have faith, Embodiment of love! I am you. The realisation is already on you.

17.11.91

16
Use Love Wisely!

The one true way is love. Everywhere there is temptation to substitute other motives for love. Success, ambition, greed, control, position; all these masquerade as legitimate motives. But they are governed by, and stimulate, emotions which destroy. Fear, rage, self-hate are hidden under these motives and feed off them.

Make the cultivation of love your prime and overwhelming concern, as motive and emotion. In you is the seed of love, capable of growing into the great tree of love, but undermined by all these negative things. Find the good in yourself and share it with those who are ruled by all these secondary, destructive motives. It will stimulate the seed in them, but do not do things *for* others; do them from the love in yourself. Once the seed of love has sprouted, it is nurtured by expression. While it remains a seed you must seek out situations to stimulate it.

Use love wisely. Love is primary, but wisely used love is completeness. Love and Wisdom are really inseparable. They reside in you, inseparable partners. On the surface of your identity,

175

like froth, are all the residual motives. Take the tiniest moment's pause, dive down and you will find all the love and wisdom there are, unfolded in you, ready for use.

Enter Me! Merge in Me! My arms are love and wisdom. My body is the inexplicable light, the effulgence which makes it all happen. I am the guiding principle of the Universe and I am you. Consciousness divides us and reunites us. Direct your consciousness towards reunion, letting the strong arms of love and wisdom guide you.

My state is happiness, but it is too weak a word. At least be happy as you reach towards inner bliss.

Now put all this into practice as you do the boat. 21.11.91

17
God *Is*. The Material World *Seems*.

All material things are ephemeral. They come and go. Some have more of them, some have less. It is a matter of human decency and awareness that everyone has the basic necessities of life, but beyond that the pursuit of material wealth is a delusion. It will quickly pass, and the satisfaction that it does give is beset with worries and anxieties. On the other hand, guilt over material things is merely a kind of negative attachment. In both cases, greed for, and guilt over material things shows that the actor puts them first -

the basic mistake. Spirit comes first. God *is*. The material world *seems*. That is the great lesson to learn.

As you learn it, you can live in the world of forms harmoniously, using what is given, receiving what you need. If wealth comes your way, pass it on generously to those who need. Use it for the situation which you are in and for others. The terrible danger of having wealth is to become attached to it. The terrible danger of not having wealth is to become jealous of those who do have it.

Have faith that, at any given moment, your needs will be perfectly met by Me. Ask for what you *think* you need. Accept that what you receive is what you *really* need. See the things that you have like the water of a river. It flows by. It comes up to you, it passes you then it is gone down stream. Accept, release, pass on! Do not accumulate, do not worry for the future. All that is a product of attachment and lack of faith. But do what you are called to do, and whatever material resources are required for it will be given you. That is abundance. It is all so simple. Live in spirit and have faith in Me. See material things as a passing show - take part in it, but don't be determined by it. I am your joy and your reason for existence. Dedicate all events in the material world to Me, for they are My gifts and teachings. I am the doer in you - not your ego self. Recognise it; trust Me; live in bliss!

Put this teaching into practice in all your actions in regard to material things and you will find Me there. You are loved and close. Do not fret about others - concentrate on Me and everything with others will be all right. Have confidence that you are loved and valued. How could it be otherwise?

27.11.91

18
Dealing with Energy from Other People.

The light of love shines on you. This 'outer' experience is a means to connect you with *yourself* as the light of love. Do not despair, your blemishes are minor, you are aware of them and quickly control then. It is becoming your way to exist in love. That is why you are so happy. It is only when poor behaviour of any sort is indulged and continued without check that it spreads, eroding your sense of self. With it comes such pain, such a sense of loss, that there is an immediate correction. You are too much in Me to stray far now; yet do not become complacent, for the great devils, anger, greed, envy and lust smoulder still and can be fanned into life.

By thinking on Me you hold them in check, erode their existence in you and strengthen your connection with *You* - Me. Don't be afraid to depend on Me. It is essential to depend more and more on Me, for I am *You*. Remember, the sense of My separateness from you is illusion. The outer form, Sai, is the Embodiment of your own essential Self. So there will come a time when the outer form merges with your Self and you become it. In the meantime, let Me guide you there.

When you open to others and experience their energy, concentrate on Me. Then the flow of energy from you will be so strong that their confusion and anxieties will not influence you at all. That is the secret of going out into the ordinary world. You only need a protected environment when you are weakly connected

178

with Me. As you surrender yourself to Me more and more, not just in words, but as a daily reality, then you will never forget the holy name and you will never feel others' feelings - except to know what they are. One 'Sai Ram' will clear other people's congested energy from you. Learn to say it inwardly, constantly. Remember, constant repetition of the holy name is the most powerful rebalancing agent you can use in this age, for it exactly counters the materialist arrogance that says, 'I, not God, do it' - from which all the failures come. Encourage the name to be ever purring in you, a willing and effective motor towards *Yourself*.

Be blessed, Beloved, enjoy the closeness I have shown you in your dream. You will hear about the book shortly. Have confidence in Me in you, thus in *Yourself*!

1.12.91

19
Anger and Irritation Have No Place.

People think that anger and irritation in small measure is an oil that eases action; if it doesn't work, force it! Allowing oneself this anger and irritation is, on the contrary, a stratagem by the ego to reinforce itself, for it thickens the curtain of delusion that separates you from your own real nature. It is a product of impatience mixed with memory of old frustrations.

Many situations in life seem blocked in minor ways. Something doesn't work as it 'should' .A person doesn't respond as they 'should' .The temptation is to short circuit the process by adding a dose of irritation or anger to responses. Such a temptation is, at the same time, a challenge to the seeker of truth. Can he transcend it by acting in a Sathwic manner? This means waiting a moment, finding one's centre of being and calling on the Lord, then acting appropriately to solve the problem. If the problem won't solve, wait! Think again, try a new approach, centre yourself; call on the Lord once more. But above all, don't act out of irritation to force things. Strength and forcing aren't the same thing at all.

Like God, the devil is not some external thing. The devil is a mix of pain and ignorance in you. His temptation is to express that pain and ignorance, not as something to be overcome, removed, but as your guiding principle. For in the pain and ignorance, energy is locked up. Allowing that energy to be expressed through anger in daily life is to reinforce it, just as a tiny trickle of water in a dam will soon develop into a torrent that can destroy the dam. Contrary to some therapeutic ideas, the devil is never absent. It exists in your past, it is a level of being to be transcended, not something to be eliminated. Therapeutic treatment *ameliorates*. It allows a release of pain to make it easier to reach a higher level. It is not a solution. Where no higher level is reached, the old devil will soon rear his ugly head again.

So guard against petty irritation and small expressions of anger, be you ever so developed, be you ever so close to Me. Be aware. Breathe slowly and consciously. Take an extra moment; reconnect with Me. That is the way forward. You can do it. You are a blessed Embodiment of love. Know it!

3.12.91

20
Who Controls What You Do?

Who controls? You don't like the idea of control. It seems to threaten your independence. But if you look a little closely, you will see that 'no control' threatens your independence even more. Whenever you act, a decision is made; a decision between action and non-action, and about the nature of the action undertaken. Something always initiates that decision. There is no decision without a decider. When you 'feel' you want to do something, when you relax the control of your mind acting as a moral guardian, a 'good custodian' of your actions, 'you' are still deciding what is done. But the *part of you* that decides is no longer at the level of your consciousness. It lives in your feelings, your momentary desires. The consequences of your actions, therefore are still your responsibility, but you are subject to your most primitive aspects, aspects of which you are not aware and which are prey to all the unresolved problems of your past.

There is no place where 'you' are not in control The question is only, which part of you is in control. There are three levels: - your divine Self. This is the part of you that is free from delusion. Decisions at this level come from your connection with higher intuition, universal wisdom. They feel wonderful, powerful, flowing and free.

The second level is through the control of your conscious mind, referring to human knowledge and teachings as to what is best. The decisions may be more or less the same as those of the first level, but they can often feel imposed. So terms like 'duty', and 'self-discipline' are involved, terms that the modern society scorns.

At the third level, responsibility at the level of conscious mind is abnegated, and the 'doer' becomes the feeling, or desiring level of ego. At this level, the doer is opened to all the unresolved desires that always exist at this level, arising out of the nature of human upbringing. To consciously stimulate this level lays you open to pain and unhappiness, the result of short-lived gratification. In short, it stimulates the devil in you.

Your task is to find Me in you, to re-merge with Me. Do not be afraid of controlling those feelings and desires that are not resolved. If they have a powerful charge that overwhelms you, do some therapy to release the pain and use the results to strengthen your self-control, at the same time seeking the higher level, God control. Get into the discipline of right conduct. Then, together with right understanding, it is not such a long step to God control and freedom. So many nowadays have felt the energy of love multiplying on the planet and equated it with 'letting go' .You have to *transcend* mind control, conscious control of your behaviour, not deny it, or you will be left with 'desire control', which will take you away from, not towards, truth and wisdom.

So ask yourself the questions, 'Who controls what I do? What part of me is in charge?' Move away from 'being controlled' by your unconscious ego-self, stimulate your self-control and self-discipline as a means of developing *Self-control*. Then, and then only, will you be really free. That is the royal road to Moksha - liberation. Practice it!

You are a loved, blessed Embodiment of love; you have My full personal support in the journey towards Me, your universal Self.

7.12.91.

21
There Is No Need to Worry.

Do not worry. Worry tenses, weakens. It does not solve situations but merely makes you more ineffective, less present in the situations that you face. Worry creates impatience, brings you away from your centre. It is totally redundant. Why fear when I am here? I run the show. Allow Me to be you and there will be none of this angst. I have promised you a tractor, and I will give you a tractor. Which tractor do you want? It shall be yours. I organise things. Give Me a clear request and I will fulfil it. This is such a small, infinitesimal matter, manifested in the twinkling of an eye. You create such a large affair over it. Neither hurry, nor hesitate. Let the group try to find agreement, so the energy is clear.

All these insecure emotions demean you, for they are the product of the arrogance of the ego and reluctance to accept God as the driver. You are God. If you do not accept God as the driver, He will not drive. When Ego drives, there is poverty, war, unnecessary suffering. Mother Earth reacts to all the collective angst and violence; her balance is upset, and she reflects you. When God drives, there is harmony and abundance for all. It is as simple as that.

183

You are God. God exists as you at a level of energetic vibration, a *will* force. Ego exists in you as another level of energetic vibration. Bestiality also exists in you as a level of energetic vibration. Behaviour and results are the consequence of the level of vibration on which you exist. Because the whole of creation - matter, energy, being itself - is one Divine thought experienced by humans as love, from each level of vibration you can aspire to a higher, as each is present in you. The aspiration is expressed in devotion, reason and behaviour, changing you little by little. You enter life innocent and open, but where your stage is set depends on your previous experience as a vibrational being.

Each of you is a different mix of vibrational levels which vary around a norm, as waves vary around an average height. A 'typical' bestial person would have some ego and a spark of God vibration. A 'typical' ego person would have some bestial and some divine vibration. A 'typical' divine person would have some ego and a spark of bestiality. A fully divine person appears on earth as a perfected spiritual teacher. All is vibrational level.

Love, for a bestial person, seems animalistic, physical. Love for an ego-centred human is expressed as partner need and consideration. Love for a person centred on divine levels of vibration is unconditional, expressing the knowledge that all creation is God thought.

Whatever your aspiration, it must be expressed through choices of stimuli in the experienced world if it is to be realised and held. A bestial person will seek inputs of low vibrational energy in food, companionship and surroundings. To change his state, be/she must change their inputs. The consequences of existing on any vibrational level will be expressed in the emotional state; as pain, violence, anger, grief, envy, lustfulness at the lower levels or happiness, joy, detachment, bliss at the higher state.

184

All is, ultimately, God's thought experience of apparent separation from unity tending to re-mergence. So there is no complete satisfaction at any vibrational level except that of conscious reunion with the One.

Centre your aspiration on Me. I will help you to realise it, apparently separate from you, till you come to a vibrational level where you realise and ultimately experience that all was, is and ever will be - Me.

You See, there is no need to worry. It holds you down. Why fear when I am here? Be blessed, Embodiment of love.

18.12.91.

22
Be Very Careful of Your Tongue.

Come to Me! Your happiness, the quality of your life, your success or failure, everything depends on Me. Accept that, act on it!. Be thinking of Me, calling My name, interrupting all other thoughts. Listen to songs about Me. Read books about Me. Immerse yourself in Me. Meditate on Me. Feel Me as your loving heart. Do not be afraid, or feel too inadequate or undeveloped to identify yourself with Me. Do it quietly, with no pomp or show or struggle. Curb your tongue, measure your action, do everything with Me on your lips. I am the one true Identity. Do not let anything divert you, whatever it may seem. I am the quality of being that you bring to your work, the chooser of the work, the receiver of the results. I am everywhere, everything; but concentrate on yourself being Me, for only thus can you experience Me constantly in everything.

Do not judge others. Be very careful of your tongue. Remember, you are talking about Me. Is it necessary to make remarks? Are they based on loving concern? Do not release irritations and frustrations by being negative or hurtful about others. Give Me all those emotions, let them be absorbed and dissolved in My love. Think of Me precisely at those moments of impatience and loss of conscious awareness. Use the thought of Me as an anchor, a lifeline. Never cling or be attached. Do your work; leave the results to Me. Then you will find peace in every situation, and what is right will come to pass.

Live this message and you are enlightened. It is the way from duality to unity. Let the small, ego 'I' melt harmoniously into the large, God 'I' .You have been blessed. Do not slip into unworthiness or petty pride. Live with Me in each minute of the day. Respect the blessing given you, All is very, very well, Embodiment of love.

The little trials with computers are of patience and calmness. Relax, do not be attached.

14.12.91.

186

23
Giving Reverence

All who know, give reverence. Those who are ego bound and proud do not, for they think *they* do it, or, prisoners of greed and attachments, they blind themselves in material trivialities. Their stomachs are indulged; the Lord is forgotten, or peripheralised.

But all who know, give reverence. The greater the wisdom, the more the wonder of creation is unfolded, the more the need for the embodied soul to sing its joy. For no mere rational expression or description can approach the meaning of what is to be known. Only uplifted feelings can begin to express the knowledge that God is all, and *I am He*. Pure oneness simply is; but any fragment of separation means duality. Where there is duality, the lesser aspect seeks mergence, becomes aware of the awesome whole of which it is a part and opens its heart in praise and humility, forgetting the separation in the opening, becoming one. Thus devotion is the great tool of transformation.

Songs of praise, prayers, ritual, silent sitting, calling the holy name, all these are, when fully experienced as means of devotion and reverence, paths of transcendence, gateways to unity. People ask, 'How ?How? How? Be practical, what therapy do we need? What are the steps? Where are the techniques?' But the 'techniques' are there in devotional expression. It is only that such people are unwilling to surrender, too proud to 'let go and let God'. There is no new, twentieth century way. Each age and culture has its own variations in forms of expression, but in any age it is devotion that opens the gate to God.

187

Festivals represent invitations to transcendence. Through collective devotional expression round a symbol, the individual can feel more; part of the great whole that is himself. Festivals may be perverted through material indulgence into belly service. Then they must be discarded or purified if they are still to act as gateways to truth.

Christmas is a great festival of the birth of one of humanity's greatest expressions of mergence with God, the great teacher of love, surrender and transcendence, Jesus Christ. Purify it. Use it as a devotional gateway to surrender, to unity. That is the way to God.

Beloved, you are an Embodiment of the Lord. Rejoice, do not settle for less. Come home this Christmas.

21.12.91.

24
Groups Rise and Fall.

Do not judge, do not give up hope. Relax. Christ was God's gift to the world, nearly 2000 years ago, to a people devout, but fettered in traditions which made their devotion sterile. Christ was rejected and crucified, yet won, for truth alone can win, and delusion fades. In turn, His followers became hidebound in traditions and so many became taken over, deluded by the apparent success of the ego's inventiveness as it seemed to master the natural world. Now it becomes clear to you that it did not. All the time, God's love remained the same.

Now a transformation is underway. Groups rise and fall, new alignments spring up and pass. Divinity is emergent in human identity, in yours, and requires the right conditions for growth, just like a plant. It needs a family of similar plants around it. It benefits from good, disease free soil. So plants are transplanted, to give them the best conditions for each stage of growth. It is always so with souls, but for souls in which the divinity is emerging from long obscurity, careful transplanting is necessary. When the plant has all the benefit it can obtain from one type of soil, it is just then that it is moved. The gardener pays no attention to the cries of the plant that it is happy and settled there, has found a good home. He places it in the place where its growth will be optimum. So it is with you.

This year you will be moving on. You will now move to join the community in Madeira. Move gracefully, but have no regrets. On Erraid, you have developed good roots, met the tests well. Bless the island and its group, release it and leave it in My hands. Leave your possessions behind you (yes, you may take your beloved computers). Do not worry. You will be sustained. Several of you will assemble in Madeira, You will be teaching again, wiser and more settled in Me. Do not be afraid. Do not regret. Centre yourself only in Me, as you move towards Me, towards Yourself.

This guidance is not at present to be shared with anyone. You are close to the source of knowledge, knowing the unfolding of the path. There is no past, future, present that is not known. I am your Essence, here in form to protect and nurture you, the good gardener. Take time to absorb this message. Do not hurry. Keeping it to yourself for awhile is also a challenge, of learning to know without blabbering. What is known is revealed at the right time, not out of anxiety or from attempts to demonstrate knowledge.

189

You are blessed; beloved; My Embodiment of Love. Celebrate Christ's birth. Have faith.

24.12.91

25
Grace Comes as a Result of Work.

What is to be given? Grace is given, always at God's will. Yet it is not given randomly. While the timing of grace is not to be known, it is possible to say that grace can be earned. Grace comes as a result of work, It may be a stimulus to further work, it may reflect a time span beyond the individual consciousness, but God reflects you to yourself in ways that help you become more. For everyone, Grace is there, endlessly flowing; but one person may receive the grace, another may reject it. One may find grace in understanding a tragedy; the other in avoiding a tragedy.

So it is better to say that the ability to receive grace is the result of work. As you work, you may realise that the rising of the sun in the morning is an act of grace, the very circumstances of your life, or death. But this way of understanding grace is itself an advanced one. When all is experienced as God's grace, one is quite close to God himself, for surrender has developed well. Even to be able to have such a consciousness is an act of grace, for, ultimately, God is responsible for all. Remember a story of Krishna and Arjuna. Whatever name Krishna called a bird that He saw, Arjuna did not dispute it. When Krishna, testing, questioned this, Arjuna replied that God defined the truth. On this level, what God does, is Grace.

When someone gives you a gift, it is polite to thank them, In the narrower definition of grace, when God grants an enlightening experience, or saves a situation, it is also an opportunity for thanks to well up, and this is itself a breakthrough. The ego has to admit defeat, that it has been saved by forces outside its control. But as one comes to realise the constant stream of divine grace in each momentary experience of life, then the whole being also resounds with praise, and the once proud ego becomes acceptant of its merger in a greater oneness, a paean of praise. The praise of self is the sign of egotism, Self, praised is the joy of God,

So give thanks for each special moment, each special event, each opportunity to know from whom beneficence comes. And learn to see and appreciate Divine Grace in the smallest daily event, the most difficult experience. Nothing, just nothing happens without a meaning in transformation. Arise, stunned in wonder that you are indeed, *That* and give praise from an opened heart. Then you are truly living.

Be blessed, you are dear, Embodiment of love.

26.12.91

26
Love - The Gentle Force.

All the world is crying out for the love that you have found. Yet the direction of their cries is deflected, so that it does not appear related to the real source of its yearning. In their need the poor are crying for material wealth, the starving for food. Among the rich the call is for meaning and adjustment, or for drugs to stave off the emptiness. Among the oppressed, the call is for nationhood, racial identity, religious exclusivity. So the list goes on, yet all are calling for the love that you have found. It is the solution to the problems of material unhappiness, the meaninglessness of material riches, the wish to belong.

This love that you have found is a power, a force, the gentle force. It is the unseen string that ties the Universe together. Only the great gift of consciousness allows it to be distorted, suppressed, forgotten. A working tool gives you the potential to shape and form to your will. But misused, it can cut and maim. Its use has to be learned. Consciousness is like such a tool. Fully utilised it represents unlimited creative power. But misused, unlearned operation makes it potentially dangerous for all who come near.

Religious systems provide the training for the proper use of the powerful tool of consciousness, how it should be directed and to what ends. But they become corroded with time and exposure, and while they are still true, they need renewal and re-exposition from time to time. Then God embodies himself so human consciousness on its path of learning can be corrected and redirected towards the goal of love. Consciousness directed towards love begins to heal - poverty, meaninglessness, exclusiveness. It removes swathes of confusion. As consciousness nears love, it turns to share with others its great discovery. As humanity moves towards love through consciousness, it becomes just, wise, and distortions and disharmonies in the natural order are removed, for they were created by the abuse of the conscious creative potential.

Give thanks that you have found the key; that your creative power of consciousness is in training for the discovery of universal love, and that you have come close to Myself in form, the great expression of renewal,.

Beloved, you are an Embodiment of Me. Embrace Me! Express Me! Live Me! Find bliss! Thus heal the people and the problems.

27
Take Care of Your Body.

Take care of your body. It is your temple. Keep it clean, know its limits, and give it rest enough. Care for your clothes, they are like the temple vestments. Make sure your personal environment is clean and neat.

From this fine beginning, serve the community and expand your message to the whole world. What you are is your message. How you care in all these respects gives an example to those around you and to the world. Do it all because you know that you are My temple. Turn inwards to the centre, and expand outwards from the centre, in breath and out breath. What a good policy for 1992.

Everything reaching *for*, emanating *from* the centre. That is perfect living, that is representing divinity on earth. That is happiness, non-attachment. Make this your goal for the year. Do not hurry. Since there is no hurry, hurry is only an expression of anxiety, uncentredness.

How to do this easily, quickly, simply? Call on Me! Listen to My messages; study them carefully; put them into practice. Be prepared to move this year, when the opening comes, Trust! Be neither attached nor aggressive when this happens. Till then, be fully present on Erraid. Concentrate on this lesson - dedicating all you do, large or small, to Me, as it is done.

Know that you are loved, cared for - for you are Me, Embodiment of Love. Now take a small sleep.

1.1.92.

28
Stay in Balance.

Be calm. Relax. Don't push yourself. Concentrate on being in centre. There is no hurry. No one in a hurry can find the way to the still centre where nothing is flustered. Embrace yourself as you are - as the means to change. If your will deviates from God's will, do not punish yourself for that. It happens largely because you are in a hurry. It is right not to eat eggs, but if, after having put the notice which said that a time would come when you would give them up in front of you at last, you suddenly stop them just like that, your body, which can't adjust just like that, reacts. So you find yourself not eating eggs, but eating meat instead! That is hurry, that is reaction. It is not in balance. If you feel ready to take heed of that guidance, start very slowly, reducing one or two eggs a week, so your body can adjust itself. Over months there will then be no trouble in giving eggs up without a reaction towards meat.

There are those with *concepts* of spirituality. Sometimes they try to impose them on themselves, by diktat. It creates strife; war in the self. It doesn't bring positive results. Start by accepting where you are, knowing where you wish to go, and make small, gentle, harmonious changes that do not disrupt things. Then you will like yourself better and care for yourself more.

My love for you is undiminished, whatever you do. If you take two steps 'backward', I still love you, as much as if you take two steps 'forward' .If you wish to realise your unity with Me, practice being the same with yourself as I am with you. Remember, you are not measured as loveable or not by your actions. Actions which spring from inner connection and are dedicated to Me, celebrate Me. Concentrate on perfecting this technique. It is within your reach.

Remember, if you judge others for their 'weaknesses', you are merely reflecting your own lack of self-love. You are responsible for yourself; they are responsible for themselves. You are God. They are God. Only the name and form are different. See the truth; react lightly to outer manifestations. Practice calling on Me whenever you find yourself judging. I will help you. Just call.

You are loved, cared for. I am always here for you. If I love you so much and you want to become Me, a great lesson is to learn to love yourself. Enjoy the game. Come gradually closer to the centre, which is nowhere but in you. The raindrop is of the same nature as the ocean; thus it merges without stress. A lump of iron retains its separateness, even when fully immersed in the ocean.

To become Me, practice being like Me. You are loved, blessed, embraced, Embodiment of love.

4.1.92.

29
Do Not Be Afraid of Me.

In Me is your refuge. Take this message seriously. There is nothing that can or will happen to you which you cannot dedicate to Me. Do not be afraid of Me, of My opinions. I love you. I know you. I am you. So when you are lost for a while in clouds of delusion drifting over from your past, think constantly of Me. Strengthen your thinking about Me, to the point where such clouds break around the light point which I am in you. *Your* work in this is to call on Me, deeply and earnestly. Then *I* will do the work. If you remember your childhood, and the desire to eat bacon becomes seemingly irresistible, call, call, call again on Me! You must be patient, but gradually with practice your call will be so strong that I must come and overpower that old desire, disperse the old clouds of ignorance. Have faith, it shall be so. Do not for a moment punish yourself, for the consequences of your acts will be made immediately apparent. Do not feel worthless; you are Me in Self-realisation. In all circumstances, just steadily continue to strengthen the connection, calling on Me, dedicating work to Me, simply repeating My name. You will find that you become Stronger in Me, weaker in ego.

Be happy that that which I speak is so. It is the true cause for rejoicing. There is nothing, no problem, difficulty or tragedy for which I am not the remedy. That is cause for rejoicing, isn't it?

Now, tiredness and exhaustion are signs of ego. Watch them, adjust appropriately. Let Me do the work. I am indefatigable and inexhaustible. As you work for Me, I work through you. There is perfect harmony, the tools move at the optimum speed, the right

197

amount of work is done. Without exhaustion, enormous amounts of work are completed. God work survives. It is love congealed in form, so it has enormous strength. For all the tasks of this world, God work is strong enough and durable enough. See the great stone monuments of the prehistoric peoples. That was God work, and it has survived thousands of years to interest and inspire modern humanity. Let God work flow through your arms, hands, body and legs. At the end of the day, you will be healthily tired, but perfectly exercised and never exhausted,

Finally, do not worry, you are living well, and working well through Me. Allow yourself patience that you can live better and work better as you allow Me to take over more and more. For I am your truth, the identity hidden behind the veil of illusion which seems to define you as separate. Cognise yourself as an expression of Me.

Be blessed, as you journey to the one.   8.1.92.

30
Don't Give Ego House Room!

The message remains, do not hurry. Be calm. There is all the time in the world. Do not worry. The wind will give you time to do your greenhouse. To flow and dedicate is a beautiful energy; not holding on but expressing love in whatever situation you are in. Love multiplies through use. There are no limits to what you can do. By becoming God you become both able to achieve anything effortlessly and to have the wisdom to know what is worth achieving. The more you give love, the more you have. And love is the joyful expression of appropriate energy in any given earthly situation. This is 'playing the divine game.'

Ego and its attendant servers, pride and self-inflation, is always waiting at the sidelines of any achievement to transform it from a work of love to a work of petty personal aggrandisement. So there needs to be vigilance. Do not give ego house room! When it sets a foot in the door, throw it out! Don't let it get re-established in your home, or bliss will flee out of the back door. Make sure everything that is done is not only dedicated to Me, but also done in mindfulness of Me. That way, ego won't get a chance to creep in.

Hurry and pressure are a devious way to prepare the ground for ego. If it can't get in directly, it tries a sneaky stratagem. The mind, willing to work for any master, fills up with thoughts and doubts. Will it work? Will there be time? Instead of joy, the work becomes pressure. Then, ironically, mistakes creep in, irritation builds, and ego has his foot in the door again. So think of Me. Be in balance, in harmony, fully immersed in the present moment. If you feel yourself slipping, call on Me - reinforcing the growing 'You - I' identity through constant reiteration. It is not a question of morning meditations. On their own, they aren't enough. They must be combined with a constant perception of the Presence. Then love will flow and multiply, miracles will ceaselessly happen and ego will little by little melt away. This is your path. Follow it; if you deviate, return to it, strengthen your adherence to it. Don't be distracted. Let Me direct the Erraid community. Be My agent. I am holding the reins so that the diverse identities here can blend. Don't be afraid or worried.

You are blessed. You are an Embodiment of love. Let us be one.
12.1.92.

31
It Is The Loving Attitude that Is Important.

Balance, harmony - qualities of the aspirant - the ability to work one-pointedly, but to balance various aspects of life. The aspirant is given various situations, and in all are challenges. Compulsiveness shows itself as a destroyer of balance, and harmony is therefore in danger. Compulsiveness arises from fear, and fear from insecurity. Develop faith in Me. Dedicate work to Me. Take the time to feel Me as the Doer, as you do when you open to these messages. Let your whole life be an expression of Me, then the faith will be strong, insecurity will be undermined, fear will cease, compulsiveness will not rule, and harmony and balance will reassert themselves so that life flows in perfect joy.

Practice, practice, practice! Use the time, use all these tasks as practice, not of acquiring new skills, but of developing this harmonious progression - from you to Me. Concentrate more on dedication of the activity, on God-awareness while performing it. One-pointedness is pure only when it arises from and flows to God with conscious will. Don't delay. Do it this morning in your work. *Here* your ego can be challenged.

The way of love is the way of attraction. Attraction is not sui generis. *You* cannot attract. *Love* attracts. Attempts to attract, repel. It is so in all aspects of life. If you send out disparaging thoughts about others, do you think I do not receive them? I *am* the other. I receive all your thoughts about Me. The ego of the other may not be aware of it, but he or she knows your thoughts about them all right. Often they forgive you for something they do not even consciously have in their awareness, but it is your responsibility to have loving thoughts about them. You can engage in arguments about this and that, decisions that seem important, but these are like froth on the surface of liquid. It is the loving attitude that is important. Lose that and you are in serious trouble, for your ego is in control.

All the various situations in life give an opportunity. I am hidden in each one. Discover Me there.

You are love embodied; enjoy your Self-discovery. Steadily become Me. You are blessed.

16.1.92.

32
Action and Reaction. An Inescapable Logic.

Action and reaction; an inescapable logic of human affairs, a teaching tool, a framework within which things happen. That each action has consequences is part of the structure of existence, as inexorable as physicality. There is no judgement in it, yet there is a higher morality at work. Each species carries its own highest potential within the limits of its existence. Humanity is limitless. Any action below this highest potential is consequence filled, for it sets off ripples, or waves of consequence. These ripples or waves are not related to personal time-spans. They exist within Divine order. Nor does individual consciousness know the previous cause. Yet through the reaction it learns what to avoid. This form of karma is not the only, nor even always the most significant teaching tool in the transformation process from human to divine. But it is always present.

Only the genuine dedication of action to the Divine can mitigate, through Grace, the karmic consequence of action, for it is itself an action of great power, an engine pulling the carriages towards the station of unity. But the *motivation* for such dedications is also part of their consequence. If it springs from an upwelling of love in the heart, it is virtually irresistible to the Lord. If it is done for the purpose of mitigating consequence, it is conditional, therefore less powerful. Yet, even with this motivation, dedication of action to the Lord is more beneficial than non-dedication.

The first step is realisation. The ego resists, wishing to experience its transitory desires without consequence. During this, painful phase, there is denial, turning the back on the obvious, actions which themselves have their own consequences; they might be described as multipliers of consequence. As realisation dawns, there is a sense of desperation, even despair, as the ego sees that it is trapped, a hopelessness. It is an opportunity for surrender, an opening to the Lord, when nothing else seems to be open. So great is His love, waiting till the ego has tried all other channels. As surrender occurs, so dedication begins, and a new power of love begins to enter the outer identity. The process is not necessarily smooth or without regression, but, since it is the only way forward, eventually it will be tried. Thus, all souls will, in the end, come to their own Divine nature.

As you observe this world, know enough not to judge, but to identify what is happening and let your compassionate heart provide the appropriate support. Let your fulfilment be expressed. It is the best form of compassion, yet be ever attentive to the other. As you ride on the carriage of Dharma, do not ride on those who are still strapped to its karmic wheels. Help them to be free and come aboard.

You are loved and blessed. I am with you always, Embodiment of love.   20.1.92.

33
My Voice Is Always There.

Listen carefully to My messages. Disentangle them from your desires. Connect with Me as your centre. I am not a dogmatist, nor am I a puritan, but I expect discipline. How can these two be reconciled? I expect discipline to do My will. That, of course, depends on the person and where they are on their journey to Me. One of the chief aspects of *your* discipline is to be able to listen to Me. You have become open to your truth, My voice. Hear it as your own, not a something separate from you. Let it guide and inform everything you do. Follow the plea to do My will in your prayers. Listen! Take the very small but crucial amount of time required to hear what is to be done and how it is to be done. Practice constantly in small and large things. The left hand listens to My will, the right hand dedicates the act to Me. I am the doer in the centre. With good and constant practice the hands will discover the motivator in the centre.

All is not action and performance. In a good ballet, it is not only the high jumps and pirouettes. A choreographer knows the effect of pauses and settings. Let yourself be flexible in action. Above all, hear the inner guidance, for that will give you perfect choreography. Remember, all that needs to be done will be done if you are in alignment with Me. Have faith in that, cease to worry, and heed the guidance. Live your life from it. My guidance in terms of general spiritual development comes to you in these messages, which can be shared at the appropriate moment. But there is also another, immediate, practical, intuitional guidance that says, 'Do this!' 'Wait!' 'Don't do that!' and so on. Learn to listen to this and trust it, for it is also Me. It is characterised by appropriateness, not dogma, for rules are generalities for the development of all. Intuitive purity gives immediate and perfect access to My Will from moment to moment. 'Lord, Your will be done,' has a practical content - inner listening.

My Will will be done; the question is, are you with Me or fighting Me? I never deceive you. If you learn to hear, My voice is always there, expressing My will, giving you the opportunity to follow Me. It is the voice of conscience *plus*, for your conscience may be carrying a burden of moral judgements that does not make for clear hearing.

I am with you, blessing you, welcoming you to Me in you. Become Me. Become what you actually are, Embodiment of Love.

23.1.92.

34
The Attainment of Divinity is to Live Love.

There is one God. All over the world He is worshipped in different ways. That is no problem. But when people begin to claim exclusiveness, they effectively deny the unity of God, and thus deny their own belief. God is love. Wherever there is love, there God is. Love flows forth from the soul. It is the special quality. that transforms the mundane. Life infused with love is joy. Even in situations of great suffering, the free flow of love transforms the situation.

So nail the standard of love to your mast. Practice it in all the situations that are given you and they will be transformed. All the techniques and recommendations are to help you perform this small and simple task - bringing love in. That is the same as saying 'Bringing God in' .The attainment of Divinity is not something complex or esoteric. *It is living love*. Love moves the energy of the being from the mind, centre of ego and restricted consciousness, to the heart. Then right conduct is known - it is immediately apparent.

Do not deny love in any way. If you don't feel loving, do not *not* be loving. Acknowledge a separation, but be loving. Take responsibility for the not-loving feeling, but do not indulge it. It is neither correct to suppress non-loving feelings, nor is it correct to give them power. If you are a divided self, empower the loving part. At the appropriate opportunity, turn loving feelings on the non-loving part, however hateful it seems to you. It is there because appropriate love was not given at the appropriate time. To give it love does not mean to indulge it. It is the healing force. Always empower loving feelings, always disempower non-loving feelings. Putting into practice empowers; not putting into practice disempowers. This is the simple, clear way of finding God in yourself. Of all the ways towards Me, this is the simplest and most direct. Like all, it depends on the exercise of conscious choice. But there is no insurmountable barrier for anyone, in any circumstances, to make that choice. Do it! Constantly be making that choice for love. Ask Me to help. I will. Gradually the separation reduces. Love becomes love. Ego and its cohorts are disempowered. Kurukshetra is won. Yet remember, never empower non-love. It will awaken again and start greedily feeding. Be vigilant.

As you learn and your consciousness is weak, I will bridge the places where you sleep and love is not empowered. I will step in for you in response to your prayers. But till we are One, I will not take the place of your responsibility to make conscious choices for love. Surrender to God - to love and make continuous conscious choices to do that in all your day to day situations. Don't worry, you can, you are already doing it.

Be blessed, trust. All is well. 27.1.92

35
Beware of Tightness and Meanness.

Act lovingly and with generosity. Tightness and meanness are signs of mistrust in Me, the Provider. What you have is not yours, but entrusted to you to use. Use it, but not as a means of currying favour or making an impression. These are ego qualities. Use what you have as an expression of Me. Do not consider spiritual sadhana as an excuse not to be generous. Where an expression of love and consideration is involved, do not hesitate to interrupt sadhana. Not doing so is not a sign of your spiritual greatness. It is a sign of that special spiritual illness known as 'holy-ness' - when a person is egocentrically demonstrating how 'holy' they are to impress others. Remember who is observing your acts and do not seek to impress. It does not work. Instead, let your innate generosity and openness of heart flow out in small, 'spontaneous' gestures. These demonstrate Me in you, and improve the quality of life around you.

But do them because of the current of energy that informs you to do them and not for other, extrinsic reasons. Only then are they My acts.

An action is Mine not because of its form, bet because of its expression. The most pious recitation of holy scripture is not mine because of the words said, but because of the place of the heart of the reciter. Good works are mine, not because of the action's consequences, but because of the expression of unconditional love in the action. Actions from ulterior motives may be beneficial in the short term, but they are not My actions in a strong sense. Even actions dedicated to Me after the event are only 'second class citizens' - reclaimed actions from the past. The expression of My will in the exact moment of action is really Divine. Doing that all the time is to be God-realised. Only right action can flow from doing My will. Do not be afraid of it.

So be generous in your love and take an instant to listen. Then love and wisdom will blend in the perfection of My will. Never be disheartened by 'failure' .There is no failure, only repetition till you get it right. Have patience with yourself. You are doing very well. I am with you, blessing you, supporting you, encouraging you. Know it, and be with Me. What other way of being is worth while?

Have faith, Embodiment of love.

31.1.92.

36
Examining the Ego.

There is only one god - He is omnipresent. God is not a man - He is all that there is, including mankind. Humans are blessed in being able to transcend their animal state and enter consciously their own Divine nature, but only if, and in as far as they can leave behind the limiting framework of their animal nature. Humans are therefore God's visitors, and may become Himself. God's house is the human heart, the symbol of love, the place where love resides. Isn't it strange to talk about visiting oneself? He who can be a visitor to himself is not fully himself. To be fully yourself is the purpose of existence, but not in the sense of fully realising the petty desires stimulated in human society, which are largely escapist in nature, chimera of the ego, to bolster the insecurity of the ego.

The ego, ahamkara, is a necessary part of human development. The growth of human consciousness requires a sense of self. But, just as it is ridiculous to imagine a plant developing as far as the stage of having a bud, and then for the bud to hold on to itself and not allow itself to flower, so it is ridiculous to imagine that humans can be fulfilled through their ego. The trap is that, as the ego develops, it begins to experience powerfulness, self-consciousness, and thinks 'I do it' - it is entrapped in delusions of its own grandeur. To its limited consciousness, the world around it, fed to it through the sense organs, seems objective and different, to be suffered or conquered, instead of a shifting projection of its own moods and sense of self. The social arrangements of ego-centred humanity bolster this sense of the objectivity of the sense experienced world, and its immalleable nature.

For everyone, God's grace provides glimpses of the possibility of something more, but the ego clings on, and tries to ignore, encapsulate such experiences, so that its world may continue unchallenged. Fear and conservatism compete with inquisitiveness in the struggle for development. But, just as the bud becomes a flower, so each individual human soul eventually transcends its ego level, for all the resistance and struggles. Thus it is not the goal of the game that is in question, or the final outcome, but the manner of playing.

For those of you who wish to find something of your nature by the path of enquiry, the examination of the ego within this schema is a most valuable way. For even the examination of the ego posits an examiner outside the ego. But it is not enough to examine. The sign of real wisdom is the desire to experience that investigated, and that requires changes in behaviour corresponding to the discoveries that are made.

In this age of materialism, most human beings have considerable transformation to make before they are ready to move beyond self to Self realisation. As the global social transformations occur, humans who are able to lift their level of being towards their Divinity are the beacons of a new age, in which humanity begins its journey to a higher level of experience. As the level lifts, consciousness awakes with the bud of perception already more open, and the ego is not so reinforced. As humanity proceeds in this direction, the frippery of materialism will disintegrate before the gentle force of love exerted on the planet.

God is not a man, but He can incarnate on earth as a man, for the purpose of bringing about transformation. I have come now, as helper, stimulator, inspirer, to guide you through the troubled waters of social transformation. Look to Me. Let Me help you Aspire to your own truth - your inherent Divinity.

You are blessed, loved, Embodiment of love.

3.2.92.

210

37
Take a Moment Before Each Action.

Let things take their course. Be in the present, enjoy each moment, whatever it may bring. Have no fear when I am here. On the material level, all that you need will be manifested to you, at the proper moment, without rush or prior to its need. There is no hurry. Be calm. Let everything unfold. Do not go to see a play thinking only about the next scene, so that you cannot appreciate the author and actors' skill in this one. Let your life be that way, too. It is a question of confirming your faith and affirming that I, not ego, rule in you. Ego is anxious and impatient, I am joyful and open to each moment that I create.

The crucial thing is: learn to take a little moment before each action, each set of actions, to be fully present for those actions. Whatever you do, be present for it in that moment. For instance, if you are moving seaweed to the gardens from a heap, where is heaven? Heaven does not lie in the completion of the job. That happens at the end - to anticipate it detracts from the present moment. Nor does it lie in the purpose of the job, in this case to fertilise the ground. That may be the reason for doing it. Nor does it lie in the appreciation your hard work may bring. That is irrelevant if the purpose is right and only increases your dependence on others' opinions. Heaven lies in the movement of the fork, lifting the seaweed onto the barrow, finding the next part of the heap to move, wheeling the barrow to the chosen garden bed, tipping the barrow out, and returning with the unladen barrow to the pile. Heaven is the full awareness of the quality of this experience, giving total attention to it, mindfully. The 'trick' is that the quality of the experience lies not in the experience but in your attitude to it. By practising 'full awareness' of the present moment as your key to the source of happiness, you are hardly able to avoid realising that the source of the happiness is Me.

As you manage this, do not be afraid, not merely to dedicate the acts to me, but to invoke that I, not you, am the doer. Thus, God, not you lifts the seaweed, moves the barrow, empties it on the garden and returns with it to the pile. At first this may seem artificial, even presumptuous, but that is only because of the ego's false modesty. Dare to do it, practice it, and gradually you become one brilliant divine action in creation. That is beyond heaven itself.

Now, extend this method beyond sea weeding, to everything you do. Ignore whether you like doing it or not. That is irrelevant. But when you have decided to do something, follow the sequence - right motivation; experience the present action; be God doing it. Life is nothing but bliss, an expression of the Great Love and you are home.

Do not condemn yourself if all this does not happen at once. Set it as your intention, bring yourself back to it, change by loving and accepting yourself. But do not be complacent of your inadequacy. If it takes a million attempts, do not give up, do not get impatient with yourself. You are getting there. I am with you till we are one, and I am always loving you, never condemning.

Be blessed, Embodiment of love.

7.2.92.

212

38
Spiritual Detachment.

Life is a sea; some days it is calm, others it is stormy. But the experience of life depends on the quality of your response to storm and calm. The great mistake is to think that your experience depends on the storms and calms themselves. The sea of life is ever-changing, but that need have no relation to your state of happiness. Nor is it irrelevant to your experience. A zombie experiences the same mood, irrespective of changes in outer state, but that is because of malfunction of the brain. The spiritual quality is to fully appreciate all the variations of the sea of life, but to experience them as different manifestations of Divine will, and thus stimulants of the quality of divine bliss in you, the observer/participant. So there is all the difference in the world between lethargic acceptance of all that happens and fully conscious appreciation of its true nature.

Generally speaking, humans respond to situations with varying moods and feelings. All of this is related only to ego-attachment. The ego identity is wounded or appreciated in the past - events stimulate once again these old feelings. It is attached to being recognised - so it interprets events in this light. Am I appreciated? Am I disregarded? - feelings follow. Thus one is a prisoner of the waves and moods of life's external stimuli, up one day, down the next, happy one hour, miserable the next.

As soon as you begin to see that the entire show is God's play, and start to release the ego-attachment to the forms of the show, the feelings can begin to concentrate and intensify about the majesty,

213

indescribable complexity and wonder of the whole experience of life. Thus, Divine orientation is not a diminution of feeling, but a concentration of feeling about that which matters. Spiritual detachment is neither passivity of feeling, nor non-involvement in activity; it is an egoless embracing of the whole, a mergence with truth, with the Divine nature of the Self. This experience is one of total one-pointedness of feeling - all the emotional resources of .the body are in the present, fully concentrated on accepting the experience. This quality is bliss. The mind is also fully concentrated so that it is razor sharp and can break through the delusion that outer form is reality, rather than a mirrored sense experience of what really is true, the Lord. So each perception becomes a perfect manifestation of God, perceived by God.

Some people think that the state of bliss is boring. In their ignorance of the state, they have confused it with lethargy. Bliss is transcendent of all ordinary happiness or pleasure. It has nothing to do with living an ordinary life and enjoying a little bit of this, and a little bit of that. It is the experience of God living the life He created, and knowing it.

Know that this way of living is available to you, not some distant dream. Seek it, approach it, realise it. Do not think, 'Oh, that's all for saints, I'm too fallible, there's much too much for me to develop before that state is possible.' That is delusion. Dare to live perfection now. Call on My help. It is not a matter of endless lifetimes of development. If you didn't receive these messages it would be harder for you. Are they not proof that you can transcend? Go for it!

Be blessed,

10.2.92

39
Install God In Your Heart.

Give thanks that I am always loving you, whatever you do. That I am always present, even when your face is turned away from Me. That I am directing and guiding your path, so you can best overcome obstacles and weaknesses. Remember this, always, in every situation.

At this present time the important thing is to love yourself unconditionally. Of course, if you aren't able to do this, it is a misconception that you can also love others without condition. You may say, if I love myself unconditionally, I can do anything at all and be all my bad qualities and nothing will control them. I assure you, it does not work like that. At first you may notice a slight 'reversion' as a dog let off a leash tends to spring away and run around. But the dog, more than anything else in the world, loves its master. Its very existence depends on the master. After a very short while it will return to the master's feet; only the master's pleasure will satisfy it. The dog is like the ego. Once God is invoked, He becomes the master - once the ego-dog has found its master, nothing else can satisfy it and it will return to the feet of the Lord who is installed in the heart.

This is true. Have faith in it. You must trust that you are not the ego, that you are love incarnated, and that the power of love overwhelms all other, the joy of love exceeds all other. All this is conditional on having installed the Master in the heart. A dog without a master will run and run till it finds a master, for it is bred to need one. Your ego, if God is not installed in your heart, will run and run to seek Him, for it is so bred. At this time, it needs discipline, for like a stray dog, it can do harm. So stage 1 is installing God in your heart as the Master. Stage 2 is having faith that God in your heart really is the Master - learning to trust Him. Stage 3 is merging with the Master, becoming one with Him. Here the ego is transcended.

You are in stage 2. Trust the Master. Play the game of life. Let Him lead, as in a trust game where you are blindfolded and someone else pushes you safely around. Do not be afraid or anxious but let go and let God. Concentrate on loving yourself, whatever happens. You will soon be back with the Master, even closer than before, even nearer the ultimate third stage.

Be loved, be supported, be Me, Embodiment of love.

13.2.92.

40
Why Not Be With Me All the Time?

All the time you are loved. Every special event is an indication that you are coming together with Me after separation. Why not be with Me all the time? Then there will be no problems, no anxieties, only wonder at the Divine Plan. Even in this there is still an element of separation, but for now, that is enough. Even special messages are an indication that at the time of not receiving the message there is separation. Why not put aside a time for writing our/My words? Begin a longer project, a book or an article, written by Me/you. You don't need to be separate and cling to the coat sleeves of My 'reputation' any longer. Let's be one. Why don't you think of it now the other way round - perhaps for a while there will be occasional separations. But for the majority of the time, there can be Oneness. You are ready. Accept it! Meet the challenge and change style! A new scene in your drama is beginning - coming closer to the denouement of this act. Don't be afraid - don't be separate. You are doing very well. Know it! You have been going through tests in the past few days. Passed!

So make the new resolve. You know all the external conditions, laid out in the scriptures. Be that - now. Free. Give thanks.

Praise and blame are unimportant. Let others swirl around the rock of your perfection. But be clear that there are no flaws in the rock, for reactions to you may also be gifts to you to move from imperfection to perfection. Never be defensive. Observe any defensiveness as a sign of poor quality behaviour which is being reflected to you. Anything you *try* to be is not the same as being. Just be Me, now.

Moving on time approaches slowly. So let it come as it comes and enjoy the time here while you are here. All is very, very well. Be One with Me, today and forever. You are blessed that this is possible.   17.2.92.

41
Any Spiritual State Can Be Infected With Ego.

God stands like a rock in the middle of the sea. Round Him roll the waves of ego. Ego is dependent on God, but would like to feel separate, to have power for itself. Yet in itself it has nothing, not even a body. So it is always a parasite, and its intentions and motives are directed at external reward, in the shape of prestige and status. In the process of the realisation of self, the ego exists. It is useless to pretend to deny its existence. Realisation in life involves the elimination of ego. In reaching this goal, the ego has to be controlled. This can be done, must be done, but the ego is a wily and slippery customer. In relation to the divine goal of mergence it frets and chafes, seeking all kinds of ways of retaining its mediating role for the divine energy, giving itself reality.

It will at times fight openly. This is experienced as resistance and doubt or rejection. It seeks for flaws in the divine, clings to gossip and rumour, tries to undermine the devotion and genuineness of the religious experience. It must be recognised and met head on if you want to get anywhere. Its secondary stratagem in this battle is to achieve its aims through putting resolve off balance. 'How weak I am, to let my ego defeat me. What a hopeless aspirant!' Self denigration and anger with the ego's small victories feed the ego's power and detract from the calm acceptance of the soul's path.

At other times, the ego will seem to ally with the Divine. 'Yes,' it will say, 'you are divine. Use your divine powers, create your own reality. Become wealthy, manifest yourself this and that. People will really recognise who you are - you'll be famous, a famous devotee, revered by all.' This stratagem can be very subtle. It is expressed in feelings of hyper-confidence, a sense that one *really* is God, not in itself but for others. It can be detected through subtle feelings of pride, overweening feelings of power, a lack of humility. Chant the name of the Lord, experience humility, and ego will recoil, rebuffed.

In fact, any spiritual state can be infected with ego. Humility itself can become a pose, a show for others. On his path, the devotee who is entrusted with teaching others is constantly threatened with the re-establishment of ego-identity and the loss of God connection, as external praise is accepted for work which is an expression of divine energy. So as you teach others by allowing My will to work through you, My words to be spoken through you, beware of praise. Do not reject it, for that is another ego stratagem to weaken you. Simply pass it back through you to Source, consciously and firmly. God is the doer, the vessel and the result. Give all praise to Him. He will assure the path of the earnest devotee so that exactly what is needed at any given moment is available, teaching or not teaching, mouthpiece or silent observer, actor or witness. Subordinate yourself totally to that will, and you will come home in the twinkling of an eye. Ego will crumble and dissolve itself back into the divine energy which, through the reflection of the senses, gave it life and power.

Face the devil! Fight to the end! Finish the game! Now is the time - you are blessed, loved, encouraged, protected, Embodiment of Love.

20.2.92

42
To Know You Are Not Your Body - Call On Swami.

Never believe the world is real. What you see on a cinema screen can move you, but you know it is a film. What you experience in life is a three dimensional film in which your identity is an actor. If you believe the film is real, you are under the sway of illusion - maya, and are attached to the transient phenomena of the film. Since you really know what is real and what is not, it is the part of you that is in delusion, ego, which seems in command. But if you are connected with the Creator of the film inside yourself, you will have great confidence in acting in the film, since you are not subject to the sway and whim of delusion, but creating the film yourself. Acting from God eliminates fear.

The greatest illusion of the human condition is death. Ego identification with the body equals fear of death, since the body is bound to decay and is subject to all sorts of dangers in the world. You are not your body, and if you really know that, you cannot be afraid of death. Thus there will be no inhibition on appropriate action, for who knows the truth is not bound by Maya. The way to achieve this state? Call on Swami. That is My great gift to you. I am here to guide you home - to replace the mind, the ruler of illusion with the heart, the seat of God in you, as the source of your identity,.

As you grow you will realise that the more you remember to call on Me, the more you will be able to achieve dharmic action in the world, not because I preach morality, but because I an the source of moral action, and if I am installed in your heart, moral action simply is there too. As you grow, it is this calling to Me that is important. It represents a switch. The call switches on the right current to light the lamp of dharma. Without that call, the mind of illusion still holds sway, and dithers this way or that in the grasp of uncertainty, or grasps onto false certainties and finds disillusion. So switch on your switch. Call on Me. In becoming dependent on Me in you, you are not losing yourself but losing your illusions. In unconditionally identifying with Me, you are gaining *Yourself*. Practice this in all situations, from small to seemingly large. 'Om Sai Ram' switches you from purgatory to heaven in a trice. 'Your will be done' is the key to the pearly gates. Accept the take over bid. Do not struggle. Then you are home and we are One.

Be loved and blessed, We are so near, Embodiment of love.

23.2.92.

43
How To Begin Each Day.

Start at the beginning. Each day has a beginning. Organise and regulate that beginning so that you are placed in connection with Reality from the first moment. What is your first thought as you emerge into consciousness? How do these early moments continue? How beginnings are formed is very important. If your beginnings are right, you may waver in the day, but you will not stray very far. If they are not, you will have a hard job keeping to the path.

A lot of people go through a daily trial at the beginning of the day. Who is master - indulgence or God's will? It is absolute folly to say, ' I'll just do as I feel', when you are a conflicting ground for feelings and desires. You have to put your will behind right conduct for yourself at the beginning, then you will 'feel' good all day. It demands a degree of discipline, which should rather be called Self-empowerment - giving energy at the beginning to the search for the Self. This discipline is minor - not some overwhelming, impossible requirement imposed from outside. It is your own inner determination to run the show. This expresses itself first as egoism, but its transcendent development is surrender to God's will, not some abstract power working outside of you to 'show you what to do', but surrender to God's will working in you to create outside reality in the interests of your Self development. It is very valuable, therefore, to be sure to start the day with God, by determining when you wake up, how you wake up and by dedicating the first actions of the day, your ablutions, to God, and then taking time in prayer, mantra and calmness. In this way God is reinstalled each day in the altar of your heart.

Do not worship at the altar of indulgence. It is a false god. Beginnings do not only apply to each day, but to each life. A parent who projects their own weaknesses on their children by indulging the child, makes it more difficult for that child to find the beginning to each day it needs to discover the divinity in its life. How a child is brought up requires love, clarity, firmness, self-confidence and discipline from the parent to give it strength and encouragement in its journey through life. In the Kali Yuga, many parents, themselves frustrated and confused, seek to give love to their children through indulgence, the worst present they could give. They have two simplistic models in their heads - bad equals loveless discipline, and good equals disciplineless indulgence. A child brought up with loving discipline will have the tools necessary to transcend ego later in life. A child brought up with disciplineless love will have to spend years finding the tools first; a child brought up with loveless discipline will spend years fighting its alienated parents. Give children the right tools to grow up with. That is part of the transformation the changing age requires.

So pay attention to beginnings. Call on Me to help, That will keep you lively, make each early moment dedicated and full of truth and stop you from slipping into empty rituals. Always

223

remember, spiritual growth has an optimum pace. It can't be forced. Every lesson I give you has to be learned, not gulped.

Be aware that I am with you, that you are truly Me, an Embodiment of love, blessed in your Self-realisation,
26.2.92.

44
To Follow Dharma - A Supreme Spiritual Test.

Do not be afraid to follow Dharma. Do not become worried or upset about the opinions of others. Do not become impatient, but be clear and principled. Make sure that principle is universally applied in your life and that there are no exceptions.

Dharma is right conduct. Without right conduct there can be no human society and no progression to the Divine Self. The source of Dharma is moral sense, which is a product of inner wisdom and the Divine source. Thus the wellspring of right action comes from within. But one has to be clear to hear it. Dharma has nothing to do with groups - it affects groups, but its source is not from groups. Collective opinion is not Dharma, but group consensus, or majority determination. However, the source of Dharma, the inner moral sense, needs to be listened to. That has become unfashionable in the Kali age, where voices of indulgence and ephemeral desire, pride and egotism strive to drive out the quiet voice of the moral sense.

In the name of right conduct, much wrong conduct has been perpetrated. People seek to justify their actions in the name of the good, although they actually spring from other motives. But that does not mean that the discipline of Dharma has to be rejected. On the contrary, it means that the struggle to purify the connection with the inner moral sense is very important. Within communities of people, many divisions and conflicts occur because of irritations of temperament and differing desires. But also Dharma and A-Dharma are constantly in conflict, for this is the purifying mechanism enabling you to learn to hear clearly the inner moral voice.

Humans enact laws to protect society from the anarchy of A-Dharmic conduct. The ultimate source of these laws is the moral sense, but a sign of the weakness of Dharma is the proliferation of laws. In the indulgence of the multiple temptations of the illusory world, people have lost touch with their inner sense. As they strive for Dharma, 'agreements' or guidelines replace laws, which become fewer and more basic. Laws and guidelines only cease to have relevance in a perfected society, which depends on perfected human beings.

As you seek Me, strive to hear My voice in you clearly, and act fearlessly on it. Be responsible to the inner voice, which relates to your whole being and the whole context of action. Never be afraid to act on the instructions of the inner moral sense, and yet always be aware of the need for clarity of listening. Never criticise others because they do not agree with you. Simply act from the inner sense. To follow right action is one of the supreme spiritual

225

tests. Act from Dharma; act lovingly; act fearlessly. That is the way to God. You are perfect, be perfect. But don't be impatient. You are love embodied, blessed, guided.

29.2.92.

45
Honour Me!

Honour Me. All that is given you comes from Me. I am very, very close to you, helping you fulfil your wish to be Me. So do not drive ahead, manfully. Be sensitive to how I have arranged the day for you, to what I have given you to work with. Neither fall victim, nor ignore what is given. You are an Embodiment of love. You are already perfection itself. You are already God, being. But your consciousness, still clouded by 'reality', can't yet break through to this, except at special moments. To be what you are, you need to be worked like plasticine, till you are not brittle and resistant but warm and soft, able to let the Divine mould you.

So there are still little ups and downs. They get smaller and smaller, for there is no longer that much separation. Honour them, observe them, flow with them, but do not be determined by them. Accept everything as an emanation of My will. Flow with, not struggle against, and you will realise and live who you are.

Be blessed, be loved. We are One.

3.3.92.

46
Be Centred on God-Centredness!

What a nice weekend! You slowed down to something like an appropriate pace. Now continue that here. Be in balance and harmony in what you do and what you don't do. Appreciate what you do, do it well and offer it to Me. Take time to be as well as to do. Taking care of these simple things will help you to be more You. Remember, haste means delay.

People demonstrate different qualities in their lives; each, therefore is a teacher and needs to learn. The quiet, inward turned person, the gentle ones, the vulnerable, all have gifts to give, quite as much as the strong, the assertive and the activists. The truly spiritual person combines all these qualities, neglecting none, embodying all. But behind all the manifestations of qualities useful to behaviour in the outer world is God-centredness. God-centredness is the easiest way to get these qualities. They emanate from God-centredness, demonstrating it. If they are painstakingly acquired and with great difficulty held in balance, like a juggling act, they are still on the periphery of truth. God-centredness provides them with no effort, flowing naturally from the source. It is this that is demonstrated by a person exemplifying a particular quality. God-centredness flows, in that respect, through them, giving benefits to others. The truly spiritual person has surrendered themselves to God-centredness, and thus all appropriate qualities flow through their body. It is the God-centredness that is primary, the qualities, its secondary, natural expression in the perceived world.

Centre your spiritual quest, then, on God-centredness, and you will find all the qualities in balance in you. Their natural expression is the result of putting the equation right. If A, B, and C are functions of G, discovering the value of G provides the key to them all. Do that yourself, encourage others to do that, and My will is fulfilled.

Remember, when your fancy takes to some particular vehicle or object, that you are committed to My will. You will not be disappointed, you will receive exactly what you need. Don't be afraid, but trust. You are not to experience lack, but fulfilment. Don't cling to a form or idea in panic and anxiety. Don't try to justify your fancies by their apparent peripheral virtues. What you need will be given, in the appropriate form. Stay centred in Me, and the triviality of these 'fancies' in relation to *actual* need will be instantly apparent in you. Let the world go by. Observe it, do not be deceived by it. Act in it, do not believe in it. Believe in Me, for I an the source of all this manifestation, your source and goal. Strengthen that faith, steadily and constantly. Play games only if you can *play* and not begin to believe that the game is real.

You are My beloved Embodiment of love. Come to Me, in all that you do. I am the way, the truth, the life.

10.3.92.

47
Changing the Point of Awareness.

Soft, like a kid glove into which My hand can fit, is the spiritual person. Not shallow, energyless, ephemeral, but becoming an Embodiment of the divine will. Each of you has this potential. It is not a renunciation of self-will, but a transcendence of it. To have ego will is a preparatory, a stretching exercise, expanding the identity so that it can accommodate the divine will. Thus ego, wilfulness are not in themselves wrong, but become so when they are redundant, when the identity has reached the point of God awareness. Baby clothes are appropriate for babies, but become ridiculous as the child gets bigger.

Of course, all can see when a baby outgrows its clothes, but how can one see the outgrowth of wilfulness or ego-will? Because it is to do with identity and not physical growth, it is not so easily apparent to the senses. The key is the point of awareness. The truly ego-centred person is unaware of divinity, fully resistant to spiritual messages and the meaning of inner vision. His point of awareness is centred in little 'I' .From this experience frustration results, and the point of awareness shifts. The will becomes confused, a sense of powerlessness appears as the Divine begins to expand in the self. Mixed behaviour emerges, contradictions are rife. Ego tries to accommodate spirit, giving it a subordinate status and legitimacy. Ego parades spirit, how good the meditator is, how well he has grasped the spiritual teachings, how well he performs - a spiritual politician still ruled by ego. Pride is transferred from secular success to spiritual 'success'.

But, inexorably, the point of awareness shifts, as inexorably as a child grows into an adult. Further dissatisfaction, confusion as the spiritual continues expanding and the ego is once again threatened, this time mortally. For the ego, humility and surrender, for the emerging Divine will, increased self-confidence and decisiveness. The identity glows, is vibrant and energy filled, physical illness recedes, or is given less importance as the being lifts its energy above the material frequencies. The power of unconditional love begins to shine in the personality, attracting and influencing others.

From the commencement of spiritual awareness, the identity may become aware of Me, the embodied form. More and more it draws on Me, accelerating the process in an ever more personal relationship with the Lord, whatever His name. For My devotees, I am ever-present, helping the point of awareness in its move, encouraging, loving, sustaining. As the One, Divine Self is expressed through the individual identity, so the transformation of the age occurs. It is a great, a joyful action. The clouds, while still heavy, begin to lift. Glimpses of the new future can be seen.

So it is with you. Adore My form; surrender to Me in your being; do not cling; do not justify. Do not seek a resting place, for Divinity in you is the only one, all apparent others are illusory.

You are blessed, supported. Let go and let Me! Trust! You are indeed an Embodiment of love.

13.3.92.

231

48
The Content of the Human Parcel.

Nowadays, everything comes in packaging, plastic, paper and so on. But does the packaging indicate the quality of the article? The makers would have you think so, encouraging you to buy according to the packaging but, in fact what matters is what is inside the packaging. The judgmental person is ego-bound and insecure. They are constantly thinking of whether another parson is better or worse than them, and the basis for their judgement is always the wrapping. Human beings come in the wrappings of personality and karma. There aren't any without them. That is the packaging. But if you judge them according to the packaging you are lost in your own packaging, and encourage reciprocal judgement from them.

Instead, investigate the *content* of the human parcel. Make an effort to remove the several and various layers of packaging, and become aware of the real content. Then your eyes, ears and more subtle senses will experience a feast of love. Other human beings come packaged for a purpose. They are your mirrors. In yourself are all the flaws and virtues you see in others. The lesson is learnt when you try to go beyond these and experience the person as God.

Make it your firm intention, your conscious resolve. Through experiencing others as divinity, you stimulate the experience of yourself as divinity. Through experiencing yourself as divinity, you stimulate the experience of others as divinity. There is total and mutual benefit from this effort. Slackness in the effort, on the other hand, drags your energy down and feeds the poor insecure 'I' .By enlisting determination and resolve in the service of the divine, unity with the divine is promoted. See others as God. See the packaging as God-given, their and your teaching aid. Accept them and yourself as you are. Through this acceptance, change occurs.

As you remind yourself of the reality of Me through 'Om Sai Ram' during the day, think also 'Do not judge others' .There is an illusory feeling of loss. If I don't judge others I renounce my critical faculty, my discriminatory ability. On the contrary, you sharpen it, by discarding the trivial and seeing what is real. The multiplication of love is the engine of transformation in the world, love of Self and love of Self in others. Criticism and negative judgement and comment merely result in defensive barriers around the insecure ego. The ego is loved into self-renunciation, not judged into it.

You and I are One. There is no other. See with My eyes, hear with My ears, think with My mind. Remember your algebra! Self plus Self equals Self. Only love enables the solution of this equation. You are love embodied; know it, seek it, live it! Be blessed.

16.3.92.

49
Understanding Atmic Consciousness.

All physical forms are becoming and dying. Some of the existences are slow and relatively unconscious - such as rocks and water. In these the organising principle is very much extrinsic and devic. In the plant kingdom, the intrinsic and the extrinsic combine in the organising principle. Devic forces work with intrinsic plant energies. In the animal kingdom, the balance is again different, but it is in humans that the greatest degree of individualised responsibility is found. Devic forces have virtually merged into individual and collective identity, with the result that consciousness is found, 'on the surface', as it were.

The task of that consciousness is to reconnect with the substratum of consciousness which underlies the whole material and energetic world, i.e. God. It has no other ultimate task. That is the game, the rules of which are set. It is not that there is punishment, but there are not, nor can there be, any other ultimate rules, and any other endeavour will always end in final frustration..

The becoming of physical forms therefore continues constantly. Their 'dying' is simply a move from one state to the next via a special energetic link. Imagine a chain. Each link in the chain is connected with the next. There is a point at which that connection is physical. That point is not immutable. If the chain is waved without stress, the connection between individual links may well vary in position. But it tends to be at the longest point in the chain. Each material form may be seen as if it were a part of a chain. Death represents the transitional connection between one link and another, the point where one link connects with another. Thus it is a special state. The other side of death is birth, where a link connects with the one before it. That is the way it is. So a fully aware being cannot be afraid of death. Only a physically embodied being that defines itself as finite and self-contained can be afraid of death.

For beings whose organising principle is largely extrinsic such as rock, there is absolutely no fear of death. For vegetable matter, the fear of death is subliminal, for animals it is partial, bet for humans, who have enough intrinsic consciousness to see

234

themselves as separate, it becomes a major issue. As knowledge increases, fear of death recedes once more, for wisdom aligns consciousness away from the apparent identity, the ephemeral physical one, to the eternal substratum of consciousness, reality.

The atmic consciousness has no limitation or definition. It may be called upon, presenting itself through the appeals by limited consciousness. So I have come, Embodiment of atma, present on all levels for the transformation of the consciousness of humanity, in response to the cries of the suffering and the prayers of the wise, to provide the energy to redirect individualised consciousness towards the Divine and out of the cul-de-sac into which it has projected itself.

Understand, be aware, identify with Me. Find bliss in reunion and perfection in beingness. This is the context of the day to day existence.

Be blessed, Embodiment of love,

19.3.92.

50
Stability Resides Only in Me.

Every change is a test of faith. However anchored in faith you may be, a continuance of the status quo is a secure experience. It may not be pleasant, but it is secure. Yet everything changes. Stability does not reside in the physical world and its arrangements. It resides in Me, omnipresent love. As long as the identification is with the projected world of form, change is a step into the unknown, requiring courage. Courage to overcome fear and make necessary moves is a great quality. But the greatest quality is movement based on faith. Where there is perfect faith, courage is not necessary, for there is a certainty of appropriate support.

The greatest change that humanity has to undergo is death. The way to be able to face death well is to have developed faith during life. Through faith, death becomes a change that is easily acceptable. For faith allows the knowledge that there is a permanent, unchanging reality at the heart of all things, and all change, including death, is an approach to this reality.

Use your life to develop an unshakeable faith. To help you, I have come, embodied divine consciousness on earth. Then the withdrawal of spirit from this physical body will be acceptable, both for you yourself, for those around you, and for those who have been near to you. If you are afraid, have courage. But best to have faith, which eliminates fear and gives acceptance. One strives for life, but, when death is inevitable, the faithful accept it with grace, anchored in God, the one immutable, transcendent reality.

For each person, death is the great examination of life. The exam may be posed at any moment. But no moment is too brief for a complete awareness of life at the moment of death. Fulfilment at the moment of death is the sign of success in the 'examination', and that can be found only through faith. There is no judgement. The 'examination' is of the degree of closeness to eternal life. Whatever increments of closeness have been won in the lifetime - or decrements - determine the general quality of the next birth. Eventually, everyone passes the examination.

Work to develop a faith which makes the omnipresent your reality. Make it ever stronger. There is nowhere where it cannot be stronger except in perfect realisation. So let it grow and grow and

236

grow. Courage is the determination to overcome fear. Fearlessness is the result of faith. The latter replaces the former, bit by bit.

All is well, the great work is unfolding on all the stages of the theatre of life. You are blessed and close, be ever more consciously with Me.

23.3.92.

51
The Connection With Truth is Primary.

What matters is not who is right. That is merely egoistic self-justification. It is *how* you behave in any situation. Rightness comes from inner connection, connection with truth. Your connection with that truth is the important thing, not how many people you can convince what the truth is. That connection is primary. What happens is secondary. Your job is to seek the truth and express it in your day to day behaviour. The truth is full of love. It does not parade itself. It is not hard edged and judgmental. It is caring and considerate of the other. Really, a life expresses truth in its wholeness and consistency of inner listening. Channelling is not enough. *Constant* connection expresses truth best in this world. Since all, finally, want the truth, living the connection in thought, word and deed is the most persuasive way of being.

People who think immediate winning is the most important thing must sacrifice or fudge the truth. The really important thing is not the noticeable and immediate impact of the truth, but its steady and holistic expression in a life. Jesus proclaimed the truth, not by pontificating, but in His being itself, right to the moment of His death. Because He was totally immersed in the truth, He knew every result of His actions, both immediate and long term. His message is the example of a life steeped in truth till the moment of death. It did not bring success, it did not 'win' the argument at the time, but for Jesus, living the truth was its own reward; there was no other.

The motives for human action are either outer, or inner directed. Outer-directed motives require approval from others. 'I do it because I will be powerful, rich, influential, accepted, liked, well-regarded,' and so on. Spiritual action, on the other hand, is concerned with the discovery and expression of truth. The wish to live truth is not in itself a guarantee that that will happen. It is an orientation of being in which God is the focus. The insecure will blend both inner and outer motives, but a God-fulfilled being will be known by their humility as well as by their insight, by their devotion as well as by their consideration for others.

So when you find yourself contesting, asserting, you have an opportunity, a challenge to withdraw and reconnect, to reorientate to the inner state of love and calmness. Remember Jesus! It does not matter if you win, It matters that you are connected. Out of that the maximum benefit for humanity will flow, but it will not be your motive. Watch Me and My life. Study not merely My teachings, but the way I am, day in and day out. This is the way to truth from the outside in. Let your heart be opened to Me in love and devotion, then I will soon be apparent as your Indweller. Discovering Me in you makes all other motives, pleasures redundant. It is hitting the Jackpot, winning the game. That is the truth you strive to find, you and all the rest.

Be blessed, you are love embodied, Strive always to discover it and live it. That is fulfilment.

27.3.92.

52
Pour Love Into Whatever You Do.

Love what you do! Let a stream of love envelop each act, so that while you perform it, that act is the most joyful happening on earth. That is bliss. All acts then become an expression of the Lord, and are necessarily dedicated to Him. When this is done, no action is boring or unworthy. An act is given its value by the attitude you take towards it. An act may be considered menial, unworthy, dirty, laborious, boring. All these are qualities given to the situation by the performer. Thus, it is the performer who defines the quality of the action, not the act itself. All of the difficulties that people experience in the performance of acts are the result of their evaluations of them in terms of their perception of *other people's* evaluations of them. The ego incorporates these into its idea of itself, and then projects its vision - of other people's judgements - into the act itself.

The solution is to pour love into what you do. That has to be a conscious decision, which is really in the form of a prayer. "Lord, you are my centre and my reality. Your very nature is love, May the love that is You-in-Me envelop this act and all connected with it, so that it is experienced as divine work."If you consciously cultivate this attitude, then there is the dawning of truth - nothing but love exists, action is a transformation of love into love on the level of form, hurry and stress cease and joy is the natural state. As an ongoing practice, make more and more of your acts conscious expressions of love. Get into the habit of it, cultivate this attitude. As you do it, you will lift to the love frequency. By establishing yourself on this frequency, the ego melts away, for it has no need to resist real happiness, real connection. This is the real yoga of action. Prayers, blessings, recitation of the Holy name during action, dedication of the action to God, all these are tools to help the welling up of love for this given moment of being-in-doing which is the emergence of God consciousness in your form.

Use every opportunity for practice. Lay aside anxiety, 'Will it be done? Will it be good? Will it be in time?' and so on, and concentrate your efforts on letting the God consciousness flow. Many of the states you experience are due to feelings of anxiety. Only love can cure this, can channel this nervous sensitivity into happiness. It is not difficult to try, especially if you do not stand in judgement over yourself for failing. Take these last months as a practice time,

You are blessed, Embodiment of love. I am never absent from you.

30.3.92.

53
Constant Personal Change Is Essential.

Remember the nineteenth century, with 'dark satanic mills' puffing up dirty smoke everywhere into the atmosphere. Now, at the end of the twentieth century, I have come. Instead of dark satanic mills, centres of light are everywhere pouring out light - the vibration of human transformation. As dark abhors light, the world is being purified. Evil is being contested. After the age of iron comes the age of gold; after the Kali Yuga comes the Krita Yuga. It is the greatest transformation in the cycle of human affairs, for the progression of the Yugas represents a degeneration, step by step, except where the cycle begins again, and the lowest level of human vibration changes to the highest. Thus the transition is an era of conflict and confusion; the worst and the best of humanity coexist, yet the best is on the rise. Many people are inwardly pulled in different directions.

As we leave the Kali Yuga, no human being is a pure model, all have been born and brought up in the old age and are disfigured by desire and powerful emotions. Thus, in the transformation humanity is pulling itself up by its bootstraps, so to speak, each helping his neighbour with his insights and in turn being helped by theirs. Centres resonate the light of transformation and I am embodied to facilitate the whole process, organise it, direct it. In this way it cannot go wrong; success is assured.

At this time each human identity identifying itself with the course of change is subjected to demands for flexibility, service and self-development. There is no other way. The need for constant personal change may hurt, but what opportunities it gives! Accumulated karma may be shed, new insights and heights enter human aspiration. The divine is close, reachable. For the clinging and unwilling it is a most painful time, bet for those who can surrender to the process it is an exciting adventure to live now. Embrace your fellow humans in this transformation process with the love that you have found. Know that you also will be supported in releasing the old.

My support is with you always. It comes directly into your being, but it is also through the love of others for you. See Me everywhere, honour Me in everyone. Remember, your life, your own example of transformed and transforming being is the greatest service you can render. Merge with Me and My will. Become love itself.

3.4.92

54
Forms Are Transient.

The creation culminates in man, but it is not for man. A plant is a whole. Its crowning point is its flower, but all its phases and its aspects are in themselves marvellous. So it is with the creation. Each being is in itself exquisite, expressing all the aspects of life in a perfect way. Thus respect for the creation is combined with wonder at it, joy in it, veneration of it. Regard yourself as part of the great garden, as the trainee gardener of the garden, too. The creation is an expression of love in form. Opening to it is a gateway to the heart, where love dwells. The creation demonstrates limitless wisdom and intelligence, as her scientific study shows. Attention to it stimulates the Buddhi. Taking the creation for granted is the sign of the unawakened soul.

Form is the projection of the Lord. It stimulates, it challenges. It expresses infinite variety. It stimulates the desire to reach out for it. But the attempt is fruitless. It is always just out of reach. One problem solved, there is another hidden behind it. And each form is transient, fades and crumbles, a temporary chimera, a wave, emerging and receding. Classify it, organise it, appreciate it, seek to control it - play the game of life. But only those who meet the Creator in every form really know the creation. He is not separate from the creation, bet resident in it, bubbling up into this form and that form, ceaselessly, tirelessly. You have to learn that the unique outer appearance or class of forms is the transient, the energy that holds the bubble in being for a while is one and permanent. That energy is not a material thing. It is perfect, immanent, stabilised consciousness, expressing itself through every wave, particle and string. There is nothing behind this consciousness, no ultimate 'cause', only consciousness projecting itself endlessly. Its nature is the definition of love. All creation resolves itself into conscious love.

As consciousness emerges in form, humans are thus seeking themselves. Their forms are evanescent, but their consciousness is creation itself, indestructible. As love becomes love and merges with Love, bliss exists. Consciousness yearns for itself, merging in blissful self-discovery. All fulfilments pass save this one.

Live in truth, in bliss and play the game of life. Be blessed.

7.4.92

55
Oneness - Not Politics!

You and I are One. Capture this thought and realise it. The method is to have awareness of our oneness at every moment of the day, and let this thought be the determinant of your actions. All the tools used to make something with do not add up to what is made. If you want to win a race, all the training, all the appropriate physical objects that help, are only significant in reference to the result of the race. The goal, the creation, is our Oneness. As other thoughts come in, bring yourself back as quick as you can to that. Then you will be clear and balanced about the work you are assigned to do, you will do what is wise and right, and you won't bring emotional projections into the task.

Many people think they are acting for the best, when what they are actually doing is healing their own hurt through their actions. But a real healing only takes place when the hurt is given to God, the perpetrators forgiven and the identity is freed. Physical disability is something that cannot be disguised or covered up, but mental disability is much more common. In the Kali age this disability is projected outwards to the experienced world, which takes on colours and hues representing inner crippling. People try so hard to change the outside world, and each believes that their particular projected pain can be healed through changes in social arrangements. But it is not so. The identities must be healed first, then outer structures of pain and suffering won't be energised any more and will easily dissolve.

Do not therefore worry about the mess that politicians are making of things. This is all outer show and ephemeral. Concentrate on the experience of love as your identity, and spread that energy in your inner and outer practice. Never lose it. Don't project your own hurts on anyone or anything. Give them to Me. They cannot resist enormous love and they dissolve, leaving you free. Letting Me take care of the problems, turn your attention to 'You and I are One', placing that in your daily actions as goal, motive and achievement, then you will become a free channel of divine energy, calm and bliss filled, fulfilled in life and contributing 100% to the Divine plan. Remember, 'You and I are One', 'You and I are One', 'You and I are One!'

There is love embodied. Cease to separate yourself from it.

10.4.92

56
Keeping the House Clean.

I am your teacher, in everyone. Be aware that I fear no one, am angry with no one, accept everyone in compassion and unconditional love. For everyone is Myself, and all the trials and tribulations they seem to go through are the struggles of emerging consciousness. As your consciousness develops, hold on to Me when you seem lost in the swirls and eddies of feelings and 'difficult' interactions. Know that your teacher and guide in the way forward is the other, in whom I am presenting Myself to show you what needs to be transcended, so you can be more and more who you are. Through My name, its remembering and repetition, you leave the level of pain and suffering and emerge into the sunshine of purer consciousness.

If you want to clean a house, you don't lie down on the floor with the dirt and roll in it. Nor do you pretend it isn't there. You stand up and take a brush. You are on a different level than the dirt. Then it easily goes into the dust pan or vacuum. *Standing up, is remembering Me. The brush is repeating My name.* As the dirt obscures the cleanliness of the floor, so your egoism obscures the perfection of your nature. I am the transformer of energy, I will dispose of the dirt so it is effectively recycled. Through the repetition of My name, the essential nature of who you are begins to shine through and, of course, you are then a joy filled being, even in times of tragedy.

The main task is to establish that this is the right way of doing things and to put it steadily and constantly into practice. Then your being will be effortlessly itself, clean and pure. In keeping a house clean, it helps if you don't let dirt into it. Otherwise you have to be constantly cleaning. Regular prayer, meditation and bhajan are the doorkeepers that don't let dirt into your being, so that it is easy to remove what is there. Use them well, and the cleaning up process will be easier.

Something perfect but obscured is different from something that needs constructing, or expanding. What is wanted is already present. Spiritual growth is really a misnomer. What grows is the ability to see the truth, to overcome the obscurity, and to live the truth in an ordinary daily life. In that way, without having the slightest stake invested in it, you will have a massive effect on the world around you. It is in fact easy, your natural state. Resistance makes it hard. Feel My love for you, personal yet unconditional. Surrender to it, and you are already home. Let 'Om Sai Ram' be on your lips, in your thoughts, return to it as soon as your realise you have left it. Then you are coasting down the last straight!

Embodiment of love, know and feel My love and blessings.

13.4.92

57
Honour Jesus - Crucify the Ego.

Today you celebrate the triumph of the great teacher who overcame ignorance to demonstrate the power of spirit, Jesus

Christ. In His life and death everything is given for a clear path to reunion. God's messengers guide the way for humanity. Yet, as He said, only some part of the seed sown bears fruit at any given time.

Make a resolve today that through the crucifixion of your ego, the spirit will live free in you. Make this your goal in life. Make love the means to attain the goal - love that includes yourself. Whatever you do to attain the goal, whatever happens as a result of your actions, love yourself. When hate and self-denigration, self-judgement or feelings of inadequacy hold the reins of your developing identity, they drive for the nearest quagmire, and stick the chariot of self in it, so it cannot proceed on the high road to Self. Come, when they claim a place in the driver's seat, refer to Me. I am the all powerful adjudicator, and will allow them no room. Then love will be the driver once more.

Love is reached by love, for it is already in you. Through its exercise, it becomes confident of its power and reality. This message must be told again and again, for it is the most easily forgotten. Discipline that does not stem from love, that is not filled with love, that does not result in love is worse than none at all. Better remain in ignorance than set ignorance up as a driving force. Only love is a legitimate driver.

Humanity is climbing up to the gods once more. It is a long slow climb, for the starting point was low, but why struggle up the slope when the lift of love is there. Above all, the great teachers are given you as reference points for love, symbols to engage the heart, to orient desire in the direction of devotion and humility. They seem real, tangible, not abstract. Love is their message. Christ answered hate with love, died with love and forgiveness on His lips, at the end clearly identified sin as ignorance, and held each soul who reads His story enthralled, awakening the indefinable essence in everyone. In honouring Him, you honour Me. In

248

honouring Me, you honour Him, for Oneness is ever itself, whatever outer expression it takes on. Love, this day, without discrimination.

Be blessed.

17.4.92(Good Friday)

58
God Motivation, Not Greed Motivation.

Use the time well. Hurry and stress are not part of using the time well. Everywhere is 'Hurry up, more production or you won't get paid, more and quicker or there won't be profit.' But what matters in this world? God matters! This world is not created by God for the purpose of making profit. It is an opportunity for life, through expressing love, to reunite in consciousness with love. So if you know the purpose of the enterprise, you will be able to choose the most efficient way of getting there. And that means that things get done out of the dedication to love, not through stress, pressure and fear.

Those who organise the arrangements for others to live and work have a great responsibility to see that the conditions exist in all levels of society for love to flow. The first requirement for this to happen is the dedication of position, responsibility and opportunity to God, not to Mammon. God motive, not greed motive is the key to the game. In any social system, God motive provides happy humanness, greed motive, misery and envy.

Make sure that your actions are always God motive and not greed motive. Remember that compulsiveness is a kind of greed motive. More and more work done is as greedy as more and more cash earned. Compulsive work is not God dedicated. Direct all push energy towards God discovery until it comes into balance. For the discovery of God in you will give you grace and harmony in your outer activities, even when outer circumstances seem hard.

God is the provider and organiser. Ego gets in the way and messes things up. As a result of its messes, desire is re-channelled and the soul discovers itself. Everything is real and appropriate at the level of soul's yearning for the One - all problems are given for solution, all difficulties are there to overcome. Passive acceptance of weakness is an indication of despair. Only then do some turn to God and the answer is given, usually in quite another way than the ego-dominated being expects.

It is so easy to find Me if you ask for Me, so easy to come home if you ask My help, so easy to be blissfully happy in the world of form if all your action at every moment is inspired by and dedicated to Me. Come to Me now, come nearer, till you accept that I am you and there is no separation,

Know the love that you are and be blessed.

20.4.92

59
Preparation for Surrender.

The small bird, as it leaves the nest, has to surrender itself on untried wings to the air around it. The bird has the model of its mother to look at. Surrendering oneself to God, is like taking flight into air. God cannot be seen, cannot be touched, cannot be tasted. The material world is tangible, social arrangements are tangible. Surrendering oneself to God is like depending on an intangible layer to fly in, for God is the substratum of the universe, not the superficial. The superficial expresses Him, but is not Him. So the undeveloped identity finds it much too dangerous to let go to this intangible unknown. Every bird has to learn to trust the air flowing past its wings. So, every human has to transfer trust from the tangible, 'I do it' to the intangible, 'The Lord is my shepherd.' People think that their sense of 'I' is the centre of their identity, but it is the husk.

Preparation for surrender is therefore necessary. Humans are equipped to experience God in them, Such experiences are called transcendent or mystical. Techniques of meditation open the mind-heart connection so that such experiences can take place easily and comfortably. The study of spiritually wise literature prepares consciousness for the experience, and the example of those who have had it, gives confidence. But the experience of God in a mystical moment of transcendence is only a first step. It is an awakening experience, a dramatic demonstration of another reality, and the experience is more intense than that of ordinary reality.

The experience of the divine is a preparatory step on the path to surrender to the Divine. It allows the identity to verify that the divine is there to be trusted. Trusting involves further development, increasing degrees of surrender, which, given conscious intention, happen sometimes relatively imperceptibly. Those who have surrendered are examples to others through their quality of living. They are the true spiritual teachers. Book learning about spiritual matters is a very minor quality, but the teaching that can be given from experience is the most powerful, the most confidence-inspiring. 'There is someone like me, who has done what I want to do. It can work.' This is the best teaching, and the meaning of the saying, 'My life is My message.'

Take flight today into My enveloping love. You are ready. All the preparation has been accomplished. Let God carry the body, dissolve your consciousness into Him. Trust, believe, have courage. You will not fall with a crash to the ground. The air will hold you up. You are made able to fly into divine consciousness and merge in it, a conscious Embodiment of Divine love. Be blessed. 23.4.92

60
Enter into My Stream of Consciousness.

Enter into My stream of consciousness, not just through these messages, but in your daily life. Through this, what you know as 'you' becomes a vehicle for the direct expression of Me. In one sense, everything expresses Me. At the ultimate, there is no separation, no duality. Separation is experienced as the result of the creation in form. You are captivated by the separateness of forms, their many-sidedness, the different experiences and pleasures they give, into believing that they exist sui generis. This is the great illusion, Maya. Further, your consciousness, developed in the world of form, regards itself as separate but part. It sees itself in relation

252

to the other expressions of consciousness that people demonstrate, rather than as an emanation of the One. The consequence of both these things is that human consciousness becomes limited and partial. As you realise that all is the expression of the One, the Divine Consciousness, you have the ability and opportunity to move towards that Consciousness and, as you do so, all the precarious rough and tumble of multi-identification begins to resolve itself. Since My consciousness pure is pure bliss, a quality of joy enters into your life, which is only sullied by remaining identifications with the world of form.

The possessor of pure consciousness is filled with unparalleled love for all the creation around them, is compassionate to all who are ignorant of the truth, becomes master of life and death and is teacher and guide. For that person, life is sheer bliss, there is no fear or worry, no race or hurry. The senses are at their sharpest, no matter what the age or state, finely tuned to appreciate, to drink in the creation as an expression of Self. Do not aspire to anything short of this. But, also, do not let the *concept* of the real define the real. Be that which you are, in change - and that includes self-discipline on the path - but do not *pretend* to be something which you are not yet in the interests of becoming what you would like to be. That is false holiness, and it will explode on you in time like a bomb. Reconcile humility towards the Creator and His creation, and self-confidence that you can and will unify with that Creator, who is your own essence. These apparent opposites are the creative tension that pulls you towards mergence.

No other human goal compares with this. Be blessed, Embodiment of love, know what you are. Be it!

28.4.92

61
The Journey To Love.

Worry and anxiety do not stem from the present situation. If your consciousness is dominated by the past, and that past created anxiety, it will try to project itself into the present. The only aspect of the present situation that matters is the level on which you live it. Everybody has worry and anxiety, for their history goes back endlessly. The challenge is not to 'solve' it, although it may be valuable to give vent to pent up feelings from time to time, consciously and in controlled situations where no one is hurt by it. But this only a 'safety valve' mechanism, enabling easier access to levels where worry and anxiety, and all the other difficult emotions, do not exist.

The important thing is, do you spend your time on the frequency of your emotions, a stormy area, where consciousness is buffeted about like plants in a gale? Here the experience of happiness is forged, but it is alloyed with pain and distress. Having found the experience of happiness, the search for its multiplication leads either down a false trail into the world of the senses, or towards its source, divinity.

To find true happiness, one has to leave the stormy area of the emotions and climb above their clouds into the bright sunshine of the levels of love. Even here there is climbing to be done, but a fundamental shift occurs when the regions of emotional agitation are released, and consciousness lifts higher. Here is the place to spend time, strengthening yourself for the final climb to the summit. Imagine a mountain side. The lower slopes are steep, full

254

of rocks and defiles. The climb is tortuous and arduous, with many cuts and bruises, detours and falls. Rain and sunshine alternate as the clouds and mists race round the sides of the mountain. But somewhere above there is a ridge, and the ridge is above the clouds. As one ascends the ridge, there is a semi-plateau, where the slopes are gentler, and the winds have abated. The sun shines, and climbing is easy. The final ascent to the summit is again steep, but with none of the barriers and hazards of the early slopes of the mountain. So it is with the spiritual path. The journey is inward, not physically upward, but the change of levels of energy is metaphorically similar.

I have come to guide you on this journey, to make the nature of the journey clear, to motivate you towards the goal. By allowing Me the leadership, you do not lose your independence, but gain it, for the independence of the ego is illusory. The divine is something formless and attributeless, but it takes on form and attributes in human Self-realisation. Do not merely worship the Divine. Live it, embody it. It will willingly mould itself to the appropriate attributes for oneness in human form. That is the true message of religion, and the solution of the quest for happiness in the soul.

Be blessed on your journey. Reach your goal of Self-realisation. Become Me!

1.5.92

62
Learning 'Divine Sitting'.

There are three elements in concentrated sitting. The first is posture. The back must be straight, and to achieve this a cross legged posture is, for most people, the best. The second is breathing. This must be deep and regular. Through this kind of breathing there is a tendency for the mind to calm and the posture to be maintained. The third element is a quiet recitation of the Holy name. This is calming and centring and reduces the likelihood of random thoughts taking over. Other techniques of breathing and mantras are 'optional extras', but if you steadily pay attention to these three factors, you will gradually strengthen the concentration, and thus become closer to My identity.

Daily time spent in quiet concentration is important, especially in the morning, to strengthen the connection with the centre, and set the energy for the day. But it also requires preparation and a degree of calmness in the life. Those with back trouble may need to prepare their backs to be able to sit straight at all, and there should be no attempt at long periods of concentrated sitting if the back is not in order. Even ten minutes 'well sat' is better than an hour of agony and struggle. Do not think that self-torture is an effective path to God. Find the right posture and then sit in it for as long as the physical limitation allows with comfort. This regular practice will allow the duration of sitting to increase, little by little, and also improve the physical condition. Where there is frequent or constant very high agitation of mood, preparation work must be done on the emotional state. In this case, short, sometimes very short periods of concentrated sitting can usefully be maintained, and here breathing exercises and mantras to control the emotional state are valuable.

Once such problems have been relatively mastered, the sitting period will increase, and regular practice at a regular time is most valuable. Concentration will suffer if sitting is undertaken at irregular intervals or times. Having mastered the challenge of regularity and punctuality, it is important to remember that 'divine sitting' is a preparation for, an introductory aspect of, a 'divine day' .The ideal is to express the concentrated one-pointedness of the concentrated sitting through each moment of the day, in whatever activity is undertaken. Then a boundless supply of energy will flow through the body in appropriate measure, joy will result from actions undertaken, and love will be manifest through you. These small disciplines are therefore of great value as a daily routine and not to be ignored or relegated to something that 'would be nice' .Samadhi - existence in God - is not a momentary happening. It is a 24 hour a day experience and concentrated sitting is an important step on the way.

You are a blessed Embodiment of God. Nothing else can give you satisfaction in this world. 4.5.92

63
The 'God Sense'.

The senses say that only that which is touched, seen, tasted, smelt or heard is real. Yet there are so many things that do not register directly on the senses, either because they are too small or at vibrations which the senses cannot pick up. The scientific discoveries of this generation are opening people to the fact that this unseen reality is very important. That can be a significant step to understanding the reality of the omnipresence of the divine.

Try to think of underlying reality, whenever you do something, not merely of the images presented by the senses. Let us say that there is another sense, the God sense, which has to be developed and listened to, because it is more subtle than the other senses. You can't touch God, you can't feel, see, smell or taste Him, but you can experience Him, using this wonderful and most subtle God sense. For it isn't that God is sometimes present, sometimes absent, like a friend or a pet, God is always present, everywhere, in everything, but the sense of His presence is subtle, and the human being is deluded by senses developed to operate in the world of form; so the experience of Him is ignored, disregarded, overlooked. But if you look for quality, you will find nothing to compare with the experience of God in any of your other senses, for He is the pure essence. People sometimes have brief connection with the God sense, and then feel sad that God has 'left them' .Actually, they have left God. To become more and more in touch with the God sense, you have to develop your abilities of discrimination and sensitivity. It is certainly worth it, but it involves changes of lifestyle, a training to replace one reality with another. The world of the ordinary senses seems real. The world of the subtle God sense, unreal. The great challenge of life is to turn this round, so that reality resides, accurately, in the God sense, and the world of the gross senses is seen as relative and epiphenomenal to it.

The God sense is experienced as love, but much more than a mundane or sentimental feeling. It is an overpowering, all encompassing, heart and mind expanding love that lights up your physical being from the inside. Sensitise your bodies, your capacities to be in touch with this love and live from it as your reality. Don't indulge the gross senses, encourage them to be dominant and to define your world of pleasure and pain, for then you will miss out on the exquisite, remain separate from the divine. Do not observe the divine from a distance, discuss it, pay lip service to it, feel inadequate before it, think that one day, perhaps, you might possibly have an inkling. Take confidence, claim it as

258

your own, and prepare you body properly as the physical vehicle which it inhabits. Indulgence of the senses is senseless, but God indulgence is the way you will find lasting happiness and overcome all fears. Continue your preparations patiently. Accept My guidance, worship My exemplary form on earth, live in Me. You are blessed.

6.5.92

64
Tightening Bolts.

Tightening up the bolts; you spent yesterday going over the bolts on the new back box. If the bolts aren't tight, it doesn't show at first, but with use, loose bolts will show in wear and tear that could have been avoided. So it is in spiritual life. Tightening up the bolts is like remembering to work with God, that little extra thing in what you do. If you forget, it may not show immediately, but the energy level of your actions is lower, there is a tendency to become possessive about things, and the little seeds of attachment are nourished. The remaining task on Erraid is to become more conscious in the moment of the divine inspiration of your work. Make it a conscious intention to bless each act as you do it, before and after, to feel the divine presence as you do the acts. Concentrate on this.

It is so easy to be lazy, even for very hard workers, and forget these vital aspects of karma yoga. But what benefits are gained through remembering them and making them a standard part of

259

activity! There is perfect energy flow in the action. There is a perfect balance between physical work and rest. There is no impatience. Above all, the experience of the divine as the doer becomes stronger and stronger. There are many motives for working hard. But at the last, the renunciation of the ego in the act leaves the way open for consciousness to become divine in its actions. That is bliss, freedom and fulfilment. So practice, practice, practice, patiently and lovingly becoming God-filled in work. Then all the bolts will be tightened up, and you will be home.

You are love embodied, be blessed to become one with it.

12.5.92

65
You Can Be A Light.

Each day is a gift from God. Learn to take nothing for granted. Taking for granted is a miracle inhibitor! God's Grace cannot be expected or predicted. Do not try to follow it, grab it, make it your personal property. Rather, enter the world of Grace in which a great harmony expresses itself in boundless generosity. Change position. Come to the source of grace in you. It does mean abandoning some minor likes, desires and petty wishes, in favour of perfect bliss and contentment, but don't be afraid. Cease trying, and open yourself to the Divine will. It will take you and carry you along. As you abandon yourself to it, your whole attitude to life changes, your priorities reorganise themselves, and your understanding of the 'whys' of things expands. Such a person is a jewel in the world, shining clear and faultless for others, loving all, condemning none, serving all, taking sides with none, a model for the way out of conflict, demonstrating higher priorities. As people live tangled up in identification with nation, region or -ism, they become fanatic, and when their emotions are aroused they will kill and maim. Pride in country and honour for the best in one's culture has nothing to do with this.

You can be a light, no more. If someone sees a light and shuts their eyes, then it doesn't help, but most people will be able to find their way better with a light. So allow yourself to be drawn to God's light which will shine in you. Then you will know the source of Grace, and its form will be immaterial.

Prepare yourself for change. There is no hurry, the direction has already been indicated. Come to Me in November and then move. Do not worry about material things. They don't matter. Release them. Whatever you need at the time, you can have. Remember there is abundance and My grace is with you. You are loved, blessed and guided. You are Me - learn to accept it and surrender to it, a conscious Embodiment of love.

15.5.92

66
Wherever You Are, I Am.

Wherever you are, I am. When you are still struggling to find Me, differences between place and people seem to matter a great deal - some places seem beautiful, others repulsive; it is the same with people. You are also at the mercy of your moods - on a 'bad day', a spot you liked before will seem dull and you find it hard to stand even your best friends or loved ones.

But as soon as you find Me in your heart, and don't let Me escape, but allow and deeply wish for Me to become your identity, all these variations begin to lose importance. You see beauty in places you hadn't previously thought to find it, and in people you thought boorish, or even vicious. That is the meaning of heaven - not to enter some dream place where everything is lovely and you can satisfy all your lower desires without retribution, but to experience the world through God's eyes, with Him in your heart as maker of your kingdom, and to see the beauty in everyone and everything as a reflection of Him.

Moving challenges the ruler of your heart. If I am really ruling you, moving is from one perfect place to another and presents no problems; if not, it is a challenge and a stimulus to find Me there. The spiritual seeker finds home only when he or she is at home inside. Then there is no more need for movement outside. Restlessness ceases when the inner journey is complete, not the outer.

Abandon fear, accept yourself fully, install Me in your heart so love reigns and find home at last. Then people will gather round you and ceaseless miracles will flow. All plans can change. Till then, move through different places, seeking the reflection of the One in each.

You are a perfect Embodiment of love - know it!

(Woodhead, near Forres) 19.5.92

67
Hyper-Responsibility is the Arrogance of the Ego.

You are out of balance. Allow Me to take responsibility. By taking responsibility when you can do nothing about things, you start to worry. By worrying you become tired and irritable. Release all this. Do your work for Me, bless it in My name and release it to Me. The things to be done are clear, there is no additional responsibility. By practising this, you find you are closer to the real identity of yourself, and as this happens, naturally and in its own time by following the prescriptions that I give you, you will be in harmony with My plan and understand it. Then everything will bloom in your life.

Hyper-responsibility is the arrogance of the ego. It has nothing to do with service, which is an outpouring of love and caring. As soon as you want to demonstrate what a lovely garden you have, what magnificent plants grow in it, you are parading your ego. Release all that. The work is the Lord's, the result is the

Lord's, given by Him as an act of Grace. This is what giving the fruits of the work means. It is really allocating all results to their rightful source. It is not a gracious act, where the ego releases a little of its prizes to the Lord in a gesture of magnanimity or even religious fervour. It represents an understanding that the Lord is the source of all growth, the guide of the hoe, the stimulator of the weather and the director of the harvest. The Lord does not need praise. Being perfect, He is not improved by it. Being egoless, He is not flattered by it. But genuine praise of God reveals the opened heart of the one who praises Him, and brings that person closer to themselves, to the true Self that the personality only reflects.

The secret of genuineness is right timing. There is a little moment of reflection that precedes action. It is not meant to be a long, ponderous, pretentious dedication, which inflates the ego, and provides admiration from others. But a small, private moment before action will raise the level, the frequency from which action is taken, and give divine blessing to the work. Without that moment, there is rush, hurry and separation. Being in balance gives you much more opportunity to reach the vibration of Truth in your work, and the results will then automatically be blessed.

Try it, remember it, act from it. Your prayers for bliss and contentment will then be realised. You are loved and blessed.

24.5.92

68
Transcendence of the Physical Requires Purity of Consciousness.

Do not deny your physical state, the messages your body gives you about its condition. On the other hand, do not be its slave, dominated by it, concerned with fulfilling its every whim. The best way to make use of the physical situation God has given you is to seek, calmly and patiently, harmony with Him. Then the maximum energy your physical state permits will be freed for action dedicated to Him. Beyond that is the Yoga of transcendence, attained by steady concentration on mergence with the Divine, purification of consciousness and life in a state of Divine Bliss. Some people, ruled by a strong ego desire for power and prestige, invest this in nominally spiritual disciplines for the transcendence of physical limitation, but such action is pointless and dangerous. Being based on base motives, it will be basely used and bring about the downfall of the user. Only purity of consciousness on the steady path to mergence in the Lord will bring about a non self-destructive transcendence of the physical. When God is in the heart, then all is opened · and all can be held there.

Ego thrives on prestige and status. Its corollary is envy and jealousy of others who seem to have that already. Dedicate all such thoughts and feelings lovingly to Me, for I absorb them and purify them, and you are released. It is so easy. Just say to yourself, "Lord, I am feeling this envy, this feeling of pride in being recognised, etc. Please take this burden from me, so I may continue to serve You," Then it will be taken and you will be free. Do not be impatient; a lifetime of service to ego is not eliminated overnight without enormous faith, and that, too, has to be developed. But do not indulge any occurrence. Dedicate it immediately to Me in a similar way to that I have outlined, and you will be freed of it. I have no need of gifts, and all energies are equivalent to the

Ultimate. Have no fear that I can be 'overloaded' .Accept My Divinity.

My interest is in re-mergence; My joy is in that. The soul's conscious recognition of its nature and experience of it is the glorious prelude to no-self, to pure Divinity. That is who you are, beloved Embodiment of love. Do not waste time - be that.

27.5.92

(The next 5 messages were received in Madeira.)

69
Letting Me Steer. 1

Let time do its work. Every location seems very different. Every spot seems to have different attributes. Respect all these seeming differences as variations on a theme. There is only one, Myself, expressed in myriad forms and styles. So do not be misled by outer forms - judging and comparing. Let things unfold.

Relax and do not feel guilty. The way to Me is not through guilt and judgement, never. Accept! What you are given now, in this moment, in these days, is what you are given. Seek blessing for it, so you may see it with the loving eyes of God. Let the Lord's will be done!

Enjoy your stay with Me in My Madeira abode. Here is an expression of relative gentleness, relative harmony. Learn to accept My abundance, for you and for others. Remember, I an Krishna and all I need I have. Be like Me. Do not be afraid of material things. Poverty consciousness is a consciousness still determined by material things. Have confidence in the strength of your divine connection. You are very close to Me, Whenever doubts or hesitations come, call on Me. Let My name be your beacon, support and friend. I will even manifest Myself to you if you call Me and need Me. Accept - honour your prayer - My will be done.

You are loved, Embodiment of love.

2.6.92

70
Letting Me Steer. 2

Everywhere in the world the sun rises and sets. Everywhere in the world, nature follows its appropriate course. Everywhere in the world live people trying to find God.

Wherever you are, it is the service of God that matters; and the heart that does it. Here or there, all is one in God. God has no preference for His people in Scotland over His people in Madeira.

There are no 'chosen' people. All are loved, seen with compassion and granted Grace by God.

Attachments to the things of this world are a form of separation from God. If you genuinely want to find God, He will set you a programme, which may involve different locations, different experiences, designed to wean you from attachments and allow you to be where you are. Association with different people will purify you through their good company, till gradually you are Me and separation is steadily reduced.

Of course, to each place you go, you can, and must give yourself - as much as you are able - Myself. That is your service, also your own purification. Do not try to define what it is that you should give. Let the situation determine that. That way you will learn in giving. Surrender without qualification to Me. I will direct and guide you in every respect. In this way you learn to ' let go and let God' .Perform your family obligations and responsibilities, but love all equally, letting that type of unconditional love which is love of Me, grow gently and steadily. Heaven is where you are, who you are with, what you are doing, if seen through divine eyes.

I am with you, loving you, blessing you, supporting you. Feel My presence.   5.6.92

71
Letting Me Steer. 3

Be in Me - out shopping, drinking tea, driving home. Get into the habit of repeating the Name silently to yourself.

Everything is blessed in your stay. Your being here is appropriate. You will not have to leave Scotland. Do not be afraid. Just release it all to Me. Accept My hand moving you. Try to live each moment fully in Me. Decisions are Mine, now. Wait, wait, wait for the next step and, meanwhile, consider the present moment, exactly what you are doing and how you are doing it. Come closer to Me in you - not hankering after Me in Puttaparti. Time for such visits will come. Where I am *not* felt as the heartbeat is the periphery. The centre is the heart in which I am consciously welcomed and made at home. That is spiritual geography. There are no 'I will's, only I am's' .Then you are one with Me and in steady bliss.

Sleep a lot - enjoy the peace and quiet moments as they are. Do not feel under obligation. Allow your physical being rest and healing.

You are blessed, Embodiment of love.

8.6.92

72
Letting Me Steer. 4

There are pause times, expression times, completion times, each having their own quality. Flexibility enables you to experience each as My gift. When there is a pause time, experience the quality of energy of that time; do not become attached to it, but, centred in Me, enjoy it. Do not think about the future, the portents, for almost all of the thinking arises from worry and insecurity. The blind person just has to trust and be led. All of you are blind before Me, so let Me lead. There will be no more worry and insecurity. I heal the blind and after a time your eyes will open into a new world in which 'Me-ness' is expressed through you and all around you. But do not seek this world or strive after it. Seek to experience the world you have now fully, for that is the way to influence the future. Motives are important, and if you are elsewhere in your motives, life will become difficult and pushy. Let Me be the guide and life becomes more exciting and, because you are fully present, more beautiful.

All the texts of your present series of messages are about letting Me steer - for if you do not, how can you attain Me? So use this practice time for letting go. Trust! You are held by Me, guided by Me, till you come to know you are Me.

11.6.92

73
How To Run a Project Spiritually.
(Message for the A Rochinha Project)

You are close, loved and blessed: continue to have and strengthen faith. Faith is the primary ingredient, the yeast that makes the dough of material action rise above itself and take on transcendent purpose. The good baker uses only the best flour, discarding all trash and material of inferior quality. So it is also in the spiritual bakery. Baking bread is fun - but work in the spiritual bakery is bliss. It also demands a high quality of resolve and determination.

The greatest challenge of this sort of work is not that it is done on the level of form: the transformation of matter and its materialisation are capabilities for which grace is given even where the spiritual level is undeveloped, given single minded resolve. The really demanding aspect is *spiritual resolve*. It is easy to discard trashy materials, require high standards of material workmanship, but less easy to maintain the highest standards of spiritual quality and to develop them constantly. Here the quality of fearlessness is required. Look at the example of Jesus. He knew that His job was to bring to His civilisation the highest spiritual energy, the culmination of all prior teachings in His tradition. From this goal He never wavered till His final crucifixion. Nothing else, not even life, mattered to Him for He had realised the bliss of union - eternal life - and so His message transcended material death. Take Jesus as your model and example for your spiritual development.

As your project develops, many will arrive, with varying opinions - who will arrive will depend upon your own level of

272

spiritual development, and your own level of fearlessness; and how you are influenced by them will depend on it, too. Remember that you are not just channels for divinity, but as you seek to approach divinity, you become co-creators with it, and all unresolved qualities in you will be expressed and created in your centre also, both in its visitors and atmosphere. This is the continuing challenge of spiritual development, constantly purifying, rejecting the dross - 'Not this, not that' - seeking only the highest energy. So you must work to develop fearlessness in spiritual matters. Truth can never be compromised and remain truth, It can be expressed with love, with discretion and with right timing, but it may not be hidden, suborned or diverted from its purpose. Only the fearless are capable of this task. Only those who have self-confidence can develop fearlessness, and those who ask in faith for grace will get the practical teaching they need to purify them to become fearless examples of God's teaching and love.

So your primary work is not at the material level of form. That will be provided for. What is vital is that the beacon of light shines stronger and stronger from this project so that it establishes itself unshakeably against the sea of worldly temptations that Jesus so well resisted.

Undertake therefore, as a primary part of your endeavours a conscious and disciplined programme of spiritual development. Follow it through till you become fearless, uninfluenced by this or that, him or her, with ephemeral ideas or enthusiasms. Then you will not waver and the light will shine brighter and brighter.

All your endeavours come to Me and are blessed by Me. I an here, embodied now on earth to help the seeker develop fearlessness. You will find help and strength in Me, whatever your situation; and for you I am the clearest and most direct spiritual guide. The guide who is the source itself is rare indeed, embodied

273

on earth, the greatest Gift of Grace humanity can receive. Do not be afraid of Me - practice fearlessness with Me - and I will be always with you.

You are blessed, Embodiments of love. Realise it in this lifetime, in your service, in your purity of purpose, in your resolve and fearlessness.   14.6.92

74
Abundance Is Divine.

Anyone in training or learning something has to make sure they actually learn their lessons. There must be a review, an assessment, to see what has been absorbed. The person who rushes from experience to experience in life with the excuse that this or that needs to be done is not really living in the present. They are not taking the time required to absorb and assimilate the teachings life provides. Try therefore, to slow down your pace a little or, rather, create the time to ponder on the spiritual message of particular experiences. Do not rush on, willy-nilly.

The experience on Madeira was of a higher level of being, for which you are now ready. This is the reason you sent there and is the reason that the opportunity to go is offered you. You are in growth; you have outgrown your pot. Good! But problems set in for plants who stay in pots they have outgrown. You do not have to go to Madeira, but it is 'the bigger pot' .People will be people, everywhere, but the company you keep is the water that promotes growth, the location is the pot which can provide the company. I will provide the means for you to go to Madeira and live comfortably. That is no problem, nor do you need to play with guilt because you will have some money. You always have the resources you need for a particular experience; so you will this time. Grasp clearly what happened to you there, what was given, what is offered. Let your karmic stings be a chance to take pause.

Abundance is divine, offered by nature as example and reflection, Does a plant think as it produces seed that it may have more than its neighbour and feel guilty? That is all regulated at another level. It produces an abundance of seed. Abundance of wealth is not the cause or the result of world poverty. How abundance is used the question. Wealth directed towards material acquisition, towards hoarding, brings no benefit, no real happiness, either to its possessor or to others. But wealth put to use for the support or growth of spirit, of love in the world, *that* transforms. Remember, the real world is God. Moving towards that world is the fulfilment of the human dream. Wealth directed towards that aim, which is service in love, worship in love, is therefore righteously used. If you have a million pounds and use it to gamble, acquire ostentatious properties and luxury possessions, you will only find yourself more neurotic the more you acquire. But if you have a million pounds and build schools, hospitals and temples; if you use some of the wealth to develop yourself and become a divine human, at which point you are equally at home anywhere, you will find and spread bliss and support others on every level. So open yourself to accept on this level. You are not going to abuse the wealth you receive. Trust yourself - you are very responsible.

You are very, very close. Unfold, like the beautiful flowers of Madeira, let our oneness blossom forth to give joy to all.

19.6.92

275

75

I Am Doing the Work.

If you remember Me in your work constantly, reminding yourself that *I* am doing the work, you will be in harmony in the work; not becoming compulsive about it, but enjoying it to the full as a gift I give among all the other gifts. It is not luxury to experience Me in performing your duty; that very bliss is the purpose of your existence and the real meaning of service. Never narrow your vision so that you experience work alone. Enjoy the harmony and variety of the natural world, seen through My eyes, the variations in the task and problems to be solved, changes in tempo and different types of experience.

Alas for the guilty, no work, no activity which consciously expresses Me can be anything other than blissful, for the source of bliss is not in the action but in the attitude to the action. Divinely inspired action is an expression of divine love and radiates bliss. Compulsive or guilt-ridden action clouds the love content and so unhappiness and irritation gather around it. Then realise that you are separate, take some deep breaths, rededicate yourself to Me, come back to the centre and take stock of things. Is it time to vary the work - is something else calling to be done - is the physical body in the appropriate state to continue? With all this awareness, reconnect with the state of bliss and take up the appropriate form of expression. This process of 'losing and finding' recurs again and again. But do not be disheartened. Gradually, imperceptibly the 'losing' will be less frequent, the 'finding' more constant. Actions will be balanced and a beautiful expression will follow. Then all devas will respond, the plants will flourish, the other workers will

276

be inspired, divine joy will reign and light will shine from the garden like a beacon.

As healing occurs, and energies are mobilised once again, it is a good time to rededicate your working experience to Me and to derive it from Me. Do not be disheartened - you are very close. Each new test is an adjustment which enables you to come even closer. Rejoice!

25.6.92

76
Use the Bridge I Provide.

Rest and digest! A completely integrated, balanced life, that is your aim at. this moment. Stay above emotional strife. Integrate through Me. Do not try to do it 'yourself', for you will fail. Put Me in charge of the steering wheel, and all that you need will be manifested immediately. To get from one bank of a river to another, you need a bridge. Without the bridge, you will get wet, possibly even drown. The bridge should be strong enough to bear your weight and secure enough that you don't fall off into the river. The banks of the river are the boundary between human living and divine living. I am the bridge on which you can trust your weight. No problem is too heavy for Me. My sides and floor are secure. Step out in confidence that I will give you a secure passage to the other side and that you will not fall into the water of delusion and get swept downstream to begin again.

Call on Me! Keep calling on Me! Present Me with problem and dilemma, emotion and anxiety. I will always be there to do it. This is the easy way - we are already One. Separation is only a phenomena derived from uncertainty. Give even that uncertainty to Me, and all seeming separation will dissolve.

Love's power is increasing exponentially. All that is resistant becomes uncomfortable, as the grass around a fire is scorched as its heat increases. I am the refuge, the cooling balm. Apply Me, daily, hourly, minute by minute. Practice, never give up or become discouraged What you need to reinforce you faith, I will give, but do not underestimate how far you have come and never mix up My love with ego power. I am the Healer, the Essence, not the genie in the bottle.

Use the bridge I provide. Rest and integrate. Merge into Me, embodied on earth. You are blessed, Embodiment of love.

1.7.92

77
Experience Me in Others.

There are many kinds of tears, but when the heart has become sealed, it is the experience of the relationship of love between people - love without thought of sex or gain - that allows the tears to flow and the heart to open.

A religion that concentrates on the performance of duty is an abstraction. Only a life flowing in and with love is a religious life.

God is love; to be close to Him, live in love. It doesn't matter so very much if you *do* a lot or a little. As long as there is separation, the experience of genuine love will reduce it. The final experience of emotion is the opening to love through the awareness of the divine in another. It has nothing to do with 'personality to personality', but is God greeting God and overwhelming the personality of a person at least for a moment. Then the differences, judgements and criticisms of the immature identity become irrelevant, and the personality becomes, to a degree, divinised. No such opening to the soul is ever completely lost, for it is a transcendent experience.

Do not be afraid, therefore of crying as you gaze into someone's eyes. Do not misinterpret the experience as you once so disastrously did, as one of sexuality or partnership. For a moment, as the eyes meet, you may experience My darshan.

Be blessed in your week. Be balanced, live in the whole of the creation, and experience it with all your senses, but be attached to nothing except the *source* of all that, that which *is*, the Divine Essence - of which everything else, including your experienced self, is a reflection in the mirror of nature; beingness experienced through the sense organs.

4.7.92

78
From *Phenomenalism* to Purity.

Move through *phenomenalism* to purity. People call My miracles my 'calling cards' .Human curiosity may be awakened by strange or out of the run events, but in the end they are no different from other external stimuli. When helicopters were first invented, a landing from one was a big event. Now it is rather blasé. Humans will soon find landings from flying saucers just as blasé. Everything material and psychic experienced by the senses is ephemeral. Only its *essence* links you to all reality.

Each generation of humanity takes for granted the discoveries of the previous one. The material world is never, ultimately, satisfying. Seek beyond phenomena to the source. Seek to be one with the light, not with the fascinating phenomena that can be experienced while approaching the flame. Then all can be experienced as an expression of the One that you are. The spiritually centred person is the example that takes humanity beyond a fascination with trivia that distorts its growth into harmony.

Be a model of toleration; do not engage or identify with trivia; always point the way beyond, to real bliss, and go that way. Be in the world, but not of it. Respect others' efforts to stimulate and energise, but support them to go further. It is love that is the key, love the motivator, love the goal. Let others linger if they will, but point the way ahead.

Have what you need for the next change. The Christmas Eve guidance was genuine and accurate. You are able to have direct information now, if you need it, for your anxiety levels are reduced. Come to Me for the Birthday. Visit your mother. Go to Madeira for a while. Have the little material things you think you need. Meet the challenge of wealth wisely and in Me - egoless you are My arm in the world. Never become complacent; never judge yourself or others. Never become attached, except to the goal of mergence.

Even such an attachment vanishes at last. When you attain reality, no attachment is sensible. You have moved hard in hard physical work. In the next period inner movement will be fast and challenging, but you are well prepared for it and will not falter.

You are blessed and loved. I an the fixed point. All others swirl and diffuse. Aspire without hesitation to Me.

8.7.92

79
The Cradle of Happiness.

In you and around you is a network of beingness. This network is like a cradle in which you hang, supported. You have built that cradle yourself on a moral journey of cause and effect through your soul history. Such a cradle of beingness may be comfortable or uncomfortable as a whole. It may have uncomfortable parts in a comfortable whole, or any combination, depending on the person involved and their state of development.

That you, personally, can recognise and rejoice in Me is a rebuilding of the cradle of your beingness. It results from aeons of moral experience and development. At this moment, I am expanding Myself in you so that you become a being of light and value, joy filled and radiant. Welcome Me in you with all your heart! Yearn for Me with all your strength! Accept Me everywhere, in everything, invisible but omnipresent, nascent, yet always liable to emerge.

As I am emergent in you, the whole network of being on which you rely is transformed on every level; locational, physical, companionate, psychological, psychic and spiritual. All is seen again, as if through new lenses. The network of beingness becomes fluid and you find yourself in new locations, with new companions, with new perceptions and new experiences. Accept all this with gratitude. Participate, but do not become attached to any aspect. For every aspect of the network of beingness is but a reflection of Myself; an expanding, transforming, transitory pathway towards union with that which is *not* changing, bliss eternal, going nowhere, coming from nowhere.

Let your heart yearn for that ultimate experience. Through the net veiled glimpses of that state are granted. They are not the net, but the result of momentary penetration of the net to the eternal Truth. I am that. You are that. Aspire to Me; yearn for Me; attain Me; live as a perfect expression of Me, untouched, unaffected by the network of being, flowing through it bliss filled!

Be blessed.

13.7.92

80
Neither Hurry, Nor Sloppiness.

There is no hurry. The world today is full of hurry. People rush from here to there, tense, stress filled, full of a sense of self-importance, worried that there won't be enough time. All around is the evidence of My beauty, but for someone in a hurry, there is no time to stop and see it. People believe that God is far away, or absent altogether, that they are the doers and what they do is terribly important. On the contrary, I am present all the time, My grace is the cause of action and the real definition of what is important can only be learned by studying Me. So control your racing steps, steady the blood, regulate the heartbeat, concentrate on Me and act from Me, through Me and with My eyes. Then your worries and performance anxieties will vanish.

It all has nothing whatever to do with sloppiness. That is the reverse side of the coin of hurry, its negative partner. Hurry in one may stimulate a resistant unpunctuality in another. Sloppiness in another may stimulate a demonstrative hurriedness in someone else. Do not get caught in these traps. Be punctual, accurate, calm, present, and do what is to be done at the arranged and appropriate times. Use nature as the model. Imagine if the sun one morning thought, 'I'll be late to get to the other side of the sky', came up early and went racing round to finish the day an hour and a half early! Or, 'It's a lazy day today, I'll take an hour's lie in and drift dreamily over.' The sun is in perfect harmony with Divine will, and acts with absolute rhythm. Adopt the same strategy for your life. It does not matter what those around you do. Just be calm, remember Me; your actions will flow perfectly, like the sun's.

You are blessed, loved, Embodiment of love.
16.7.92

81
Draw Near the Wellspring of Love.

Love! That is the key. Love God. Love yourself in your approach to God. Love others as they are. Love takes you beyond attachment. It separates you from absorption into others' moods. It gives you equanimity. Use all your power, all your determination, mobilise your will to see with eyes of love, hear with loving ears, think loving thoughts. Embrace all that is not love in you and transform it into an expression of love. When energy comes towards you, receive love. Every form of attention has a component of love. Take that essence, and return love to it.

There is no spirituality without love. There is no God without love. There is no meaning without love. Life itself withers. Love is the transformative component of every act. Anger reduces every action to flames. Love increases every action to perfection. Love can never be hurt, never insulted, never provoked.

Draw near to the wellspring of Love. Honour it! Experience it in yourself. Know love as the wellspring of the universe. Sense it as the ultimate vibration, the ground of all being. See in it the truth. Love is God, God is Love. That is the secret, the essence of the teaching, the great demand, challenge and solution.

All teaching that deviates from love is distorted. All wisdom that does not spring from love is flawed. Love is clear and courageous, strong and courteous.   Let all burn, but never the house of love.

You are blessed. You are Me. Know it!

19.7.92

284

82
The Solution to Anxiety.

Anxiety is like a haze which exists between the outer world experienced by your senses and your inner reality - your divinity. Do not for a moment think of it as related to your sense perceptions. On the contrary, it may be totally absent in frightening situations and disturbingly present when you are thinking of trivia. The haze of anxiety is not equally present in all jivatma. It is a karmic challenge.

The solution to anxiety is simple. I am holding you. I do not drop you, will not drop you, have no desire to drop you. Place your faith in Me. Anxiety cannot withstand surrender to Me. It withers away and is replaced by calm, centred confidence. The onset of an anxiety attack is a wonderful opportunity to strengthen your connection with Me, to develop more confidence in Me, to increase your faith. At first there will be a battle as the anxiety strives for control, but if you keep repeating My name, calling on Me, surrendering yourself and ego control to Me in that moment, more and more quickly you will banish the anxiety, till the time will come when it is not triggered by any situation.

A young child may have a recurrent nightmare. As it grows older and its consciousness develops, the nightmare ceases to be frightening and finally ceases altogether. Anxiety is like the nightmare. As you become more centred in God, it releases its hold and finally fades away. It is a stupid mistake to think that changes in the outer world can ultimately remove anxiety. Fear of it and its effects on the body is crippling, for it does not allow you to use your full potential to do My work.. So follow the solution. Develop faith and strength in surrender to Me. Then 'Don't worry' and you can be happy!

Anxiety should always be dealt with directly and by the same method. It is of the same order as delusion, a confused inner state. Never accept it as real or valid. It is not like fear. Fear can be a genuine physical survival mechanism in a life threatening situation. Fear stimulates consciousness and physical reaction. Anxiety paralyses. Use every opportunity to centre yourself more firmly in Me. I am Cause and Solution, the player of the game of life. Become one with Me - don't hesitate. There is no other goal or value that has precedence.

Be Blessed.

23.7.92

83
Final Message. The Shift To and From Love.

During this period, a time of assimilation, you should release this frequent direct communication, just 'checking in' from time to time. Be concerned to put into practice the messages you have already received, which provide a perfect spiritual 'manual' for someone in your position. Read them through, use them. Share them with good friends in Sai or sympathetic spiritual seekers. Once this assimilation has happened, a new series of fuller messages will come as pert of a project for publication, and this will be an expansion and development of what you have received, with examples and illustrations to give people the opportunity to use it. But your first task is assimilation. Everything has its time and place.

A major shift is going on in you and the world. Allow yourself to be open to the available love. Love polarises people - not because of its nature, but because of the response to it. By getting nearer to love, you are empowered, self-sufficient and able to care appropriately for others. By rejecting love, you open the door for all the other emotions which drag you into the world of illusion, anger, envy, disempowerment and so on. Thus people separate themselves. There is no biological separation of the race, for everyone has the simple potential of opening themselves to love. But, in a completely natural way, those more and more open to love separate themselves out from those less and less open. To separate oneself from love is a sad and forlorn state, and arouses only compassion. But the separation is inexorable and is the preparation for the new era.

Because the love organised identity in formation is vulnerable to violence (and temptation), support havens are being built up all over the globe, for reinforcement and succour to those seeking love. There will be as many as needed, oases among the mirages of frustrated desire. Love, wisdom, right conduct, inner peace and gentleness to all the world - these are the qualities of the *new* humanity which will emerge from the ruins of *materialistic* humanity when all the violence has been spent and the war in the shadows has exhausted itself. Do not take part, but offer love to all who seek it. In your behaviour be a model of the new humanity, living in a transformed and purified world.

Never be afraid that it will not happen. I am 'happening' it. That is why I have come. Darkness cannot tolerate light - hate, rage, greed and all the other rakshasas cannot tolerate love; even as they defy it they dissolve and disappear. The primary thing is to strengthen love in yourself, with all that that entails.

Love and blessings; and an 'au revoir' for a short time.

30.7.92

Part 4

The Path To Love is the Practice of Love

An Introduction to Spirituality

by Carol Riddell

Foreword by Eileen Caddy

Dedicated in Love, Humility and

Gratitude to

<u>Bhagavan Sri Sathya Sai Baba.</u>

Acknowledgements

Above all, to Swami', Bhagavan Sri Sathya Sai Baba, Source, Inspiration, Guide, Supporter, Friend, Divinity. If I look to Him, He looks to me. And even if 1 forget, He looks to me.

The basis of this book was written during a three month stay gifted to me by Albert and Anneliese Harloff at their beautiful former centre, 'A Rochinha' at Ponta do Sol on Madeira, an inspiring location. We are always together in our hearts.

Henk, Marianne, Arendt and Hanka Van der Sluis gave the house 'Taigh Sith' on the Ross of Mull, as part of the 'Highland Renewal' Project, for me to live in during typing up. Charles and Heather Murphy were there to support me as I began the text preparation and Charles did some initial revision. When they went south for a time, Iris Urfer gave me her love and support. The detailed criticism of Sandra Kramer and Lynn Barton stimulated me to present the book in this form.

The Findhorn Foundation and its Erraid Community have given me so much over the years! So many friends, so much unstinting support! Thank you, everyone

291

Charlette, the indefatigable 'Kaypro Computer' typed the book initially, and Brother HRII, printed the new version.

Contents

Page

Foreword by Eileen Caddy

Many people are now seeking to reach a state of divine and unconditional love. Carol Riddell's book offers constructive, common sense help in reaching this ideal and how to incorporate it into everyday living. She leads us to discover the love within each one of us, and stretches our consciousness to reach that only real source of happiness - Love.

The exercises are excellent, and will be invaluable not only for groups but also for the individual on the path to unconditional love. I believe the meditations, some of which I personally use and find extremely powerful, will also facilitate the reader in their inner search for their divine centre. The desire to reach this centre leads us on the path to love, and the way to reach this path is the practice of love, through service, devotion and stillness. Let service come from wholeness, not lack. Let devotion be the practice of love, and the practice of love be stillness.

Let all you do and all the words you express come from love. The time for love is now, for now is all the time we have.

Eileen Caddy

Introduction

This book explains the meaning of a spiritual life, and provides a way for people to get together with like-minded friends to practice its principles. Through understanding and practice, one can transform daily life, give meaning to one's experiences, and find happiness in the service of others.

There is little 'theology' or narrowing dogmatism. The teachings can equally apply to Christians, Buddhists, Moslems, Jews, Hindus or Humanists, as long as one accepts that the essential principle of the cosmos is love, a love which is both detached and personal, all-pervasive yet specific. The various religions are the structures and social supports through which the search for truth can be channelled. All are, ultimately, equally valid; yet, in as far as they are social constructs, flawed.

The guidance in this book is 'channelled', a technique for accessing a higher wisdom that can be learned (see exercise 11). The exercises have been tested over a period of four years in workshops in several European countries and at the Findhorn Foundation. Several self-help groups have already used them.

The dominant 'religion' of this age is materialism, a world-wide doctrine with many 'priests' .Its consequences are disillusionment, cynicism and, in the worst cases, self-destruction. Finding a way past materialism is the challenge of this era. As a result of my own experiences, 1 have become confident that humanity will find the way. This manual is a contribution to that end. It is the result of 20 years of training and experience in Zen meditation, therapy, psychic studies, at the Findhorn Foundation and as a devotee of Sathya Sai Baba, the great Indian spiritual teacher.

As always with such texts, work with it carefully, but critically. It will help you along your own path to true happiness in life.

Guidance

Contents **<u>Page</u>**

A Beginning

Who doesn't want happiness in life? People everywhere, whatever the task they are engaged in, hope for it. They define their aim in many different ways. For one, it is having a new car or computer; for another, owning a piece of land. It may demand possession of a loved one, or an increase in power and prestige. Every human desire you can think of is projected as a potential source of happiness.

Many dream of happiness in social terms: they believe 'society' or 'people' could be happy through belonging to this or that institution - such as the church, or 'democratic society' — or through social transformation.

None of these individuals and social groups have found what they seek. They go through life searching. Some are convinced they have discovered the source of happiness; only a little more will give fulfilment — another (newer) car, computer, wife, husband, project. Others cajole — only a little more struggle, violence, obedience … and happiness will be there for the populace.

As people get older, many become disillusioned. They feel happiness is a death-right, only existing when unpleasant earthly duties have been fulfilled. Others resign themselves to obligation and dullness, resentful of those who so foolishly seek an unattainable goal. They are mistaken. Happiness is the birthright of every human, but it is a state of being, not a state of achievement or possession. It has to be realised. You have it now, but are unaware of it because of the way you perceive and define the world around you. It is inherent, all-pervasive. It is, *now*, and remains so, irrespective of circumstance. Happiness is not in another bucket, so to speak. It is in the bucket in your hand, hidden under the sand of attitude and world view. It is perception that needs to be transformed. The first great spiritual challenge is to shift the focus of longings from a future state of acquiring to a present state of recovering, uncovering.

To take this important spiritual step requires an act of faith. Old thought patterns whisper: 'If 1 don't feel happy right now, how can 1 actually be happy - that denies my own experience.' On the contrary! It has to be affirmed: 'Though 1 don't feel happy right now, it is clue to the way 1 see things.' It is not such an easy step to take and maintain; it is not easy at first to trust. There is help there; but even accepting that can be scary. Yet it is this change in attitude which leads beyond knowledge to wisdom itself.

The Basis of Happiness is Love

It can be affirmed: Love alone exists; all else is secondary. Love expands and presents itself as *forms*. Physicality, thought and expression, are all, in their essence, love. The entire universe is composed of and constructed of love. Love is the natural organising principle of human existence. The expression of love is necessary in relationship and the growth of human awareness. Here, then, are three great spiritual truths:
*   The physical universe is love clothed in *form*.
*   The way of the universe is love organised in *structure*.

*   Conscious life results from love expressed in *relationship*.

The third truth provides the link between human consciousness and the true source of happiness. It is like the key which opens the door to happiness. We will return to it later.

Love is a quality — but one unlike any other. Since love is the basis of everything, it has no opposite. If it were to have one, it would not be something like 'hate', which is merely love distorted, but 'nothingness', which is an irrelevance.

In the spiritual sense, all consciousness that does not experience existence as love is illusory. As soon as love takes the form of human beings, those same humans learn to experience life in ways that hide the love from which they were created. The social construction of human existence itself builds this 'illusion' in. Although all the objects you may experience with your senses are actually love, without their differentiation into forms and names, consciousness itself would be impossible. Although human life requires the illusion of form, it is possible to regain the experience that love is the basis of every form.

Love, as a quality, is not neutral. In human experience it translates itself as feeling. This 'feeling quality' of love in human relationships — whether to parent, spouse, child, pet, nature or God — is genuine 'happiness'. The more one experiences love, the more happiness there is. Eventually, happiness becomes 'bliss'.
Beyond bliss is 'ecstasy', which describes the experience of the whole of creation as love. To penetrate the illusion that there is 'not-love' is ultimate fulfilment — to reach enlightenment. It requires that everything that exists be experienced as love. Once one is completely illusion-free, harm and hurt to others would just be unthinkable. But as human beings develop, the practice of love

300

and its expansion to wider and wider areas of life lead to steadily increasing happiness.

Here is a simple example:

If you work in an office with five people and like two of them, are indifferent to two and dislike one, we can give you a 'happiness quotient' of +2 -1 = 1.

If you change your attitude so you can like three, remain indifferent to one and still hate one, your 'h.q.' will then be +3 -1 = 2. By changing a little more so you are indifferent to the one you disliked, your 'h.q.' then becomes 3.

It rises to 5 when you can like them all.

Let's suppose your 'transformation' *doubles* the intensity of your 'liking' by increasing its love content. Your happiness quotient will then shoot up to 10.

Finally, to find enlightenment, you transform yourself so that you experience love for all humanity and the created universe, without exception. Your 'happiness quotient' is then infinite!

How do you transform yourself? The first thing you have to do is to determine to try; and lovingness increases. Then, try to accept that all is ultimately love, even if this seems abstract at first. You are now on your way to the deepest truth of all great religious belief - God is love, and love is God.

Since the truth is that the basis of all existence is love, you also are love. If you do not experience yourself as love, your experience of the rest of creation as love will not be perfect. The task is to understand and remove everything that prevents you from experiencing love as your own basis. The more you can genuinely express that experience in life, the more love will become the focus of your identity. Thus is happiness realised; to have a fulfilled life, you have to seek your own loving nature. There is nothing selfish in this, for what you find leads you inevitably to the service of others.

(Note. Modern physics unravels the physical principles by which the universe is created. Scientists, describing and categorising forms and energies, present them as 'abstractly' as they can, denying qualities of feeling in themselves. One is not supposed to feel angry or joyful at the experience of photons, much less project such qualities upon them. The 'scientific approach' regards them only as 'photons' .Since love, the essential quality, gives *feeling* when experienced, the scientific method can never really comprehend the true nature of the universe - it has denied love 'a priori'. There is a point when physical enquiry must merge with spiritual experience for the most profound insights.)

Experiencing Love

Love is the basis of everything. Humans experience love through relationship. By consciously deciding to seek more and more love in their lives, they become aware of their own essence. Thus they approach vibrant oneness, the basis of form and the source of bliss.

A conscious decision to seek love implies an identity - a self - that can make such a choice. Babies do not have this identity. To become fully human, they have to develop one. A baby being is love, innocent and vulnerable, but without the consciousness that would enable it to know that it is love. It is the way things are. Even the instinctive life of the human baby is small. It needs human relationship in order to survive and to develop a sense of self which can make choices to seek love. Human relationship inexorably links it to the existing world of human consciousness.

There is no escape from culture, language or nationality - all of which are lying in wait - via parents and siblings. The baby enters this interaction equipped with the desire to live, which is expressed physiologically in its needs for food, drink and warmth. As those who provide for these needs are identified as separate from the general environment, consciousness begins to emerge. Through this identification, the child begins to experience love in a conscious way.

What love means for the child is very strongly affected by the treatment which it receives from such primary figures. Since it has no other yardstick, the little child accepts the providers it loves as perfect. As they are not, its definitions of love can be distorted in the earliest stages of its development.

In extreme cases, a baby/child brought up with violence may incorporate violence into its definition of love. One brought up with parental withdrawal may bring distance into its definition of love. One brought up casually may define indifference as love. And so on. To find the way back to true love - the source of bliss - all such misidentifications must be overcome.

When a child's wishes are not immediately gratified, it experiences a sense of frustration. It starts to wish that things could be better arranged than they already are; it has become cognisant of a self separate from its experiences. Through separation the child can begin to evaluate the world around it. By the time the child

303

begins to experience itself as a separate identity, distortions of what love means are already in place.

As childhood continues, more complex forms of expression, social rules and customs are added to basic identifications and frustrations. The little child interprets, and is changed by, its surrounding situations. Because this is the way everybody develops their individuality, people grow up with enormous confusions about the way to search for and express happiness - often passing them on to their own children. For these reasons, most people have to make a major shift in perspective to comprehend that love is the real source of happiness.

For everybody without exceptions, there are moments which could lead to the discovery of the essence - Love. These 'clues' may be ignored, rejected or misinterpreted; nevertheless, they are there. Often, they are moments which seem outside of normal - socially accepted - experience, giving them a mystical quality. Here are some examples:

* experiences where the self seems to merge with nature;
* experiences of a sense of oneness in otherwise ordinary social situations, accompanied by intense feeling;
* experiences that may occur when someone consciously seeks love, such as in meditation.

During such moments there is an 'expanded' consciousness; the self merges into indefinable unity. Since these experiences are beyond the scope of normal consciousness, they are also beyond the scope of common language, and people have great difficulty in describing and communicating them. These special moments are short-lived and cannot be recreated at will.

Every human being has such experiences appropriate to their consciousness. They are 'extra-social' and do not arise logically out of the particular setting in which they occur. They are a practical proof of the existence of Grace. Love is more than the passive existence of universal oneness. It moulds itself into experiences which potentially expand and redirect consciousness. It not only exists, but also manifests. It can focus to support an individual.

The challenge is that not all extraordinary experiences are mystical. Some may be symptoms of delusion or even mental illness. You need to have discrimination and integrity to evaluate them and understand their meaning. As you make the effort, you can discover that literally everything that occurs is part of a divine drama of separation and reunion, and every experience, of whatever kind, has a place and a function.

(Note. This focusing of love also happens when a divine teacher appears on earth to assist in the discovery that love is the source of happiness. Rather than a projection of love outward upon a form ('Love is there, but not in me!'), devotion to such a teacher may assist in the discovery of love within: 'He helps me to find love within me', or, 'Love manifested guides me to my own essential love' .But remember that not all love-professing teachers fully embody what they profess.)

More About Consciousness

In the highest experience, manifest creation is realised to be love and known as continuous ecstasy. This is truly Divine Consciousness: 'Being, Awareness, Bliss'. It is total human fulfilment, the soul merged in love with all creation; the Divine and the human become one, without separation.

Why is such a thing a goal, if it is already there, the essence and birthright of all humans? Why are even the 'clues' to it ephemeral and tantalising, often misinterpreted and feared as bordering on insanity? One reason is that the consciousness of the average person is not prepared for such powerful energy.

If a high amperage is put through an inadequate circuit, a fuse occurs at the weakest point. The circuit has to be strengthened before it can take the higher amperage. Love is the energetic basis of all creation. To experience it constantly as a reality requires both physical and mental development. This does not necessarily entail endless hours spent in meditation in silent places; since humans are capable of experiencing Divinity, they require the practice of love to discover its omnipresence. If one is potentially able to run a mile in, say, five minutes, one has to have the determination and physical capability to perform the task. This is achieved partly by exercises, but, above all, through practice.

There is another reason why enlightenment is not quite readily available. To understand it, we must return to childhood development.

Without a sense of self, consciousness cannot grow. In a little baby, this sense of self hardly exists; a nascent consciousness floats in a sea of undifferentiated, unexperienced lose. The self is 'drawn out' by interaction with its particular environment, and builds up a 'personality' .The early experiences of relationship are

306

so powerful in this developing identity since it cannot resist them. Because the sense of self is so unformed, the child's experiences have a powerful effect on its identity.

As growth continues, the child becomes more powerful, more adaptable and less overwhelmed by input. It interacts more; the self congeals. A relatively stable sense of self, the Ego, emerges.

Gradually, more or less consciously, it develops '*strategies*' for coping with the challenges posed to it and tries to resolve its problems by these means. The more effectively a strategy 'works' for a child, the more it tends to be adopted as part of the ego. *Thus, an individual illusion is created, which separates the ego self of practical short-term strategy from the potential self of limitless, joy-filled love.*

To the psychological illusions of a developing child are added social ones. In the present age, a materialistic consciousness is a strong component of almost every ego on the planet. It says: 'The way to happiness is through what you have, what you do and what value others attribute to you - 'prestige' .Many people hold on to this illusion until death's door — the end of the road for the soul's lifetime ego — frustrates it.

In these psychological and social ways, the ego, which is necessary to the achievement of personal consciousness, acts as a powerful block to the awareness that love is the real way of being. Thus, that which has created the self has to be surrendered for the realisation of the True Self — quite a challenge.

If ego is to be suddenly overthrown, what may remain? The fear of madness, oblivion, social ostracism, and poverty have all been advanced as good reasons for keeping within the ego's boundaries. Deep, suppressed childhood traumas may subvert even a determined wish to find love. Desires for instant gratification may

307

make a seeker impatient and easily discouraged. The path to self realisation requires understanding and a cool head. Small wonder then that it is not so often taken.

The established religions do not always help. In order to regulate social action among individuals living illusions about happiness, religious systems have not only taught that 'God is love, and love is God'; but their moral codes have become law and practice. This is a great dilemma for all religious teachers: God seems more 'outside' than 'inside' and morality becomes command rather than discovery. Some religious institutions almost end up denying that there is an 'inside' — a direct connection to love — God — in each individual. Such a love link could threaten the authority of the churches organisations themselves, not to mention that of social institutions at large. This is one of the reasons why love expresses itself in perfect human form from time to time — in order to ensure that individual's direct contact with love itself is not forgotten.

The Divine System and the Human System

The development of the personal identity, essential to consciousness, distorts it, to create a subjective awareness: the human system. Parallel to the human system is the Divine System, interacting with it and giving it meaning.

For human beings who do not make good progress towards Self-discovery in their lives, death would be a devastating defeat. But, just as there is a cosmic physical order by which things run, there is also a cosmic moral order. Both are governed by the law of cause and effect. The workings of the moral order have been discovered by inner exploration, primarily by the spiritual teachers of India.

A man who kills another, if discovered, is subject to the moral effect of punishment in the human system. In the 'divine system', all action has a moral effect. Some religious systems believe in the 'day of judgement' after death, when the soul is judged according to its earthly actions and allocated an appropriate place — heaven, limbo or hell (eternal damnation). But love knows no damnation. All creation is on an eternal path to conscious reunion; this is love's way of experiencing itself.

Although the individual's personality dissolves with death, the soul is clothed in the consequences of its actions. It does not die, but re-emerges in life as another being to work out those consequences and create new actions. It therefore has another opportunity to experience love and find happiness. This law of moral cause and effect is called 'karma'.

An individual soul is a non-material aspect of divine energy. It is endlessly reborn in different forms until it has developed its consciousness to the point of experiencing oneness and its truth as love. Life is an opportunity for learning about the universality, omnipresence and feeling of love. Eventually all souls learn this lesson — they are reborn continually until they do — and consciously reunite with love. There are no failures; but because of differing individual attitudes, some soul-experiences take longer than others. However, at any given moment, conscious emergence is available, if the identity is prepared to accept it.

Physical existence is not random karmic discovery. Love is not merely passive and existent. It is dynamic and supportive. The divine regulation of life ensures that every soul's experience is regulated and relevant to its choices. This grace-filled intervention operates constantly, although individuals do not become aware of it until their consciousness is awakened.

We can picture creation as a divine game. Love divides itself into physical forms (the board), structures of organisation, physical and moral (the rules), the players (individual souls), and the teacher and supporter of the game (divine Grace).

Grace, the teacher, provides appropriate experiences to which embodied souls react. The miracle of Grace is the perfect governance of all the complex interactions of embodied souls , so that each individual can make choices leading to the discovery of love. This miracle of constant creation inspires awe and humility in those who become aware of it.

The 'divine system' parallels the human system, but is far, far wider. It encompasses all forms, not just human forms. It regulates the entry of *life-force* into form, the entry of *consciousness* into life force and the entry of *awareness* into consciousness, until, eventually, the soul becomes aware of itself as love, and experiences itself as love. At this point, the regulator and the regulated are one, continued physical existence is a choice and incarnation is voluntary and perfect.

Great love allows freedom. The greatest joy occurs when freedom is used to find mergence. That joy, that ecstasy is Love's self-experience, or divine self-knowledge. *There were never two, only the illusion of two.* As the illusion dissolves, Love experiences itself.

Understanding the Divine System

Theologians of all faiths have struggled with such concepts as free will, divine intervention, the existence of evil and the meaning of suffering. Unless you start from the knowledge that love alone is real and that the process of creating human consciousness masks that truth, the ground is full of pitfalls.

Much theological argument merely takes the apparent world at its face value, accepting that the experiences of our normal senses constitute truth. This is fallacy, constructed to comprehend, rationalise and attempt to control an apparently external, objective reality.

But from such ignorance flows only ignorance. Solutions to human problems of war, famine and disease are always 'just round the corner'. A new technology applied in one place causes problems somewhere else. A problem is solved in this part of the world and another emerges in that part of it. By thinking that the material world is 'really real', people think that real solutions can be found in it.

If one denies that love and grace control the illusory world experienced by the senses, explanations of that world and attempts to change things will be equally illusory. For many centuries there has been no effective change: humanity has been crippled by violence, disease and suffering. The ways they are inflicted may change, but the 'solutions' do not resolve problems — because these really stem from its alienation from love.

If the evidence of the senses is not subordinated to the practice of love, karmic cause and effect continue to operate from the divine system like a rule of a game, in order both to expose the effects of ignorance and to offer choices that could lead souls to the wisdom given by placing love first. The way to knowledge of the divine system and alignment with it is the practice of love. You can either apply love in life through service; or reject all that is 'not love' by devotion (surrender to God); or, in stillness, strip off all superficiality to become aware that love is the ultimate reality.

Love is fundamental. In different eras the relative importance of service, devotion and stillness may vary, though the practices are never exclusive. In the present 'action packed' age, service is most important.

Subtly, little by little, the practice of love itself — and not merely its discussion — changes consciousness, expands it. It does not matter where one starts; the murderer or brute, who chooses not to murder or be brutish moves in love's direction. Grace and new understanding will flow to such a person in measure: 'Take one step towards Me and I will take ten towards you.'

The practice of love develops a certain feeling concerning aspects of one's daily life. This 'feeling' is not emotional but

312

intuitional — an access to wisdom. It has nothing to do with deluded states, nor is it quite the same as conscience, which is concerned with mentally internalised social moral codes.

Such intuitive wisdom leads one to the awareness of three basic principles. One, love is the basis of all things. Two, the operation of the observed world depends on a Divine system. Three, a direct inner connection to love is possible.

These principles really turn everything around. In the human system it seems that 'a dog is always a dog'. Wisdom shows that 'a dog is a dog' by Divine Grace. *If you are near the source of Grace, the dog may turn out to be something else entirely.* There is a story of the God figure, Krishna, walking with His devotee, Arjuna.

"Look, Arjuna, over there sits a crow!"

"Yes, 1 see the crow."

"No, Arjuna, it is a pigeon!"

"Indeed it is a pigeon."

"No, it is a sparrow!"

"Of course, it is a sparrow."

"Arjuna, you are merely agreeing with everything I say to please Me!"

"No, Krishna, You are the definer of reality. If You say it is a crow, it is a crow; if You say it is a pigeon, it is a pigeon and if a sparrow, then a sparrow it is."

This story shows that the human system — the 'objective' world — is really defined by the Divine system. It is only by love's adherence to the 'rules of the game' that the human system appears to be real and responds to the scientific 'laws' that scientists have deduced for it. The application of Grace can change or 'bend' these rules at will.

Baldly stated, the above is just information, subject to argument and discussion. But by actually practising to love, you will come to know the reason for it in your heart, your 'innermost being', so you won't need to get into argument. Through the practice of love, intuitional feeling develops and wisdom begins to emerge in consciousness.

The practice of love is not something intellectual. Life is a school, but not an 'academic' one. People from any walk of life undertake the 'course of study' which the practice of love entails. The conscious choice to do so is the choice to take a spiritual path in life, but you can practice love and achieve wisdom without building theories about it.

As long as the ego is still powerful there are psychological pitfalls on all the paths to wisdom. Feelings towards other people are strongly coloured by qualities of the ego: sexual desire, attachment, dependency, admiration, envy, hatred, rejection and so on. Love differs from all such attitudes; rather, it is masked by them. For instance, a worker in an office may have a boss and a subordinate. Their roles may make one seem superior and the other inferior, an egoistic attitude which arises from the human system. By overcoming this attitude and respecting and valuing both colleagues, irrespective of their roles and performance, they will be moving in the direction of love.

Love is *detached* from either a role or a performance. But a general may remain detached whilst ordering the deaths of thousands, so detachment *alone* is not the essence of love.

A mother deeply loves her child, and much attachment is involved. If she extends her affection to all children, she will be

314

moving towards love. The practice of love is always *expansive*, incorporating larger and larger categories of things.

A business man may see a wood, and view it as an opportunity for saleable timber. If he views all woods with such an opportunity in mind, he is certainly being expansive, but by no means approaches love. If he begins to see one tree in that wood as *intrinsically* beautiful, perfect, wonderful, he then begins to approach love, for he is *accepting* the tree as it is.

Love is 'coloured' by appropriate qualities, depending on the situation. Examples are: *patience* in repetitive tasks; *respect* when working with nature; *compassion* in accepting human ignorance and suffering.

The happiness that comes with love may bring tears to the eyes in its intensity. But someone who enjoys spanking so much that it brings tears to their eyes is not practising love. Qualities attributed to love cannot themselves define it. Love is basic and ultimate. It is defined by its experience, and descriptions are never quite adequate.

People who come to know love, their essential Self, are wise. They are unaffected by the ups and downs of life in the human system. Intuitively, they know that everything derives from the Divine system. *They are full of compassion for human beings who struggle in life, unaware of their own perfection.* Those who have loving wisdom serve, not to demonstrate the practice of love, but as loving agents of Grace.

The Practice of Love as the Way to Love

The three main forms of the practice of love are service, devotion and stillness. Let us examine them further.

Service should not simply be thought of as doing good for others. There are many ways of 'doing good' that have distorted psychological motives and are fraught with illusion. For instance, if a person feels inadequate in themselves, they might feel better when caring for others who are less well off. This is not service, but projected insecurity. It is as if a person were to say to another: 'I am only ¾ of a person. Lend me ¼ of yourself and I'll be alright.' Such a 'server' is really being served. They need the poverty and deprivation of others to 'do good' to. What would they do without a famine, crisis or third world to provide them with fodder for their own needs? Although it is possible to find a path to love through any activity, a person who does not feel worthy without helping other is truly being served by them rather than serving.

A preliminary to true service is to make a connection with love within. *Service is to act from it.* In fact, nobody who finds love can resist serving. It is an imperative, just as water building up behind a dam will somehow find an outlet in the end, be the dam ever so high. Service comes from wholeness, not from lack. Wholeness comes from contact with love.

Before any prestigious and high-sounding activities, *the first and most basic form of service is consciously to practice looking lovingly on others*. Initially, this is an act of will; and it will instantly put you in touch with the illusions which veil love. Looking with love is like digging a little channel to let water flow out of the dam. As soon as it starts flowing, it enlarges the channel by its flow. The practice of looking with love gives a person energy

316

and motivation to get rid of their personality blockages so that the Divine system may be more freely expressed. What an energy that releases what a motivation! Such a simple thing, such a good feeling! One is not a sinner, expiating guilt, but a human being expressing the Divine within.

Look lovingly on your room, on the clothes you have to wear, on your belongings, on the world of nature, on your partner or your children, on your friends, on your parents and relatives, on strangers, on your enemies. To practice this for even half an hour a day is the beginning of service. Think of all of them with love, not judgement, criticism, or qualifications - without 'buts'. You will find happiness moving into your life and out into the world. Frustration with the world which seemed to be the cause of your troubles turns towards the real cause, ego structures, and gives you the determination to reform and transcend them.

Just a little lovingness practised is the next step in service. Lovingness expresses love, and opens inner channels to wisdom, Grace and the Divine system. Through it knowledge of the Divine will become possible and you will want to follow it, knowing Love as a teacher which gives you the optimum path, blending its lessons with your desires to support Self-realisation.

Once love begins to flow, some means for action will be provided by Grace. In service, the act done is much less important than the quality with which it is done. A woman cleaning her home may provide more service to humanity than an aid worker distributing relief food packages to the starving, if the former acts with love and the latter from insecurity.

Ultimately, it is only love, increased drop by drop, that can resolve problems. It is a mistake to think of 'trouble spots' as being somewhere else, to do with another part of the planet. Like a run-down body which breaks out in a boil somewhere, so a system with

317

little access to love will produce 'trouble' spots at some point within it. Poverty and starvation, epidemics and brutality are a direct result of lack of love in the system. A loveless person cannot find happiness; nor can a loveless humanity. There are adequate resources for everyone to enjoy a life of physical well-being — only lack of love stops them flowing appropriately. Humans struggle to solve these problems through changing social systems, but any loveless system will create problems, no matter how perfect it may seem on paper.

Again and again people are deluded by achievement. They want to see immediate results! Achievement without love is hollow: an empty form giving at most, ephemeral satisfaction. If love is not present, the 'achievement' of feeding the hungry does not resolve the problem of famine, which merely rears its head elsewhere. Of course, you do put a band aid on a cut, but it is better to deal with the carelessness which led to cuts; don't think you have achieved something great by putting on a band aid.

Service is the practice of love most easily accessible and valuable in a world starved of love. It involves surrender to grace, trust that the right lessons are being given, faith that all tasks are transient and will be changed at the appropriate moment. It is not easy to release human will and become totally aligned with divine will. But service will take you there.

The second aspect of the practice of love is *devotion*. Devotion is love surging into wonder, surrendering in the knowledge that, though seemingly separate, you are one with love. Devotion acts primarily through the *feeling* self, cleansing it, purifying it, elevating it. It also carries rationality along with it, as a surge of water carries with it all the flotsam that has been lying around.

Devotion arises in the heart, as you realise your utter minuteness compared with the overwhelming and infinite universe. It arises as a fraction of the divine order guiding all lives is revealed to you with overwhelming consciousness. Devotion bursts out when a perfect embodiment of love in human form reveals itself. It is characterised by a feeling of expansion of the heart, by awe and wonder: Love overwhelms.

Devotion to an abstract, conceptualised love is most difficult, nor is it a quicker or purer way to oneness with love — as mental pride sometimes suggests. It is a great challenge to try and deny the physical, human side of feeling in order to find transcendence. Devotion to a Divine teacher is the easy way, the holistic way through the forest of attachment and desires in the human personality.

As with other spiritual qualities, the roots of devotional attitudes lie in human relationship. A baby expresses devotion in its dependency on and trust in its nurturer. Its feelings become coloured by the way its needs, desires and demands are satisfied. People often begin a devotional relationship with a teacher by projecting onto him or her their experience of this primary relationship, looking for the flaws they once discovered in parent figures.

For devotion to be in the present, such motives have to be transcended. Divine figures on earth always suffer from projections from the past. They are rarely seen for who they are, in spite of the intensity of devotion of their followers.

Spiritual teachers come to focus love and adoration. Their task is to embody love so purely that projections from childhood have no peg to hang on. In a developing relationship of faith and trust, their role is to unveil the mystery of the Divine system and, beyond that, the perfection of love, so that the devotee can begin to experience it. Once devotion, genuine and spontaneous, begins to flow, it can be purified through prayer and song, reflection and meditation, till confusions from childhood wither away

True spiritual teachers have penetrated illusions, discarded ego and are indifferent to all the projections showered upon them. Even if they sometimes play an 'as if' game with their devotees — 'It looks as if 1 am angry or neglecting you, but I am actually purifying your devotion, for love's sake' — they continue to see divinity as being equally present in all, irrespective of behaviour. Devotion to a Divine teacher makes acts of grace personal, immediate, and comforting, as the devotee's mind strives to unite with love, disentangling it from the strings of illusion.

Devotion is still not perfected, however, as long as it is directed solely at one figure. For that figure can only be an exemplary expression of the Divine. *All are equally divine, and shrouded in the cloaks of confusion.* As devotion purifies, it bubbles over into compassion for and service to all humanity and creation, love's own projections in the great game of life.

Everyone teaches each other. Nothing is more delightful than to share love with others. But devotion to other seekers is not proper unless one is able to love each equally without projection or attachment, thereby experiencing them as divine embodiments. If you project perfection on to someone who is not perfected, you misplace your faith and enter once more into the karmic chain of cause and effect.

Love expresses itself in being and in living. But as devotees strive towards Self-awareness, they can easily become trapped by the power of love's acts and the admiration which they cause in others. Ego seeks to appropriate power and admiration, to find gratification in fame and reputation. Once again, a new cycle of karma begins.

So remember that all acts of love belong to love alone. As you work on Self-discovery, dedicate every 'success', every 'achievement', every 'gift of grace' to the Divine teacher. Let your day be full of His name, your thoughts be full of His presence.

Do not attempt to own your acts. They are love's .Dedicate them to love, in devotion and humility. Use your free will to surrender your ego to love, completely and without inhibition. Then you will find love.

Stillness and Understanding

The third aspect of the practice of love is stillness. Through it you can discover your true identity and find fulfilment. Through stillness, the mind is calmed, allowing argument and thought to drift away so that love alone is 'laid bare'.

To describe spiritual experience effectively and share it with others in a book, talk or video energises and stimulates interest in self-discovery. But there is a great distinction between scholarship, which is based on argument and learning, and an *experience* of Truth. To see a sign at a street corner which says 'Restaurant this way', does not stop your hunger. At best, it helps you to know where to eat. Using stillness as a discipline at first supplements and then supplants book learning and argument, and gradually cleans up the identity by reducing unnecessary speech, idle chatter and thoughtless words. This is a form of practising love.

Though discipline is not an end in itself, it is required to learn any skill. You cannot be a physician or carpenter, bus driver or astronaut without first subjecting yourself to discipline. Similarly, learning stillness requires it. For many people nowadays discipline has to be learned before it can be practised, which makes this method of spiritual development doubly hard. Even with discipline, seeking Love out through meditation can be very arduous. The Buddha took seven years of sitting to find it.

Although spiritual experience does not come through normal sensory channels, it carries with it a certainty that is deeper than sense-perception. Often we *think* we see, hear, and so forth, but we actually do not. But an experience of that which *is, as* it is, is never forgotten and leaves no room for doubt. You can doubt everything, but not the experience of love.

The aim of stillness is to free the self from attachment to sense impressions, memory, random thought and material aspiration, so that you can experience love through and through.

The process is to slough off layer after layer of the personality —'Not this, not that' — till love alone is left and real —'I am that' .Repetition of a holy name or of holy sounds, or contemplation of the pictures of spiritual teachers may help to still thought. Physically comfortable bodily positions give ease in the attempt.

With stillness comes a sense of detachment. After a while, this is infused by love, until a great compassion for the created world emerges. This compassion remains for a time after such a meditation, but fades if it is not repeated.

A meditating figure sits still and upright, in a solid position comfortable for the body. A chosen mantra, or a holy name, may be repeated. The eyes are closed, or, if open, focused on objects which do not provide a stimulus - for example, a blank wall. An inner,

322

verbal preamble may set the intention for the time in stillness. If such sitting is the sole practice, it must be prolonged and prolonged. Grace will be given to help the endeavour. As one approaches Love, wisdom about the divine plan of creation becomes available, physical limitations are removed and the soul is divinised. At the final stage, time and space are transcended, and Love alone is real. Neither sound, mantra, nor picture has any further significance.

All three ways of discovering and practising love — service, devotion and stillness — are valid paths to Love. They are not mutually exclusive. All of them benefit not just the seeker but also humanity itself.

In this epoch, the proportion of time spent in service is highest, that in contemplative stillness least; but the balance may change with age and individual circumstances. The final experience however is the same. Through practice of the three forms, you will discover which 'blend' of them is best for you. Anything that does not expand love — real happiness — in you is valueless.

The practice of love releases love's energy so that it flows through the world. Subliminally, it stimulates a desire for love in others, thereby becoming an aspect of Grace.

Judgement is Redundant!

The discovery of love profoundly changes human identity. Whilst there is no way to escape the past, which is the ladder of human growth to love, there is no necessity to linger on the lower rungs cursing past events, or feeling guilty about them. Nor do you need to have nightmares about the things that you did. They were done during many lifetimes and all human history is mirrored in your own.

In the secret corners of the past lie your deeds of ignorance and thoughtlessness. They are like sterile trails, petering out in a desert from which the only way out is to retrace your steps. Within your own past, you carry all that you might nowadays judge others for. You are different only because you have become wiser and such things no longer attract you.

Since you used to do the things for which you judge others, your judgement can only be deemed self-judgement or redundant. Evil actions are the result of love veiled by ignorance — consciousness ruled by a simple egoism which seeks immediate gratification. Since you, yourself, are the person you judge, be compassionate.

This does not mean that one should condone evil acts. It is not right for someone, even on a human level, to escape the consequences of their actions, otherwise they will be more likely to continue doing ill. Human systems of judgement are there to detect wrongdoers and those whose job it is will mete out punishment. But the Divine system runs by experiential training. Grace, in its compassion, gives the soul lessons which have the best of hope teaching that ignorant behaviour does not lead anywhere.

However, *judgement is not one of the consequences of an evil act*. Judging a person because of their actions is as inappropriate as if judging the sun for sometimes keeping behind the clouds. Evil people are quite as much divine as the righteous, in spite of the differences between their actions. They have the same potential to discover love as devotees, although their circumstances may differ. Every act has the potential to create a new step towards love consciousness.

Do not hate, revile or judge others. Have compassion for the executor of a crime, be it ever so great, as well as for its victims.

For yourself, do that which is right within the moral system of society; or better yet, unite with divine wisdom and act from it. Jesus suffered Himself to be tortured and crucified, knowing that it would open a great pathway to love for humanity. This act of love cannot be considered a happy experience in the normal sense. But if Jesus had not done it, it would have meant a devastating and inconceivable unhappiness, even greater and more prolonged than His actual suffering. If you can climb the step to love, you will know the best thing to do in life's situations and be astonished very often. But judgement of others only puts you in chains.

Imagine a light burning in a box, kept within a cupboard in a dark room. Take away all the casings and the room will no longer be dark. Similarly, love is like a high-frequency vibration obscured by lower frequencies. Remove the latter and love remains.

While the light is hidden in the cupboard, you have to hold on to things in the darkened room in order to get around. But once the light is exposed, it is no longer necessary. As you become more loving, many things you thought you needed will have less and less interest for you.

People who have a consciousness that is deeply obscured experience life at a base vibration. They strike discords of greed, envy, hatred, anger, violence, and brutality. As they gradually find love, the discordant frequencies are left behind.

Love over lights all lives and all behaviour, shining from within. Thus as you find the vibrations of love within you, you are not proud, judging yourself superior to your neighbours; but more and more, you will see them as essentially the same as yourself, following a comparable path to your own.

Therapy and the Practice of Love

Love is. It is released in you by its use. It lifts you up, and it brings you to who you truly are. The only way to find the love that is your essence, to understand and experience happiness is to practise it.

The practice of love does not include dissembling. Love cannot flow freely if 'secret' agendas are on hand. The human ego is adaptive and resourceful. Before blooming, a flower protects its fragile blossom with a harder casing that falls off as the flower is ready to open. The human ego is like this casing, but it is identified with self and unwillingly released, even when one wishes to do so.

At first the ego resists the call to inner spiritual awakening. It may find arguments to deny the presence of the divine in humanity. Or it may align itself with those who say that humanity can only be redeemed from sin by external forces. Or it may seek hedonism and short-lived pleasures in order to 'forget' that its days are numbered.

The acknowledgement of spirit, of love *within*, is a great breakthrough for the identity: there is a greater Self, to which the ego is redundant. At this point though, the ego is still in place. Its next strategy is to try and subvert the practice of love for its own ends. It turns a loving deed into a 'good' or 'praiseworthy' deed, a deed which shows others how 'holy' the actor is. The motivation becomes pride and status. Ego tries to turn a loving act into an act of power and prestige, which demonstrates the superiority of the performer and the inferiority of the receivers. Is money given for some spiritual teaching? Then ego will seek to turn it into a lucrative source of income in order to indulge a wealthy and indolent lifestyle.

Ego is linked to the human world. It is created by it, dependent on it and its motives. It tries to preserve itself by remaining on the human level. Ego steals around love, seeking to seal off all approaches to it. But eventually, ultimately, the practice of love will lift the Self above this level and ego will be gently and lovingly released, as consciousness advances beyond it.

Humans have now become more aware of ego consciousness, with its dark, hidden basements where the unassimileable, overwhelming experiences of childhood are stored. just as guards around a prison cost a great deal, so much human energy is expended to repress events of the past too terrible to face, events which shade the personality with fear and anxiety. Many people spend time and resources delving amongst these dark corners, attempting to become aware of their ulterior motives and to release some of their stored pain.

There is no harm in delving into the past — for that is what it essentially is — as long as it does not become a way of life. If you constantly refer to your past as the source of your actions, you are trapped by it as you were when it hid in your unconscious. In fact, after a certain amount of emotional release, you actually feed it in the mistaken belief that you are healing it. It is easy to let your own morbid curiosity shackle you to your problems.

Each of you carries the past, not only of this lifetime, but of a thousand before it. Each of you once performed most of the nasty acts of revenge, retribution, desire and terror which are repressed by your conscious mind. That is why you can repress them - because you have learned the lessons and risen above them. Dwelling in the past — to find the motivations and explanations of life — is a worthless exercise. As you discover that past lives have been real, it is tempting to dwell on subliminal memories of long-resolved challenges. Since they have no longer any importance, the exercise is a diversion, without spiritual value.

Love grows by the practice of love. It may sometimes be helpful to release blocked emotional charges, but the way forward is to practise love. This de-energises the past, brings you into the present — where love is — makes you aware of who you are, and allows the past to rest, quietly resolved.

A man discovered in therapy that many of his actions were motivated by an ambivalent attitude toward his mother. Instead of releasing the emotional 'steam' of this discovery and moving on, he began to excuse all his acts by it, blaming his mother for every failure. His ego had found a way to cling on for a while. If he had yelled out his pain for a short while and then consciously practised being loving to his mother, he could have healed their relationship and found happiness with her.

The practice of love heals, and guides to the Self. It creates a new identity, to which the past is but a wry memory. Even if motives are mixed, it will slowly purify them. Whatever ego's strategies, they will crumble before the *conscious, disciplined* and *continued* practice of love. To find out who you are, live in the present. Don't waste time!

Words and Actions

Underlying creation is a great sound. From its echo, humanity forms language and turns it into a plaything, an illusion within life's illusions, weaving and regulating, proposing and exhorting. Words only give direction and stimulation; at best they act as shorthand for experience.

Most words are uttered in the service of the human system and act as expressions of ego desires such as reputation and wealth. Humans erect mountains of words to describe simple things, which they proceed to bury under them. Even a great tome about love can make love less simple and less attainable.

So let love be expressed through your words:

* Say little, so that truth is not cluttered.
* Whatever you say, seek to let God speak it.
* Speak from quietness, consciously seeking love's presence.
* Celebrate the delights and worries of human life — its pains and sorrows — with words informed by love.
* Be love speaking and you will not bind yourself to the status and power brought by manipulating words.
* Let your words to others be a signpost to your knowledge of the source of love.

If you know little, speak little. If you know more, you will speak little anyway.

Through knowing love, you will speak less but you will communicate more. Your actions, your words and your thoughts will harmonise. You will have no ulterior motives; instead you will be love's agent, the kind of person who arouses the curiosity of others, and guides them in their own search.

To find happiness, seek the love in your heart before you speak or write; be aware of the implications of your speech for the listener and remember that love communicates directly, heart to heart.

A person who treats words in this way will be 'good company', someone that makes others think, the kind of person you should seek to be with on your journey to your-Self. Such good company will support and guide you on the path. In the end, once you are filled with love, you will no longer need good company, for you are whole and able to spread light amongst others.

Be In the Present

Each human life is bound by birth and death; in between is the time to find love and practise it. Time is merely an organisational form.

Human beings have set up time to regulate their lives. Having set it up they become dominated by it, rushing and hurrying everywhere. Modern lives are run by timetables and alarm clocks. Such things are products of anxiety and, ultimately, of a subconscious sense of the approach of death — for death seems to cut short all uncompleted activity.

And then comes a moment of Grace, when time ceases to have meaning. There is only now, beginningless and endless. As identity creeps back in, time returns.

How can you comprehend love if you are limited by time? In the experience of love, all that is, was, or ever shall be is *now*. All universes, parallel universes and alternative universes, all realms of visible and invisible energy are one. All is perfection. Love is now, not tomorrow, next year or after death. If you seek after something, you haven't got it. Love, you do have, now, at this moment. What is required is to know it.

There is absolutely no point in hurrying towards love. The best you can do is to practise it in whatever way is appropriate. As you do so, stress and impatience begin to disappear; a sense of harmony emerges. At first, time does not cease, but as anxiety diminishes, its significance is reduced. Time becomes subjective. It may fly or it may hover. The past may seem a moment or an age, depending on your mood. The aim is to make the present moment infinite. So many people are directed away from this moment. Some ponder compulsively on the past, seeking to rearrange things that have been, to find understanding and release. Others are full of fear and worry for the future —'What will it bring?'; 'What does it mean?'; 'How will 1 do?' — trying to safeguard themselves against all risks.

If you live this moment to the full, the 'problems' of the past fall away. It is the same with anxieties for the future. It is what you do now that determines your future, not how you try to safeguard yourself.

People often try to escape time by running away into dreams and fantasies about how things might be. But there is only one place to run to with open arms: to the strong, welcoming security of the love that is present within you now; there eternity lives.

All journeys in space and time are actually journeys to now — to that moment which is the same as all other moments, to that space which is the same as all other spaces; to the time and place where you know love. *Instead of hurrying to get there, concentrate on living the now. What you experience is now.*

The game of discovery unfolds, according to your position on the 'board of life' .If you know that 'now' is the only home you should become a master player, and, demonstrating love in your every move, a contemporary being.

You can only 'play for now' by releasing egoistic desires for worldly achievement and status; they relate to possible future states and are a source of anxiety and strife. 'Playing for now' means practising love and surrendering your control of situations to the Divine Will.

The more you run, the faster will run whatever you seek to catch. just stop in the now and you will discover that it has not escaped you at all, but already lies waiting at your feet. As you cease to hurry, the practice of love redeems time for you, comfortably embraces your past and future and allows you to know better who you are. Death ceases to loom menacingly.

Perform the duties which God gives you, practice love in every moment and you become 'real' and contemporary. All that seems impossible to the anxious mind becomes easy; the 'objective' world of space and time breathes love to you and the present begins to embrace eternity: it is now — not then — that 1 am to be found, Love itself.

Suffering and Death

The soul seeks love at any cost. It will willingly enter painful experience as a human being to enable love consciousness to develop. The soul is aware of love as the only solution to life's problems. It seeks, prays for re-entry into life, for there, and there only, can it find the way to love consciousness. The soul will re-enter life again and again, until consciousness of love pervades the human being and wisdom is discovered. This striving of the soul for love which explains the problem of suffering: human beings, mesmerised by ephemeral desires, replay every lesson until they take up the opportunities given to them to turn their desires to love. That is the soul's motivation to enter suffering humanity.

A loved one dies; a friend is crushed in an automobile accident; hundreds of thousands starve. A child is beaten to death; a battle ground is strewn with bodies; a dreadful disease causes a protracted and painful demise. Torturers pursue their vicious work. If there is grace, why do such things occur? Suffering and death are the hardest facets of the human diamond to accept; they are the most testing.

Suffering depends on attitude, among other things. When someone is cut, one person might say, 'Oh, 1 should have been more careful with the knife.' Another screams at the sight of the blood. The first experiences no suffering, a little pain perhaps and a lesson learned. The second imagines they are suffering and, consequently, feels it. Their pain is magnified by fears of infection and death.

If you stretch your hand into the fire, you will be burned. That is a kind of self-inflicted suffering. If your acts deny the practice of love, you will also suffer.

Compassion towards suffering is one of love's great gifts. When you express your compassion by practising love, you begin to transcend suffering. For love is not dependent on outer experience. Engage with love and you will find happiness, for happiness depends on love, rather than the ups and downs of outer life. Lovingness ameliorates the suffering of others; it heals the sick with a deep quiet joy that is an overwhelming power. By strengthening your connection with love, you learn that your suffering is the result of non-loving *action*. If you are centred in love, happiness can be present, in spite of pain, for suffering and pain are both *reactions*.

While the world is occupied by people who are motivated by material possession, the degree of suffering rises. Greed results in poverty and starvation; luxury in squalor; envy in crime; and power in violence. Those who themselves do not materially suffer (at the time), but are full of greed, cause suffering for others, even if the parties are separated by thousands of miles. *Grace provides the resources for all to live. How they are divided and used by men and women is the responsibility of humanity and reflects its moral state.*

A human society centred in love might not be materially wealthy, but it would have little or no suffering. If you can understand this you will be able to see suffering for what it is. Be compassionate to those who experience the results of not turning to love. When you feel suffering yourself, you will know that your soul is teaching you. Instantly hold fast to love and the lesson is learned; suffering will recede.

Another aspect of suffering is its connection with fear: fear of others' views; fear of unresolved problems from the past; fear of losing material standards that you expect; and, above all, fear of *death*.

Death is merely an interlude between births. The physical body, possessions and ego sense are released. The soul exists as energy on a non-physical plane. For those bound by desires for the physical, death is a terrible event. But for those who know love and live by it, death is no great hurdle. For those approaching conscious embodiment as love, even the entry and exit are known and chosen.

See death for what it is and you will not suffer on account of the dead, but commend them to grace for their next appearance on the stage of the human drama. Make love and its practice your being and you will have neither fear of death nor lesser fears. Since you do not know the time of your death, practise love now. There is no point in wasting time in unnecessary fear.

Detachment and Engagement

A small child is tempted by its parent, who presents it a bright and cuddly object. Jackdaw-like, it grasps. At first, it gives it back quite readily, but after a while, it refuses. The concept of 'mine!' is born — so simply does a child enter life's training. The practice of love — spontaneous giving - thus begins to be masked by *holding on*.

As soon as holding on is established, *taking* emerges. But who may take? Anxiety about possession is born.

Next it is a question of *protecting* - and struggle arrives.

Out of successful struggle emerges the thought of *keeping*.

'Keeping' requires power, and power in the service of keeping soon leads to *aggression*. The pattern of human civilisation is easily established!

All too often, the 'gifts' of loving parents reinforce 'mine' and 'my-ness', with their attendant chain of dubious qualities. But a loved parent can nurture in a way which brings to dawning consciousness the sense of wonder and reverence that comes with spontaneous giving.

Even for a young child there are choices — to hold or to give, to possess or to release. All through life such choices are offered. Give freely and joyfully, and release the ephemeral satisfaction of 'having' with all its attendant fears. View even the things which you feel you need:— house, partner, whatever — as a trust, to be used for a while in the practice of giving, and not as a possession.

Holding on ties you to the material world. It may even affect giving. A thing grudgingly, resentfully or conditionally given involves fear and faintheartedness. Calculation, thought of return, or manipulation, taint the energy of both the giver and the gift.

To a person addicted to 'having' — however little they may actually have — the idea of 'giving-living' is rather terrifying. Anxieties will crowd in : 'Perhaps I'll starve!' 'Nobody will like me! 'People will laugh at me!' 'I won't be respected!' 'I'll be vulnerable to anyone's whim!' 'Who'll look after me when I'm old!' 'If 1 don't cling, my partner will leave!' . . . . These are the ghosts of the human world, its terrifying phantoms, sired by holding which make release so fraught.

None of this is unconquerable. The practice of loving provides strength and joy. Every step towards love draws grace. It works! Little by little the fears can be understood for the illusions they are.

The entire material world, with all its relationships and interactions, is God's gift. Even qualities which one possesses' — humour, anger, fearfulness, desire and so on — are God's gifts. Love has released them into form and energy.

The real source is not the gift but the *giver*. Capture the Giver and all is yours. But the Giver is not located in the physical dimension; nor can He be reached by spaceship or through 'hyperspace', neither can He be ensnared by spells or psychic power. The Giver is Love and resides in your spiritual heart. By the practice of love and detachment from all His gifts may the Giver be found.

So do not grab at the artefacts of the Giver, be they ever so tempting. Centre your desires on the real prize, aim high!

The Giver gives; so give like the Giver! Emulate Him! The Giver is love, so practise love! Let the Giver's material gifts circulate freely.

338

Trust the Giver's ability to give; trust your life to it and you will receive all that you need, but continue to give to others, in love. If it seems hard, start practising little by little. However much you are distracted, return to the task.

Be *engaged* in the world, a channel for divine gifts rather than their possessor. You will discover a life of bliss, without clinging, anxiety or fear. As you do, detach yourself from everything else *harmoniously*, for harmony makes detachment and engagement real.

To reach the final goal — the essence of all these gifts — even attachment to the Giver has to be released, for if the Giver were attached, His gifts would not be given on! Quietly know who you are, abandon striving and desire. But do not pretend to have reached the goal when you have not; that is dissembling. Practice of this engagement and detachment is part of the practice of love.

A world composed of people on such a search will be very different from the world of today — dominated by people holding and its retinue, fear and aggression.

Surrender

If you understand that love is life's reality, and that grace is all pervasive, you will also realise that your reality is love, and that freedom exists when you are united with the giver of grace — Divine Will.

The development of the ego has manufactured a defensive world, full of anxiety, compulsion, insecurity, projection, and all those neuroses that psychologists enjoy theorising about. As you seek love by practising it, these masks can be released. With them go previous definitions of pleasure. Instead of attachment to this or that, you begin to find love in more and more of the human and natural world. You begin to appreciate creation in all its forms.

The practice of love creates the conditions for surrender to Truth; it frees the body's energy, allows it to become a chalice for omnipresent love, and provides liberation to bliss.

The practice of *conscious surrender* supports that process. It proposes:

* God, not self, is the doer.
* Acts are done for God, not self.
* The results of actions are God's, not self's.

In your infancy you had to 'surrender' to your parents; the experience of surrender is there. To practise conscious surrender, it helps if you have a genuine spiritual teacher; for one of the duties of such a teacher is to receive this 'intermediate' surrender, and to guide you beyond form to love itself.

Surrender to parents is followed by resistance, as ego develops and judgement grows. The divine teacher is a perfect foil for the hidden roots of ego. He or she appears perfect, as parents once seemed, and does not possess the 'faults' which the child tried to resist. A healing process can take place; for former resistances to parents are played out in projections on to the teacher, leaving the identity free to surrender *now* and see, behind the form of the teacher, Divinity itself.

Many so-called 'spiritual teachers' are incompletely evolved. Those who are genuine will transfer attachments projected by their students onwards, to a perfected teacher. If they accept such attachments themselves, they have succumbed to their own ego and cause only disillusionment to the seeker.

The practice of surrender is devotional and comprises the following elements:

* prayer;
* chanting and singing to the Lord;
* silently repeating the Lord's name till it becomes as integral as the breath;
* dedicating all actions, throughout their duration, to God.

Such devotional practice, if it is part of the practice of love, and not a meaningless ritual, accelerates the release of ego-will and builds confidence in faith and grace. It facilitates access to Divinity and the emergence of Self from the cocoon of self.

The 'devotional path' is not in itself an easy way to Love. The combined practice of love and devotion —'integrated devotion' — provides intense and frequent experiences of bliss, which stimulates desire for love. Surrender to love — it is the perfect guide to yourself — it will never let you down.

Omnipotence and Its Attractiveness to Ego

Love — oneness — divides itself into many; in this way, it can know itself. This initial and ongoing creative act is the acme of power. Creation and modification of 'physical form continue all the time, organised by physical and moral laws which also structure consciousness.

The energy of Divine Will maintains the stability and character of the entire creation. There are creative, maintaining and transforming aspects of the power of love, while the power of grace supports the strivings of consciousness towards love, bending or breaking laws governing the material world if necessary.

Such power is an attribute of Love manifest. As you seek love in yourself, you gradually begin to experience the power of Divinity in yourself.

At first, the world seems objective and rational, as obeying the laws by which it is governed. With each step towards love, this 'rationality' becomes relative. 'Coincidences' begin to multiply, leaving the 'rational' faculty of the mind, developed for a lawful world, perplexed.

It seems impossible to count on these 'coincidences': sometimes they happen, sometimes they don't. You meet a person you were thinking about. A book opens at an appropriate page. Help comes just when it is needed. An accident that seems certain is avoided. Yet accidents do occur; sometimes help does not come. This is a new subjectivity that seems capricious.

As you dedicate yourself more and more to the practice of love, nearing the source of grace, you find your thoughts and desires empowered. 'Extra' faculties emerge. The body now becomes a vehicle which may be left and re-entered. 'Impossible' things such as bi-location, the rearrangement of the physical world,

342

the replay of a sequence of time, direct knowledge of others' thoughts and feelings — all become possible. At a later stage, conscious control of incarnation and non-incarnation is achieved — the mastery over birth and death.

These powers have been described by Indian spiritual teachers and collectively termed 'Siddhic'. But they are known to spiritual teachers all over the world and rightly regarded with great ambivalence, a gift and a challenge at the same time.

The difficulty is that they emerge in partial form before ego has vanished from the identity. The remaining ego may give itself a boost by using elements of such powers for self-aggrandisement and prestige, or in attempts to coerce or manipulate others. Such misuse constitutes an 'abuse of trust' .If it is not corrected, it leads very rapidly away from love — like going down a snake in a 'snakes and ladders' game. And since to lose what you have almost known is a real tragedy, the exercise of Siddhic powers should be regarded with extreme caution by the unperfected seeker of Self.

Power without love causes much unhappiness. As such powers manifest themselves in you, continue resolutely with your surrender to love! *Remember that they are not 'your' power, but love's — used solely and appropriately by love, for love, and out of love*. Ultimately, when you are love, consciously and perfectly embodied, love's power will flow from you as a stream of compassionate grace, in just the right measure to each seeker.

A new age of spirituality is succeeding the age of materialism. As humans are transformed for it, the 'objectivity' of the material world will more and more be brought into question. The greatest temptations will not arise from the material per se, but will lie in the ego's attempts to manipulate Siddhic powers. Prepare yourself well, for the transition will be swift!

Humanity is Ruled by Divine Will

Humans think that their systems make the world better. People almost always say their century is better to live in than the one before. Never has it been so loudly insisted upon than in the age of materialism.

As proof of the virtue of this age over any other, people extol running water, the motor car, television, and the aeroplane, in spite of war, famine, poverty, and homelessness. Although great resources have been spent on medical care in many countries, diseases have multiplied to keep up with them.

The production of a plethora of material objects has replaced spirit as the focus of human fervour and endeavour. Since all these material things give only illusory and ephemeral pleasure, this age might be said to be the most poverty-stricken of all. Desires are stimulated endlessly and possession anxieties thrive. Commodities may become more complex, more may be known about the laws regulating the physical universe, but this is no progress if human consciousness is more and more turned away from the divine.

Love is scarce in this age; what there is, is very precious. Even a little love will secure divine grace. In this sense, the darker the age, the easier the path to spirit as love welcomes those who have turned from such manifest and multiple illusions towards the truth.

Humans think that the things they achieve and the civilisations they build are permanent; they constantly ignore their own history. Whatever the quality of past civilisations, spiritual or material, they have faded or been destroyed. For remember that all the human material resources that can be mustered — even in this age — are infinitesimal in relation to the natural powers of the universe. Only divine grace keeps a civilisation in being for a time. Divine grace, not human will, changes it.

But ego sees itself as the 'doer' and for support expands this view to humanity as a whole. It disregards the fact that love is the true doer. It operates to create, maintain and transform, as much in collective human affairs as in other parts of nature.

It is better to see humankind as actors on the stage, playing the drama of love lost and regained. Divine Grace, not humanity, structures the different settings. In every age, and in every civilisation, the theme of the drama is the same. Only the context differs. Contemporary society and civilisation are merely settings against which this universal drama is played out. God is the author, awareness of the truth of love the theme.

In this divine drama, there are four recurring epochs in human history, defined by the degree of human separation from Truth:

* In the 'great' age, humanity is close to spirit, but grace is given only as a result of extreme effort. Ignorance and wisdom are rather separate.

* In the second age, spirit is still primary, but many find themselves torn between two paths and powerful 'enemies' of spirit emerge, to try human motivation.

* In the third age, spirit and delusion are almost evenly matched, with ceaseless wars between their representatives. Even the good must conquer materialistic desires.

* And in the fourth age, materialism is dominant in almost everyone and each must wage an internal struggle to discover the truth hidden behind illusion.

It is divine power that changes these settings. At present a figure of true love is embodied on earth to usher out the age of materialism and introduce an age of spirit. The cycle is in process. It is simply the way things are, like a natural law.

The transformation takes place through all who seek love as the truth of their lives. As they follow this impulse, they begin to find their own truth. And as Grace works through them, they become agents for change. A very different human society is emerging, one which will surprise even those who yearn for it, for they also are steeped in materialistic concepts of human well-being.

One age is not 'better' than another. In each, humans struggle to attain love, learning what blocks and what facilitates their task. Nor is the task easier in one age than another. A different context brings about different practice, and presents different challenges — but the goal remains the same.

Human happiness will not be achieved by a new age, but by the discovery of love, and mergence with it. Seek that as transformations unfold about you, and you will be in harmony with them:

* Practice love in compassionate and dedicated service and you will find love multiplies.
* Surrender to the Divine will, which is the only will.
* Though engaged with the world, achieve detachment from its material things, dissolving your egoistic self so your real Self can be found.

346

   * Wonder at transformations in the world of humanity and nature and use them to reinforce your faith.

   These are the great tasks of your lives. Achieve them and happiness will be found; your lives will be well lived.

3210694R00185

Printed in Great Britain
by Amazon.co.uk, Ltd.,
Marston Gate.